C000109454

Frank McClean

Frank McClean

Godfather to British Naval Aviation

Philip Jarrett

Seaforth

PUBLISHING

TITLE PAGE CAPTION

Frank McClean's Short S.40 moored on the Thames, with the Houses of Parliament providing an imposing backdrop, following his dramatic flight up the river on 10 August 1912. This study epitomises McClean's persistent determination to make the government and the British public aware of the fast-growing capabilities of the aeroplane, and of Britain's aviation industry, in the early years of the twentieth century. The advertisement for the *Daily Mail* on the side of an omnibus on Westminster Bridge is ironic, as that newspaper had promoted the intended flight up the Thames of French aviator *Lieutenant de Vaisseau* de Conneau, who had to call off his attempt after a mishap in France. (ROYAL AERO CLUB)

Copyright © Philip Jarrett 2011

First published in Great Britain in 2011 by
Seaforth Publishing,
Pen & Sword Books Ltd,
47 Church Street,
Barnsley S70 2AS

www.seaforthpublishing.com

British Library Cataloguing in Publication Data
A catalogue record for this book is available from the British Library

ISBN 978 1 84832 109 0

Published in association with the Fleet Air Arm Museum

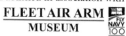

All rights reserved. No part of this publication may be reproduced or transmitted in any form or by any means, electronic or mechanical, including photocopying, recording, or any information storage and retrieval system, without prior permission in writing of both the copyright owner and the above publisher.

The right of Philip Jarrett to be identified as the author of this work has been asserted by him in accordance with the Copyright, Designs and Patents Act 1988.

Typeset and designed by Neil Sayer
Printed and bound in China

Contents

Introduction

Mention the name Frank McClean to most aviation historians and you might spot a glimmer of recognition, or perhaps something a little more positive from students of British naval aviation's early days. His role in instigating and facilitating the training of the first Royal Navy aviators is readily acknowledged, but few are aware of his many additional achievements.

It would be easy to number him dismissively among the moneyed flyers of the pioneer years who bought aeroplanes and flew them for their own sport or pleasure, but Frank McClean invested his vast inherited wealth in Britain's national security, and also became heavily involved in aviation safety and in promoting aviation through membership of several Royal Aero Club committees. Nor was he afraid to take an active role, though he seldom sought the limelight unless something or someone urged him into action for a cause. After first becoming an aeronaut and then teaching himself to fly, McClean became the Short brothers' voluntary unpaid test pilot for several years. Seeking greater safety, he pioneered the concept of multi-engined aeroplanes, paid for them to be built, tested them, and then made them freely available to naval aviators.

Although a few of his more public exploits drew attention to him, such as the aerial photography experiment over the sunken *Oceana*, the flight up the Thames to Westminster, and the painfully protracted expedition flight along the Nile, much of his work was carried out quietly, away from the glare of publicity, which he generally shunned. The aeronautical press of the pioneer years often commented on his desire for privacy and lack of response when it sought information. He was happiest when he was flying at Eastchurch, well away from crowded public venues such as Hendon and Brooklands, and this meant that reports of his activities were sparse. He seldom wrote anything for publication at the time, and wrote only two brief accounts of his early flying days subsequently, and they were not widely broadcast. When he did put pen to paper he was dryly witty, and never afraid to have a joke at his own expense. All who knew him held him in reverence, valued his friendship and were impressed by his modesty and even temper.

Although he had no dependants at that time, McClean usually declined to take part in competitions and races. Ironically, when he entered for the round-Britain seaplane race of 1913 his Short S.68 proved a troublesome non-starter. Unlike many other aviators he did not need prize money to finance his flying, and there can be little doubt that the deaths of his close friends the Hon. Charles Rolls and Cecil Grace heightened his awareness of the increased risks entailed in flying competitively. These tragedies did not deter him from flying, but merely led to his becoming involved in accident investigation and in seeking ways to make flying safer. His part in subsequent investigations into the fatal accidents that befell other fellow flyers, such as H J D Astley and S F Cowdery ('Colonel Cody'), contributed to the effort to pinpoint causes and prevent recurrences.

In some ways McClean's modesty worked against him. When he was awarded a later pilot's licence than he clearly merited, owing to his absence when the first British licences were allocated, he made little of it at the time, being more concerned with progress than vain protestation. When his pioneering achievements were belatedly recognised with a knighthood, the honour was bestowed so late that many of his fellow pioneers had passed on before and were conspicuously missing from the celebrations. And, like other pioneers who lived to a good age, he was unknown to many of those who read his obituaries.

But Frank McClean was never one to complain. He was a big man with broad shoulders, and philosophically accepted whatever befell him. He was most active in the early years of the twentieth century, not only ballooning and flying but making long expeditions to remote Pacific islands in attempts to witness eclipses. He evidently enjoyed life, and enjoyed sharing its pleasures (as the ladies he frequently treated to flights were doubtless aware).

Although McClean was never one to sing his own praises, he merits wider recognition for his significant contributions to British aviation in the pioneering era. Without him, the Royal Navy would not have got into the air as early as it did, and it would certainly not have been as prepared as it was when the First World War broke out. Without his patronage and support the Short brothers' young company would have struggled to survive in the difficult pre-war years. Without him, and others of his ilk, lackadaisical and short-sighted politicians and military leaders might never have perceived the vitally important role that aviation would play in future international conflicts.

I was given the impetus to write this book by Grahame Mottram of the Fleet Air Arm (FAA) Museum, who gave me access to the McClean material donated to the museum by Sir Rupert Carington, and Michael Oakey of *Aeroplane Monthly* magazine. Although McClean was known to me, in the throes of researching his involvement in the pioneer years of British aviation my eyes were opened. The extent of his commitment, and his farsighted generosity, were truly extraordinary but had gone largely unrecognised. Even many histories of British naval aviation make only a passing reference to his part in its birth.

This account concentrates on Sir Francis Kennedy McClean's life as a pioneer aeronaut and aviator in the exciting pre-First World War years. This was by far the most active and significant period of his life, and, as the record shows, a time of intense and constant involvement in the fast-developing new science of aviation, and in its applications. While his contributions to astronomy, both as an investigator and a benefactor, and his activities during and after the First World War were also noteworthy, it was in the flying world of Edwardian England that Sir Frank made his mark, so his subsequent achievements are summarised in the concluding chapter, in which significant episodes and events are spotlighted.

As a private owner, Frank McClean purchased an extraordinary number of aeroplanes between 1909 and 1914, and these, plus some that were ordered but either unbuilt or uncompleted, are listed in an appendix, with brief histories. This is the first complete listing of what must have been one of the biggest fleets of privately-owned aeroplanes in the world at that time, though they did not all co-exist, of course.

One difficulty I encountered was the question of how to address my subject in the text. In the pioneer era he was Francis McClean in the popular press, but to his friends and often in the aeronautical press he was Frank Mc-

Clean. It would certainly be wrong to address him as Sir Frank when writing of his work during this period. After he was knighted in 1926 he tended to be referred to formally as 'Sir Frank' rather than 'Sir Francis', but, as many later quotations in this volume show, he bore the accolade lightly and his friends and acquaintances still called him Frank, which was evidently what he himself preferred.

Another minor problem was the spelling of Egyptian place names. The important thing is that the phonetics are correct, the sound of the Arabic name, but in the throes of research one encounters alternative spellings that are equally effective in conveying those sounds, such as Assouan and Aswan, or Wadi and Wady. I have generally adopted those forms currently in use.

Acknowledgements

This account would have been much the poorer (and less accurate) without the valuable contributions of friends and fellow researchers. First and foremost among these is Gordon Bruce, who unselfishly shared information gathered by him on early Short aircraft in his researches in various archives, including notes he made from the Shorts order book during his time as Secretary at Short Brothers Limited and during his own researches into the aviation activities of the Hon. C S Rolls. In addition, Gordon patiently responded to my deluge of queries over several years, and clarified many points during our lengthy correspondence. This process also unearthed many errors and inaccuracies in previous accounts of Short's formative years, particularly concerning the company's first aeroplanes. Some questions may now never be fully resolved, and we have only vague mental impressions of some of the aeroplanes, such as McClean's enigmatic Short No 3 and the S.46 'Double-Dirty', but hopefully their known histories have been set straight.

Others who made welcome contributions or provided helpful assistance were the staff of the FAA Museum, especially Grahame Mottram, Moira Gittos and Catherine Cooper; Peter Elliott and the staff of the RAF Museum archives; the staff of *Aeroplane Monthly* magazine, and particularly Michael Oakey (who also provided some Egyptian expertise), Tanya Caffrey and Amanda Stroud; Andrew Dawrant, a trustee of the Royal Aero Club Trust; the staff of the Cheshire Archives and Local Studies in the Cheshire Record Office; James Rait for his researches into the flying experiences of the Hon. Maurice Egerton; Eric Harlin; the staff of the County Library Headquarters of Cardiff Central Library; Jack Woods for material relating to Sir Frank's lineage and ancestors; Barry Gray, and Mark Wagner of Aviation Images, for photographic work; G Stuart Leslie, David Browning and, very especially, my wife Marilyn for her patience and forbearance.

I am also grateful to Murdo Morrison, the present editor of *Flight International*; Chris Male, editor of *The Aeronautical Journal* of the Royal Aeronautical Society; and Andrew Dawrant of the Royal Aero Club Trust (the RAeC published the *Royal Aero Club Gazette*) for permission to use extracts from their respective (and much respected) publications.

Philip Jarrett
February 2011

CHAPTER I

A Pioneer's Origins; First Flight

In 1955, shortly after the death of Sir Francis Kennedy McClean at the age of 80, his old friend and fellow aviation pioneer Lieutenant-Colonel Alec Ogilvie wrote: 'He was a wealthy man for those days and he was prepared to spend his money freely in getting to the bottom of things which interested him and in which he could see benefit to the country.' This tribute really understates the massive contribution that McClean made to British aviation, because he played so many parts. As well as being an aeronaut and a pioneer pilot, he ensured the initial success of Short Brothers as an aeroplane manufacturer, served as the company's first test pilot, and, in the words of that great naval aviator, Air Commodore Charles Rumney Samson, his generosity 'started the Navy flying'.

The reader will have gathered already that McClean must have been a rich man. Born on 1 February 1876, he was educated at Charterhouse, Clifton College and the Royal School of Mines, and then spent three years training as a civil engineer at the Royal Indian Engineering College, Coopers Hill, London. Then, aged 22, he went to India in 1898 and served in the Public Works Dept of the Bombay Presidency, India, for three and a half years, returning to England in 1902 with the intention of joining the family business and pursuing a career in engineering. In 1902 McClean became a director of the Cannock Chase Colliery Company, a post he retained until the company was nationalised in 1948, and was elected a Fellow of the Royal Astronomical Society and a member of the Royal Institution. In 1904 he

Frank McClean, in a white shirt and wielding a hammer, samples the labours of a collier in the Wheal Grenville Mine.
(FLEET AIR ARM MUSEUM)

became a member of the board of Powell Duffryn Associated Collieries, and remained so until 1948. Upon his father's death in 1904 he retired, aged only 28, considerable independent means enabling him to pursue his personal interest in astronomy. To learn how those means were accumulated it is necessary to go back two generations.

Francis K McClean's grandfather, John Robinson McClean, was born in 1813 in Belfast, Northern Ireland. He was the third son of Belfast merchant Francis McClean and his wife Margaret. After attending Tillicoultry School, Clackmannanshire, he continued his education at Belfast Royal Academical Institution. In 1834 he went to Glasgow University, where he gained high honours in mathematics and natural philosophy. At the same time he undertook practical studies in mining, engineering and surveying, with the aim of qualifying as a civil engineer. John married Anna Newson in 1837 and that same year a son, Frank, was born.

Adrian Long, J R McClean's biographer, says:

> He was a remarkable man, with great vision, who lived an extraordinarily active business life much of it spent on projects in Staffordshire embracing railway engineering, water supply and coal mining. His achievements in and around the Brownhills area have been considered to be equal to those of Isambard Kingdom Brunel and Thomas Telford.

It is impossible to list all of J R McClean's accomplishments here, but especially worthy of mention are his improvement of the Birmingham Canal and his work on the Tame Valley Canal, England's last main canal; and surveying and contract work on the Thames embankment and Belfast Docks, all done during a

seven-year pupillage with Walker and Burgess of Westminster, London. After becoming an independent civil engineer in 1844 he was appointed engineer to the Furness Railway Company, and two years later he became engineer to the South Staffordshire Junction Railway (SSJR), opened in April 1849. He then leased this railway, this being the first recorded leasing of a railway to an individual. When it was taken over by the London and North Western Railway in 1861 McClean received a payment of £110,000 in compensation for the unexpired part of the lease. He compensated members of the staff with up to two weeks' pay following the change of ownership.

In 1854 J R McClean and R C Chawner, chairman of the SSJR, were awarded the lease for the Hammerwich and Uxbridge collieries from the second Marquis of Anglesey, and built a branch railway to the pits. The pits were eventually purchased by their newly formed Cannock Chase Colliery Company, and its first steam locomotive was named *McClean*. Formally inaugurated in 1859, the company eventually owned ten pits and a brickyard. The collieries were a major source of McClean's wealth, and as well as building a church at Chasetown he had boys' and girls' schools built and maintained there, plus an institute containing a library and leisure facilities, shops and other services, including a doctor. This benevolence attracted some of the area's best miners to the town.

McClean's other West Midland enterprises included the Birmingham, Wolverhampton and Dudley Railway and the West Bromwich, Wednesbury and Bilston Railway. He was also involved with Cardiff's East Bute Docks, Newport's Alexandra Docks, the Ryde Pier Company and the Eastbourne Water and Sewage Works (presaging F K McClean's Eastbourne connections decades later), new docks at Barrow in Furness, the Devonshire Dock, and the Buccleugh. He was instrumental in establishing fresh water supplies into the Black Country, and in 1849 submitted a scheme for the supply of fresh water to London and the draining of the Metropolis that was adjudged the best and most practical scheme submitted.

In 1851 J R McClean was instructed by Emperor Napoleon III to report on the practicality of introducing the English system of public baths and washhouses in Paris, and in 1855 the Viceroy of Egypt invited him to join an international commission to consider the practicality of building a ship canal linking the Mediterranean and the Red Sea, later made reality as the Suez Canal. He was also consulting engineer for the La Coruna, Santiago de Compostela, Vigo and Orense railway system in Galicia, north-west Spain, and for the system in Moldavia, east of the Carpathians in north-east Romania. In addition McClean was engineer to the Lemberg-Czernowitz Austrian Railway and the South Eastern Railway of Portugal.

He was a vice-president of the Institution of Civil Engineers from 1858, and its president in 1864 and 1865. He was also a Fellow of the Royal Society and the Royal Astronomical and Geological Societies, among others, and a lieutenant-colonel in the Engineering and Railway Volunteer Corps. In the 1870s deteriorating health caused him to retire from active engineering, and he spent more time in leisure pursuits, travelling several times to Egypt and also visiting India, China and Australia. He died in Ramsgate, Kent, on 13 July 1873.

John Robinson McClean's only son, Frank (F K McClean's father), was born in 1837 and went to school in Westminster, thereafter studying at Glasgow University (1852) and then at Trinity College, Cambridge, in 1855, where he was a wrangler in the Mathematical Tripos, LL.D, FRS in 1859. While Bachelor Scholar of Trinity in 1859–62 he was involved in improving the drainage of the Fens, and in 1862 he joined his father's partnership. Frank was resident engineer of the Barrow Docks and Furness and Midland Railway from 1862 to 1866, and then worked as an engineering consultant in London until 1870, when, aged 33, he retired from professional life. Having married Ellen Greg in 1865, he lived with his growing family at Ferncliffe, Tunbridge Wells, Kent, until they moved to Rusthall House, a new large residence in the same town, in 1884. There were three sons, of which Francis Kennedy was the second, and one daughter, Anna.

During his retirement Frank indulged energetically in astronomy and other academic studies. He financed telescopes and observatories and promoted studies of them, and was awarded the Royal Astronomical Society's Gold Medal in 1899. He also endowed scholarships at Cambridge. Frank McClean senior died in 1904.

Aerostatic inclinations

It will become evident that, in addition to his father's fortune, Francis Kennedy ('Frank') McClean also inherited some of his interests, but his fascination and involvement with things aeronautical originated outside the family.

Frank McClean made his first balloon ascent, from Battersea, London, on 12 July 1907, with The Hon Charles S Rolls (later a cofounder of Rolls-Royce Ltd) as the 'pilot', the balloon descending at Langley Park, Bromley, after covering eight miles in an hour and a half. Another ascent, with Oswald Short, was made on 16 July, when an altitude of 4,800ft was attained before the balloon descended at Dorking in Surrey, and on the 25th McClean made

The Shorts' balloon works at Battersea, London, in 1909, with the *Venus* (left) and *Continental* No 2 ready to ascend. The close proximity of gasometers containing coal gas was an asset for such sites, but the area was very confined by elevated railway tracks and was thus unsuited to aeroplane production and testing. (AUTHOR)

an ascent from the Crystal Palace with Frank Hedges Butler and 'Miss Gorst' and the balloon came down at Kenley. Although he made no further ascents in 1907 he clearly caught the 'bug', as that same year he was elected to membership of Aero Club (later the Royal Aero Club, RAeC) as an aeronaut, and then unanimously elected to replace Frank Hedges Butler on the Main Committee. The Aero Club had been founded in 1901 by a group of wealthy and enthusiastic balloonists, with the object of uniting aeronauts and obtaining balloons for members to fly. In 1938 McClean recalled:

The Aero Club Members in the years before 1909 were a quiet, sedate, genteel body, whose only vice was to be considered by the hoi-polloi as amiable lunatics. They consisted of city gentlemen, lawyers, wine merchants, Peers of the Realm and their offspring, and

they dined together once a month at Jules' in Jermyn Street [London]. The Club was at 166 Piccadilly, and their guide and secretary was Harold Perrin, of happy memory.

They became more hard-bitten with the advent of mechanisation.

In the early years of the twentieth century ballooning was a fashionable sport, though it has been estimated that there were probably fewer than a dozen privately-owned balloons in England at that time. One owner was Griffith Brewer, a patent agent who had made his first ascent in 1891. Brewer had also become a prominent member of the Aeronautical Society of Great Britain (ASGB, later the Royal Aeronautical Society), founded in 1866 with heavier-than-air flight as its *raison d'être*.

In 1907 Brewer was selected by the Aero Club as the English competitor for the second Gordon Bennett balloon race, starting from St Louis, Missouri, in the USA. His companions on a trial run from Battersea Park in London on 25 August were the Hon. Claud Brabazon and Eustace and Oswald Short, who had begun balloon manufacture in 1901, made their first balloons for sale in 1903, become established as leading British balloon manufacturers and were appointed aeronauts to the Aero Club in 1907. Brewer and Brabazon competed in the event on 21 October and managed to cover 350 miles during 25 hours aloft.

Membership of the Aero Club brought Frank McClean into contact with these men and several other prominent balloonists, including Charles Rolls and J T C Moore-Brabazon (later Lord Brabazon of Tara), and also Eustace Short. These contacts were to have far-reaching effects in the years ahead.

McClean had inherited his father's abiding interest in astronomy, and was also a member of the Royal Astronomical Society. One consequence of this was that he organised expeditions to witness eclipses in remote parts of the world, the first being to Flint Island in the Pacific, some 390 miles north-north-west of Tahiti, to observe an eclipse of the sun scheduled for 3 January 1908. Although his efforts to assemble a party in England were unsuccessful, he set off on 3 October 1907, taking some fifteen cases of equipment. He hoped that he would be able to find colonial astronomers to accompany him, and when he reached Colombo he received a telegram from C J Merfield of Sydney, Australia, offering assistance.

In Sydney McClean was introduced to the astronomical photographer James Short and W E Raymond, both of whom worked at Sydney Observatory, and retired surveyor Joseph Brooks. This group, plus New Zealanders Henry Wincklemann and the Reverend F W Walker, made up McClean's party. Reaching Flint Island on 23 December, they negotiated the channel blasted in the coral reef encircling the island and set up camp near a better-equipped party from the USA's Lick Observatory, led by Professor W W Campbell. The day of the eclipse dawned fine, but by 10am it had clouded over and there was a heavy rain before totality. Fortunately it cleared in time and the group succeeded in exposing a good number of glass plate negatives of the eclipse, then hastily packed and departed on the *Taviuni* that afternoon. Immediately upon arrival at Auckland, New Zealand, McClean sent a cablegram describing the eclipse to England, and details were published in the 23 January issue of *Nature*. He subsequently wrote an account of the expedition.

In May 1908, having returned from Flint Island, McClean again took up sport ballooning with his own gas balloon, the *Corona* (50,000 cu ft capacity, probably built by Short Brothers). He recalled that 'with good gas it could carry four persons, and it made many voyages from London to various points in England but never beyond'. On 28 May he visited the Balloon Factory at Farnborough, and on the 30th, with *Corona* entered for *The Car* Cup, he ascended from the Hurlingham Club at Fulham in London with Rolls, who was described as the pilot, 'Cruickshank' and 'Lady Pajet', and descended near Twyford (he does not say which Twyford) three hours later. Several more ascents followed.

Three categories of ballooning were practised by the RAeC members. As described by Mc-

Frank McClean's first gas balloon was this one, the *Corona*, of 50,000cu ft capacity. It is seen here after descending in open country at Upper Halling, near Rochester, Kent, at 4.45pm on 10 April 1909. (FLEET AIR ARM MUSEUM)

Strongly laced into the inside of the basket about a foot above the bottom was a rope, 'to which passengers could cling in a crouching position with no part of their anatomies showing above the top'. This was only for use in a rough landing, and to guard against this eventuality a trail rope some 300 feet long, weighing from 50lb for ordinary balloons to 90lb for large ones, was hung from the hoop above the basket. Once this rope had touched the ground it slowed down the rate of descent by easing off the weight, and its friction acted as a brake to the balloon's horizontal speed. An anchor was also provided, but, McClean wrote '. . . it had bad habits and was really useful only for hedges and strong fences. It bounced on hard ground and caused telegraph lines to go all hay-wire, while the job of retrieving it from tree-tops was of interest only to acrobats'. Lastly there was a ripping panel in the envelope to allow gas to escape in seconds when landing in a wind to prevent the balloon being dragged along the ground.

'It will therefore be seen,' McClean stated, 'that there were ample safeguards against trouble on landing, while on starting off from the ground troubles that did sometimes occur were mostly due to lack of care.'

'In fact, it may be said that, given ordinary habits and instincts of self-preservation, there was little danger to those in the balloon.'

However, ballooning was not without its incidents and mishaps, as McClean recounts:

Clean, these were: 'The afternoon trip with no objective except pleasure, peace and quiet, and a view of the landscape unattainable at that time by any other means'; 'Competitions to land nearest a given spot. This introduced problems of wind direction at various heights, maintenance of stability at any altitude considered best to reach that point, and a possible rushed landing'; and 'Long-distance International Races, such as the Gordon Bennett Race, with the necessity of conserving gas and ballast, finding the strongest winds and avoiding the open sea.'

The balloon envelopes were made from cotton or silk doped with varnish or rubber, and 'stood a lot of rough usage in the process of getting back to earth'. The basket, 'or, to be more accurate, the standing accommodation', was always made of wicker, because 'a rectangular wicker basket can, and does, take up any shape when violently impacted but resumes its original rectangularity when it comes to rest'.

Ordinary ballooning, as opposed to long-distance races, was a quiet pastime punctuated with incidents. Starting from the grounds of the Crystal Palace on one occasion, a flukey wind had given the balloon a false lift which petered out, and it made straight for the glass edifice. By pouring out bags of ballast (fine sand) the obstruction was cleared, but below the torrent of sand was an ample lady gazing up with open mouth, and the last seen by the aeronauts as the Palace was surmounted was of two companions beating her on the back to help the ejection of unwanted matter.

On another occasion, at Hurlingham, with a large number of balloons starting on a point-to point, the *Corona* got out of hand in the wind and had to be ripped [on 11 July 1908, see below], while another in getting away tore open the top of one still on the ground.

Once in the air the occupants were themselves at peace, usually, but the middle of a cloud lit up by flashes of lightning was poor for the nerves and there was nothing to be done about it.

People and things on the ground were not so secure. The trail rope could, and did, do extensive damage to greenhouses and suchlike, which had to be paid for, and on one occasion after it had climbed over the telegraph wires on the side of a road it swung clear and hit a woman on the large of the back, resulting in damages claimed by an irate husband.

But incidents of any magnitude were rare, and those in the balloons looked down on those who were earthbound while those below looked up to those above them, and the world was at peace.

He ascended from Hurlingham in the *Corona* on 24 June with 'Ld' Royston and Jim Lockyer, alighting at Milford, near Godalming in Surrey, and on the 29th, when the *Corona* rose from Battersea, his companions were Hedges Butler and Jim Lockyer and they travelled to Crondall,

near Farnham in Surrey. Another ascent from Battersea, this time on 6 July and again with Hedges Butler and Jim Lockyer, ended with a descent at Hainault Forest in Essex.

Corona was entered for the Hedges Butler Challenge Cup event at Hurlingham on 11 July, but the take-off was abandoned owing to bad weather and the balloon was ripped on the ground to release gas quickly. Instead, McClean ascended in the balloon *Britannia* with Rolls (who probably still owned it at that time), Cruickshank, Westland and Simon Lockyer. He recorded that they covered 75 miles in 1 hour 56 minutes and reached a maximum speed of 49mph before descending at 'Brandon'. He subsequently purchased the *Britannia* (78,500 cu ft), from Rolls, who had commissioned it from the Short brothers for the first Gordon Bennett Balloon Race in 1906, its capacity being the maximum permitted for this event. By the time McClean acquired it the *Britannia* must have been approaching the end of its useful life, as the life of a cotton balloon was two years, or three at best. *Britannia* was entered for the third Gordon Bennett Race, in October, held under the auspices of the German Aero Club, because the 1907 event had been won by a German and hence the 1908 race was to start from Berlin. McClean was to act as Griffith Brewer's aide.

Brewer's account of this event, including technical details of the participating balloons, was published in the 24 and 31 October issues of *The Field*. Describing the gathering of balloons, he wrote:

All the twenty-three balloons in the race were spherical in form, the original pear-shaped balloon now being obsolete. All the German balloons were of rubber fabric, and many of the foreign balloons were of similar manufacture and material, being coloured a dull yellow. The British balloons were all of varnished cotton, and the *Banshee*, a beautiful translucent balloon with its luxurious car [specially built by Short Brothers for the event], looked not only a worthy supporter of British aeronautical honours, but, with its padding and soft carpet, seemed like a Pulman [*sic*] car in comfort, compared with the bare provision of absolute necessity in the tiny baskets of rival competitors. One balloon stood out from the rest in its beauty, being covered with aluminium paint, which glistened in the sunshine like a ball of silvered glass.

McClean's account

Fortunately McClean also wrote a very complete account of the event. His use of the present tense in certain places suggests that it was written shortly after the race, but it was apparently not published until shortly after his death in 1955. It is a graphic first-hand account of what it was like to participate in one of the world's greatest ballooning events:

In August of 1908, having purchased the balloon *Britannia*, it was arranged that I should act as assistant to Mr Griffith Brewer in the

The essential features of a typical gas balloon of the era are shown in this working drawing of the 77,000cu ft *Banshee*, built by Short Brothers and the winner of the 1908 Gordon Bennett Race. The key is as follows: A – 36in-diameter wooden butterfly valve; B – waterproof shade or umbrella to protect the valve; C – rip panel extending from near the valve to the balloon's equator; D – rip cord; E – breakable stops which break at a tension of 50lb and enable the rip panel to be torn away downwards when the rip cord is pulled; F – valve line attached to underside of the valve doors and extending right down through the balloon; G – the appendix, a varnished cotton pipe about 12ft long and of 36in diameter, open at the base; H – an auxiliary pipe attached to the underside of the balloon to enable gas to be added immediately before an ascent, after the appendix has been disconnected from the main gas pipe; J – leading lines, which divide and become network as they approach the balloon; K – drip band to cause rain or moisture to fall clear of the car and hoop; L – hoop forming the foundation of the balloon, with 36 small toggles on its upper side to receive the 36 leading lines of the net, and eight large toggles on its underside to receive the eight car lines; M – car lines supporting the car or basket; N – wicker map table attached to the side of the car and projecting outwards; P – grapnel rope (independent of the trail rope on *Banshee*); R – coir trail rope 300ft long and weighing about 90lb, seen in the form of a bundle, which can be dropped from outside the car and allowed to unravel as it falls; S – the car, 6ft 6in long by 5ft 6in wide, and about 3ft 6in high. Also provided were a cone anchor for checking balloon's speed in the in the event of a descent into the sea, a sea anchor, and a canvas bucket to allow water ballast to be taken up. (AUTHOR)

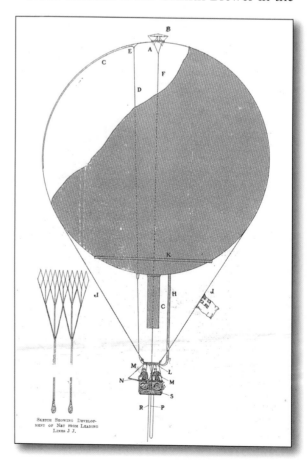

Gordon Bennett Race starting from Berlin on Sunday, the 11th of October.

Many arrangements were necessary, the race being a long-distance one and the few preliminaries usually required for an afternoon run would not suffice for a possible two days in the air. First a minute examination of the envelope of the balloon was made both for pin-holes and to see that the ripping panel was in order. This envelope is of cotton with several coats of varnish. Then the net and

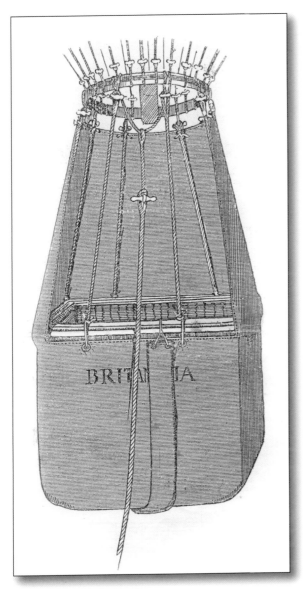

valves were examined and the car and type of trail rope chosen.

The car used was the one belonging to my other balloon, the *Corona*, which although rather small, is very well made and comfortable. The trail ropes were composite, the first a coir rope 100ft long connected to the hoop by 60ft of strong fine rope down which the anchor could slide, and the second 25ft of very thick rope which would float in case of landing on water and known as a 'serpent' suspended by 80ft of ½-in rope. The possibility of crossing the sea also necessitated the carrying of life-belts and a waterproof cover to put round the car so that it would float.

The principal instruments taken were the usual three, the statoscope, the aneroid and the barograph.

The statoscope is an instrument for telling if you were rising or falling. By pinching the end of a short open rubber tube you enclose air at the pressure at that moment, and the difference of pressure between the inside and outside of this tube due to rising and falling, immediately moves the indicating needle one way or the other. The aneroid is simply the ordinary barometer marked for altitude, while the barograph is also an instrument in common use but with the drum rotating at a greater speed.

In addition to these we had several compasses and instruments for map following

To guard against the possibility of a 450-mile run over the unbroken water of the Baltic Sea, the three British balloons were provided with waterproof canvas covers which could enclose their cars on all sides and extended up to the hoop above the car on the three sides away from the trail rope. Thus the front of the car could strike the sea without admitting water, and if the balloon were becalmed it could sit on the water for days until a wind sprang up. (AUTHOR) and electric hand lamps. The maps to be taken had to be very comprehensive, as until the last moment (and not even then as it turned out) it could not be known in what direction we should travel. Large-scale maps round Berlin and two fairly large-scale maps of North Germany, as well as one of Denmark and Scandinavia, were, however, obtained at once, that being the dangerous direction and the one that would bring us most quickly to the sea. At the last moment we obtained maps of the whole of Eastern Europe.

Food was almost entirely tinned or bottled, and consisted of sardines, tongue, chicken and fruit, with bread, butter, cheese and chocolate, while in addition to a large supply of water we carried a little beer and whisky and milk.

There were three English balloons competing, the *Banshee*, carrying Messrs. Dunville and Pollock, the *Zephyr*, with Professor Huntington and Captain the Hon. C. Brabazon, and the *Britannia* with Mr Brewer and myself. They were taken over to Germany by Short Bros., aeronautical engineers to the Aero Club, and by Mr Perrin, the sec-

retary of the Club. We followed on Thursday, the 8th, via Flushing, arriving in Berlin the following evening. Very little remained to be done except to get the bread and other perishable supplies, which were got on the Sunday morning.

On Saturday there was a point-to-point balloon race of which we watched the start. The wind was then almost due south and the probability of an over-sea passage to Sweden seemed likely, but the following morning by daybreak it had veered round to the west and it was then that we got a map of Russia and some of the competitors obtained Russian money. During the morning it became west-north-west, and at 3 o'clock when the first balloon was started it was almost due north-west.

The starting ground was at Schmargendorf, a suburb of Berlin, and was very rough and sandy. A squad of soldiers under a sergeant was detailed to each balloon to fill it and take

Balloons massed at the Schmargendorf gas factory site in Berlin in October 1908 for that year's Gordon Bennett Balloon Race. (AUTHOR)

it to the starting point. The lift of the balloon was twice tested before the start so as to make certain that there was sufficient but not too much buoyancy.

Inside the car there was none too much room although we had things hung on pulleys to the leading lines and all round the outside of the basket. A wicker shelf for laying maps and other things on was ready to be fixed outside, and the basket containing food was also outside as well as the grapnel and serpent and a large number of sandbags.

Owing to the number of men helping it was possible to start the balloons at very short intervals. Some got away well but the majority evidently had not sufficient lifting power, and after rising a little came down almost on to the heads of the crowd of onlookers. The balloon that started ninth was the American *Conqueror*, which hit the wooden fence behind which the crowd was watching, and then went straight for a tower after a close shave with another balloon which was awaiting its turn to start.

In the meantime, the *Berlin* had been sent off and we in the *Britannia* at No.11 were receiving our final directions when a shout from the crowd made us look up and we saw the underside of the *Conqueror* get slack and then rise up to the top of the net. Our send-off was temporarily forgotten and all eyes watched to see what would happen next. At first clouds of sand were in the air above the descending balloon showing that they were discharging ballast to lighten their fall. Afterwards we learnt that they took to cutting away the bags complete, a somewhat dangerous proceeding for anyone below. We could see this burst balloon turning round and round sometimes looking a complete parachute and at others showing enormous rents almost up to the valve at the top. But it came

down slowly, slower even than one often brings down a balloon when intending to land, and the only danger was the fact that they could not choose their place to come down on. They hit the top of a house, knocking down a chimney and making a hole in the roof, but escaped uninjured. As a matter of fact the probability is that a burst balloon will parachute but it is not an experiment most people would care to try. Another balloon also appears to have burst during the race with the same result.

The cause of this accident was probably that the neck of the balloon was not large enough to allow the rush of gas out when they rose very quickly to clear the tower.

When the *Conqueror* had fallen out of sight, we were again given our directions, and at 3.45 the order of "hands off" was given and we rose easily but gently away from the crowd and noise. Our direction was south-east, and at the height of 1,900ft where we found equilibrium the wind speed was about 12mph. First we crossed houses and saw below us the wreck of the *Conqueror* with its envelope lying across the roof and the car hanging down the wall. Crowds had collected in all the streets and on all the house-tops and more crowds were running in from all directions. A possible accident is really the reason why many people collect to see balloons start, and they are generally disappointed; and even when there is not an accident you often see wonderful tales in the papers, as on the occasion when, at Hurlingham, owing to the strength of the wind the *Corona* had to have its ripping panel opened, and several papers the next morning described the tearing in pieces of the balloon.

After leaving the town we kept south of the river Spree, crossing the Walzigar See at nightfall, after which we had a meal of sardines and pears. The sardines proved too oily when mixed up with maps and sand, and we did not try them again. It was at this time that the wind commenced to veer round, and when we had finished supper it took some little time to find out again where we were. But the numberless lakes around us reflecting the moonlight enabled us to locate our position. Steadily our course became more south except for a short period when a vertical current of air had taken us up from 1,000ft height to 2,500ft, and a long halt over one spot followed by a very slow drift to the east made us impatient. We allowed the balloon to drop to 700ft, and our course became south-south-west. If we had not done this we should have had a good chance of winning the race, but we could not tell that the wind would go right round and we wanted to be moving all the time. We passed a few miles to

the west of Kottbus, the lights of which were visible to us for five hours and helped us to locate our position all that time with ease.

Still trending more to the west we passed low over a large manufacturing district and over numberless quarries, passing chimneys which nearly reached to our own level. We had a light cord 200ft long hanging below us to give warning of rising ground, but it only once touched. If we had our trail rope out it would have been impossible to have kept so low for fear of doing damage. We then rose to between 1,000ft and 2,000ft height, and at half-past three we passed to the south of Finsterwalde going due west and at not more than three miles an hour. This course contin-

Frank McClean (left) and Griffith Brewer in the basket of the *Britannia* at Berlin in 1908.
(PRESS ASSOCIATION IMAGES)

ued till daybreak when a low ground fog began to cover the country and for the time it was impossible to tell in what direction we were travelling. During the night Mr Griffith Brewer had managed to get in four hours' unbroken sleep curled up among the sandbags and other paraphernalia in the bottom of the basket. When the sun rose I turned in for a couple of hours and had a good sleep in spite of the discomfort. On waking when I looked over the edge of the car I found clouds everywhere below but clear in the distance. From any height you never have an horizon but simply see the country disappear in blue haze. For this reason if you wish to take any altitudes of stars or the sun you must use an artificial horizon, but we did not carry any instruments for this purpose.

Gradually the clouds broke up and in a gap we saw a big river with steamers and barges and knew we were somewhere over the Elbe, but not until 9.15 did we find our exact position when we passed a few miles south of Wittenberg. From there till we crossed south of Magdeberg at one o'clock, 8,000ft up, all was easy. The sun warming the gas gave us a steady rise and the river below us made our map-reading easy. From then on it was different as we got into open country and finally lost our position when putting out the trail rope. A network of railways showed clear below us but apparently they were only minor lines as they were unmarked on the map.

All this time we were falling gradually until at sunset we crossed a fair sized town at some 500ft. We shouted out to people below and were told it was Gifhorne. The wind had now risen considerably and we reached a town which we afterwards discovered to be Celle in just over the hour, travelling low and over open ground, and here we got rid of tins and bottles and other heavy articles to save ballast.

At half-past eight when the moon had risen for some time but not enough to make the landscape clear, we suddenly found the appearance of the country change. For the moment we thought that a gale must have got up and hurried us to the North Sea, but on dropping low we found that it was heather-covered country with occasional woods. Knowing that we could not win, as any balloon to the north or south of us could get further than us, we now decided to land, and Mr Brewer held open the valve while I stood ready to cut the anchor free when he gave the word. As the 150ft trail rope touched, he called me to cut, which I did and then held on tight to await the bump. It came, and again we were up in the air at some 30ft, and looking over the car to see what kind of a place we should hit next. Then as we came down he pulled the ripping cord and with the next bump and a final struggle to rise again the balloon *Britannia* collapsed slowly on to the heather at 8.46pm, or almost exactly 29 hours after it had left Berlin. The car lay on its side and we crawled out through the tangle of ropes on to the heath none the worse for our 25 miles an hour bump. Then after lighting pipes, eating some chocolate and covering up the instruments, we rolled the sides of the balloon envelope over on to the middle, so that less surface should get wet during the night. Then, getting into our sleeping sacks we put our heads and bodies into the upturned basket, leaving our feet out in the heather and went to sleep.

At six the next morning we woke to find a thick white fog hiding any landmark that might tell us our position so we got back into the basket and had some breakfast while the mist cleared a bit. Then we found that just ahead of us was an area of mud and water, but to one side were wheel ruts which we followed till we came to a regular track. It was still too misty to go far from the balloon so we went back and packed the small things and unfixed the valve and hoop, and as we finished this a cart came up with two men who told us we were 10km from Langwedel and that we could get assistance from some farmhouses a little way up the track. So I went in search of them and with some difficulty, owing to lack of German words, made the owner understand that I wanted a cart to take the balloon to the station. With the assistance of four men we got the balloon packed and into a cart and left our camping ground at half-past eleven for Langwedel Station. For several miles there was only a track,

and after being jolted in the cart for a bit we got out and walked.

At Langwedel we had two hours to wait for a train to Bremen, from which place we despatched the balloon by boat to London and ourselves caught the night train to Flushing, reaching London on Wednesday night, the 14th of October. In the same train were Messrs. Dunville and Pollock, who in the *Banshee* had landed on the borders of Denmark, and at Flushing we were joined by Professor Huntington and Captain Brabazon who had landed near Brandenberg.

So ended a most interesting trip. The *Britannia*, although two years old, proved per-

Seven ballooning enthusiasts in the basket of *Britannia* during trip No 13, on 7 November 1908. This photograph was taken by Griffith Brewer, using a camera suspended from the balloon's network. The rear four men are, left to right, McClean, Dunville, Hunt and Lockyer, and the three in front are Pollock, Brewer and Bidder. (FLEET AIR ARM MUSEUM)

RIGHT
Wilbur Wright in typically serious demeanour in his Flyer at Le Mans in August 1908. His demonstrations of fully controlled flight astounded spectators, many of whom had hitherto dismissed the Wrights as *'bluffeurs'*. (AUTHOR)

fectly gas-tight and after 29 hours in the air we still had eight bags of ballast left. This would have been sufficient for the whole of Monday night and would have compensated for the contraction of the gas the following afternoon when if we had been able to continue we should probably have had to land about 3 or 4 o'clock.

The *Banshee* did better but was a brand new balloon only having had a trial trip before the race. They, I believe, had 12 bags left after 37 hours in the air, which probably would have taken them for another 36 or even 48 hours. The *Zephyr* descended early [near Brandenberg] owing to a tear in the envelope.

Thus the *Banshee* and the *Britannia* beat all previous records for duration in the air previously made by British balloons.

In November McClean made three 'local' balloon flights, two in the *Britannia*, descending at Ashchurch on the 7th and at Chelmsford on the 14th, and one in the *Corona* on the 15th, when they descended near Godalming.

A fascination with flying

In August 1908 the aviation pioneer Wilbur Wright visited France to demonstrate the aeroplane invented by himself and his brother Orville, and proceeded to astound Europeans with his demonstrations of fully-controlled heavier-than-air flight. Brewer introduced himself to Wilbur at Le Mans at this time, and eventually became the British Empire agent for the Wrights' patents. His fellow Aero Club and ASGB members were well aware of what was happening. On 8 October Brewer and Rolls were among those privileged to fly with Wilbur at Pau. Oswald and Eustace Short had already, in September, announced their firm intention to turn their factory over to the manufacture of

Wilbur Wright's biplane outside its purpose-built hangar on the Hunaudières race track at Le Mans, where the first demonstrations took place. (AUTHOR)

aeroplanes, and when they heard of their customers' experiences in France they decided that they should begin building aeroplanes straight away. Shortly thereafter they were appointed 'Official Aeronautical Engineers' to the Club.

Wilbur kept no log of all his flights in France, but a syndicate composed of Aero Club members under the leadership of Lord Royston, and accompanied by Eustace Short as the syndicate's engineer, visited France in the first week of December 1908 and inspected the Flyer. All syndicate members were formally introduced to Wilbur Wright by Brewer, and given flights of five to eight miles' length.

On 3 December McClean travelled to Paris, and two days later he travelled by train with Brewer to Le Mans and then back to Paris, having accidentally missed Wilbur at Le Mans. On the 6th he lunched with Wilbur Wright and then went again to Le Mans, this time with Wilbur and Eustace Short. On 7 December he first saw Wilbur make a solo flight, writing: 'All being ready, Wilbur Wright first made a trip by him-

self, circling round the ground, sometimes almost touching the tufts of grass and at other times far above our heads. I should say that 40 feet was about the highest that morning.' To compensate for the previous fruitless journey, Wilbur then took Eustace Short aloft. After that it was McClean's turn, and he was given a six-minute passenger flight, starting with a catapult-assisted take-off along a launch rail. He wrote:

Then, with a very slight jerk as Wright loosed the wire catch [this means that the weights (some 1,000lb) at the top of a pylon 25 feet high, were released and gave by rope and pulley a starting impetus to assist the engine thrust], we glided forward along the rail. The engine without any silencer made a terrific noise close to one's head, but this was soon forgotten as, without effort or shock, we left

Wilbur aloft in France. The Flyer was a demanding aircraft to fly, requiring constant inputs from its pilot, but Wilbur handled it with great skill. (AUTHOR)

the rail and on a perfectly even keel raced across the plain. As we came to the far end Wright steered in a sharp curve with the machine at an angle of 10-15° from the horizontal and the tip of the left wing only a few inches from the sand. Righting her again we rushed with the wind, rising this time to some 20 feet from the earth. All the time Wright was moving his two levers and the elevating planes in front never seemed at rest. The ground flew past below our feet and the wind whistled through the wires and supports. . . . After two rounds lasting six minutes and covering some three miles we returned to the starting point and, with the engine stopped, slid gently against the ground, coming to rest within 20 feet of our first point of contact.

The speed of the machine was 25mph.

Wilbur then gave flights to Professor Huntington and Roger W Wallace, the RAeC's Chair-

man. When Eustace returned to England, he and Oswald invited their elder brother, Horace, to join them, and he did so at the end of the year. McClean said that it was after the flights with Wilbur that 'the Aero Club became heavier-than-air minded'. Brewer later wrote that: 'Wilbur never took a fee for any of these passenger flights, and when it is remembered that many people were willing to pay hundreds of pounds for a flight in those early days, these four special flights were a favour of no small character.'

Rolls had decided months earlier that he wanted a Wright Flyer. In this he was in company with McClean, J T C Moore-Brabazon and Alec Ogilvie. Ogilvie ordered his aircraft from Wilbur on 30 December, but at that time the Wrights had yet to decide who would handle their British business.

CHAPTER 2

1909: The Struggle to Fly

In January 1909, as Oswald Short's entry in the company's order book records, McClean ordered 'One aeroplane complete (Shorts No 1)' from Short Bros. This was to be the first aircraft designed by Horace for the company.

In February the Aero Club's first 'aerodrome' was opened on a tract of level marshland between Leysdown (Shellbeach) and Shellness Point (also called Shelness Point and later Shell Ness) on the Isle of Sheppey, Kent. Through

The Short Brothers' aeroplane works at Leysdown, Sheppey, in 1909. The site soon proved problematical and the factory was relocated to Eastchurch. (AUTHOR)

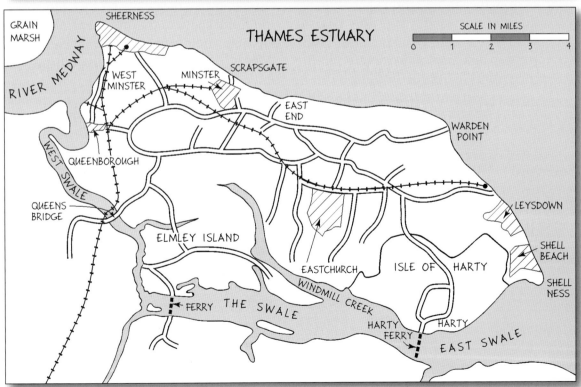

McClean's Short No 1 under construction. This was the very first aeroplane built by the Short Brothers, but unfortunately it proved not to be the success that was anticipated. (AUTHOR)

A three-quarter-front view of McClean's incomplete Short No 1 on display at Olympia in March 1909. Although the skeleton looks quite complete, most of the fabric covering has yet to be applied and the engine and the chain drive to the propellers have yet to be installed. The triangulated supports for the propeller shaft are temporary wooden struts, replaced by tubular steel structures in the finished aeroplane. (AUTHOR)

A three-quarter-rear view of McClean's incomplete Short No 1 at Olympia in March 1909. The outermost of the twin port rudders has been covered. The aircraft was completed in July. (AUTHOR)

Brewer the club leased 400 acres of land from a local estate company, then sub-let half an acre to the Short brothers for their factory. McClean bought the farmhouse Mussel (or Muscle) Manor (now renamed Muswell Manor) for use as the club house, together with flying rights over several hundred acres over the adjacent marshes. He also paid for the work to prepare the airfield, and had a private aeroplane shed erected on site. It was also reported that the coastguard station was being converted for sleeping and other accommodation. Late in March the uncovered airframe of Short No 1 was exhibited at the first Aero and Motor Boat Show at Olympia, London.

Nonetheless, McClean was still eager to obtain a Wright Flyer, and asked Brewer to pursue the matter during the latter's planned visit to the brothers at Pau, France, in February. By 20 February the Wrights had decided that, owing to the small British market for their aeroplanes, they should run the business themselves and subcontract the construction of the aircraft. They therefore broke off negotiations with the various syndicates and asked Brewer if he could recommend a contractor. Unhesitatingly, Brewer proposed the Short Brothers. Brewer returned to England, and on 3 March he wrote to Wilbur and Orville at Pau, saying:

On my return to London Mr McClean was very anxious to find if I had succeeded in getting him a Wright aeroplane. I told him that I had not done so, although as you had decided to have six machines manufactured in England I had no doubt this would enable you to take his order. He says that if the price does not exceed £1,000 he would like to definitely order the first machine that is ready. If he cannot have the first he will willingly take a subsequent one, but I think he deserves the first machine, if it is available, as a reward for his persistence. Would it not be possible for you to accept orders for machines in rotation* (*giving each machine a number) without specifying any date of delivery. If you could do this and also definitely settle on a price, I believe I could get you direct orders for one or two machines beyond that of Mc-Cleans' [sic].

Before leaving Pau I propounded a little plot with Eustace Short and which I can let you into in confidence. This was to get Shorts to hustle with the first machine so that when you passed through England on your way to America and you possibly came to their erecting shop on the Island of Sheppy [sic] to inspect the work, that an aeroplane and starting apparatus should all be complete and only require one of yourselves in order to fly in the air. Given that the day was calm I should think you would be unable to resist the temptation and would try the machine, thus creating a further step in English history.

I am obliged to let you into this secret so as to induce you to see that an engine is supplied for the first machine to enable them to fit it on its bearers and get the flyer in flying order.

On 18 March Orville wrote to Brewer from Paris, saying: 'In regard to the machine for Mr McLean [sic], the first and second machines are already taken, but we should like to enter his order for one of the other six now under construction.'

Horace immediately went to France and made a set of working drawings of the Flyer, and in March the contract for the construction of six Flyers was let to Shorts, the order following immediately after McClean's aeroplane on the Short's order book. Brewer later wrote: 'In advancing this project McClean gave his generous support and probably it is due to him more than to any other English sportsman that Short Brothers were able to carry through their somewhat ambitious effort to start aeroplane designing and building in England.' On 31 March McClean ordered one the six Wrights, at a cost of £1,000 (£200 downpayment), and was allocated Short-Wright No.3. Moore-Brabazon also ordered a Wright, but sold his slot to The Hon. Maurice Egerton before delivery.

On 27 April McClean was given permission to make solo balloon ascents, and made several in the small *Comet*. (Curiously, he did not enter these ascents in his log book of 'balloon voyages', perhaps not considering them 'voyages' in the true sense of the word.) On 18 May he was awarded RAeC Aeronaut's Certificate No 11.

On 4 May the Wright brothers visited Shellbeach; they were to do so twice more in 1909, on 17 August with their sister Katherine, and on 25 October, but they never made any flights there. On 7 May Ogilvie, who had expressed a desire to join the Aero Club, received a letter from McClean, enclosing a member-

McClean's Fédération Aéronautique Internationale (FAI) Aeronaut's certificate, No 11, awarded 18 May 1909. (FLEET AIR ARM MUSEUM)

ship application for Ogilvie to complete. Mc-Clean wrote:

Dear Ogilvie,

I enclose an application for membership of the Aero Club. Will you fill it in, together with the name of your seconder and return it to me.

I have the promise of the third of the Wright machines which Shorts are building.

They will probably all be ready about the same time (a couple of months?).

Rolls, who has one, is going to be taught how to drive in France. I am trusting to luck and any experience I may get with my Short machine.

McClean was still making occasional balloon ascents, and on 22 May he took his sister Anna

Orville and Wilbur Wright visiting the Short factory at Leysdown on 4 May 1909 to see where the Short-Wright Flyers would be manufactured. Wilbur (left) and Orville are the central figures in bowler hats. Second and third from the right are J T C Moore-Brabazon and Griffith Brewer. (AUTHOR)

Orville (left) and Wilbur Wright leave the Short factory at Leysdown on 4 May 1909. In the doorway are Horace Short and (right) Griffith Brewer. (AUTHOR)

This famous group photograph was taken outside Mussel Manor, Leysdown, on the occasion of the Wrights' visit on 4 May 1909. Standing, left to right, are: T.D.F. Andrews, the owner of Mussel Manor; Oswald, Horace and Eustace Short; Frank McClean; Griffith Brewer; Frank Hedges Butler; Dr W J S Lockyer and Warwick Wright. Seated. Left to right, are J T C Moore-Brabazon, Wilbur Wright, Orville Wright and The Hon. C S Rolls. (AUTHOR)

aloft from Hurlingham with two other passengers in an international balloon race, but descended near Romford in Essex. Anna would soon be making aerial passenger flights of a somewhat different nature with her brother!

First attempts

The Short No 1 was delivered to McClean in July, and he began testing it at Leysdown in August. Although evidently Wright-inspired, the biplane differed in several respects, most notably in having rigidly-braced three-bay wings, whereas the outer bays of the Wright Flyers' wings were able to be twisted ('warped'). The airframe was principally of spruce, covered with rubberised Continental balloon fabric. Lateral control was achieved by warping extensions of the wing trailing edges at the outermost bays. A biplane elevator with a fixed fin between the surfaces was carried on booms extending forward from the wing cellule, but there was no tail. Instead, four rudders were fitted between the warping extensions at the wingtips, two on each side. The pilot controlled the elevator using a lever in his left hand, the rudders with a lever in his right hand, and the warping through a foot control. The single engine drove a pair of 10ft-diameter laminated spruce two-bladed pusher propellers through a chain drive. The undercarriage comprised a pair of robust ash skids attached to numerous struts; there were no wheels. Launch was to be achieved using a starting rail.

Accounts of McClean's attempts to fly Short No 1 are scant, and have been confused with his later initial flights on his Short-built Wright. The Wright-type, French-built engine was still awaited in July, so McClean bought a second-hand Nordenfeldt car and had its engine installed in his aeroplane. This was far too heavy, and when the first trials were made in August and September the aeroplane could not even reach the end of its starting rail. However, the *Morning Post* of 12 August reported that McClean had 'fluttered' on the aircraft on 7 August, and *Flight* for 14 August reported vaguely that he had 'carried out tests'. Three days later,

the day of Orville Wright's visit, he performed 'balancing feats', making runs down the launch rail to get the feel of the machine. When a reporter from *The Aero* visited Shellbeach in November he inspected the machine in McClean's hangar, stating: '. . . in the light of the development of the last few months even, it looks tremendously massive and unnecessarily heavy,' but adding 'However, it has shown its ability to fly with an ordinary Bariquand & Marre engine, and it is to be considerably lightened, so more will be heard of it later'. The nature of any 'flight' it might have made is unknown, but it was unlikely to have been more than a brief hop.

McClean wrote in 1938 that:

No suitable engine of light weight was obtainable and the motor car engine installed proved too much for the planes to support; in other words, it would not fly. By the use of a catapult it had to go into the air, but

McClean in Short No 1 on its launch rail at Leysdown, August/September 1909. The fuel tank is above and behind him, the tall vertical tube radiator is behind him on his right, and the chain-and-shaft drives from the engine to the propellers are plainly visible. The heavy construction of the skid undercarriage is evident. (AUTHOR)

Short No 1 after a run along its starting rail at Leysdown on 7 August 1909. It proved incapable of flight. (AUTHOR)

being unable to remain there, it returned hurriedly to *terra firma*, the consequential damage being localised by deliberately weakening the undercarriage. Perhaps it was just as well that the engine was heavy and did not give the centre of pressure and the centre of gravity a chance to come to loggerheads in the air.

In 1950 he wrote, in similar vein:

[The Short No 1] never flew as its motor-car engine (installed in place of a non-existent aero-engine) failed to keep it in the air, after the momentum obtained by dropping 1,400lb of lead from a height of 25 feet had died out. Luckily this loss of momentum happened very quickly, as otherwise the damage due to re-contact with *terra firma* might have extended beyond the undercarriage.

The aircraft was probably soon abandoned, as McClean was already trying out his new Short-Wright biplane. Nothing more was 'heard of it later', but, if *The Aero*'s contemporary report was correct, and McClean's late-life memory at fault, the French-built Wright engine in his Short-Wright No 3 could have been 'lent' to Short No 1 to give McClean a trainer. There are 'windows' for such a transfer both immediately after delivery of Short-Wright No 3 on

16 October and then after a major smash on 6 November (see below).

Meanwhile, evidently aware that his Short No 1 was too heavy and cumbersome, on 3 August (as the Shorts' order book confirms) McClean ordered a new machine, designated Short No 3. The intended engine was not specified.

Back to ballooning

On 3 October McClean, still an enthusiastic aeronaut, piloted Mortimer Singer's new Short-built balloon *Planet* (78,000 cu ft), which had a cotton and rubber envelope (known as Continental fabric), as the British representative in the fourth International Gordon-Bennett race, starting from Zurich with Singer, a 'most capable pilot', acting as his aide. The task had fallen to McClean because the Aero Club's first choice for pilot, Griffith Brewer, was too ill to take part. The *Planet* had made only one previous ascent, and its equipment 'included every possible necessity for a long-distance trip'. The balloon was taken to Zurich in charge of Oswald Short, and re-

McClean makes a brief take-off from the rail in Short No 1 on 7 August 1909. He was reported to have 'fluttered' on this day, but nothing resembling a true flight was accomplished on this machine. (FLEET AIR ARM MUSEUM)

mained in his care until the ascent. McClean was usually frustratingly quiet about his own accomplishments, but he made an exception in this case and provided *Flight* with a first-hand account of this eventful voyage. It appeared in its issue for 27 November 1909, and is given here in full.

Starting at 3.59pm, in beautiful weather, with a gentle wind of 15 or 16 miles an hour, we travelled in a north-easterly direction, and passed low over Kloten and Wulflingen. But the sky behind us was watery, and before long there were clouds in every direction, and the occasional rain that fell was a forerunner of the storm that caught us during the night. We had been warned not to travel too close to the ground, owing to the danger from high-tension electric wires, and we kept our trail-rope up for some distance to avoid possible contact with them. About a quarter-past five we came close to the American balloon in charge of Mr Mix, and found that they had used 4½ bags of ballast as compared to our 5. This cheered us a little, as we had up to then feared that there was something wrong with the balloon, but we were unable to accept their very kind invitation to come over to dinner. They rose to a considerable height and went ahead, so we followed to over 4,000ft in order to get the same wind.

At 6.18, when it was getting dark, we were over the Zeller Zee, an arm of Lake Constance, and were moving in a more northerly direction than any of the other balloons, of which there must have been ten or a dozen in sight. As we were rising, we now had dinner, consisting of cold chicken, cake, pears, and white wine; but before we had finished we plunged into a cloud at a height of 5,200ft and a quick drop followed. We finished our thirteenth bag of ballast at 8 o'clock at a height of 3,600ft. It was raining but fairly clear, and the lights of hundreds of villages twinkled up at us from the ground. But they were unrecognisable one from another, and all we could do was take our direction, which at this time was about 15° north of east. From 8.20, when the moon rose, till 2 o'clock, we took alternate periods of rest. All this time it was raining hard, and at intervals we were enveloped in cloud. The light from the moon was almost negligible, but we could see enough to mark our direction as about north-east to east-north-east. Till 11.30 the *Planet* never attained equilibrium, and in order to save ballast we poured away our water, and at every available opportunity threw away food and stores, but only when near enough to the ground to see that all was clear.

At 11.30 we passed some distance to the north of a large town, which presumably must have been Munich, but at the time we thought we were further north still. Then after trailing over some high ground, when we rose to 7,000ft without the use of any ballast, we crossed a large river running north and south, and our troubles began. In front of us was high ground, and the balloon seemed unable to make up its mind on which side to pass it. First it tended one way and then the other, but very slowly, and for nearly half an hour we remained in doubt. Then suddenly we made straight for the highest point and over it into dense cloud. We could tell that we had reached another valley by the precipitous fall of the balloon, and then the trail-rope touched and another tree-clad mountain rose right in front of us and far above. A bag and a half of ballast only cleared us by some 50ft, and again we were in dense fog, while the wind whistling through our ropes showed us that we were in another ravine. For over an hour this continued, and when at last we saw land below us, we were travelling at some 40 or 50 miles an hour in a direction only a few degrees from the north. It was this period that upset all our calculations, for we took it that north had been our course all the time, whereas it must have been nearly south to land us where it did.

With dawn we sighted one other balloon to the north-east of us, but the downpour that followed blotted it out, and we were left in solitude, with a bleak and lake-strewn land below us, through which wound a river in a deep and rocky gorge. This river we followed for hours, at one time clearing it easily and at

another rushing at express speed right into its chasm. All the time ballast was required, for the rain literally beat us down. It poured in rivulets from the rain-band, but much followed down the leading lines, and prevented any possible sleep in the car, which quickly became soaked through and through.

We had entirely lost our position, as we judged ourselves to be between 100 and 200 miles further north than we were; in fact, we were looking out for the Baltic Sea. Our belief in this was confirmed by the lagoons we passed over at about 8 o'clock, with muddy, sloping banks, and every appearance of being tidal.

In view of the new rule disqualifying anyone who descends in the sea, we consequently attempted to keep within sight of land, and when at a quarter to nine we again entered the clouds, we valved sufficiently to drop once more into the open. This was the beginning of the end, for we again came on to the trail, and it was only with the throwing of much ballast that we cleared the next hills. Then after crossing some cultivated land at a speed of not more than 15 miles an hour we plunged suddenly into a thick white mist, so thick that we could not see the ground even when our trail rope was touching, and here, although we still had some ballast left, we came to earth so gently that we sat on the same spot till assistance arrived and we were lifted into a patch of grass alongside. A crowd soon collected, among them a policeman with fixed bayonet, but all were good-tempered and willing to help in the packing. Luckily one man could speak French, and he showed us the way to the village, where we got the Mayor to sign the 'Livre de Bord'. We were naturally annoyed when we found we had landed far south of our supposed position, and were at Remenin in Bohemia, especially as we could have lasted an hour or two longer.

During the storm it is probable that we travelled south instead of north as calculated on by us. This would account for our very big error in position, as our speed at that time was tremendous.

The greater part of our food and drink had gone overboard, but the locker remained, and our spare clothes and sleeping sacks, in addition to a certain amount of sand.

The Bohemians were most delightful people to land among, though somewhat inquisitive. The process of changing one's socks gave them the greatest joy, in spite of all protest. Most of them were barefooted.

Having got the *Planet* into a cart, we walked to the house where the Mayor lived, and from there took a carriage to Kopidlno station. Once again difficulties of language arose, but in the end we found ourselves at Prague with the balloon safe, and we celebrated our return to civilisation by a hot bath and a Bohemian dinner.

McClean later looked back on the adventure as 'an unpleasing trip with obnoxious moments'.

Self-taught aviator

On 6 October the Shorts wrote to the Wrights, stating that, apart from the engine, 'the No 2 machine is completely ready . . . We should like to know if you could let McClean have the machine because he has his shed adjoining our works . . . he is very cautious and we are sure it would be to your advantage that he should have one of the earliest machines . . .'. In the event Short-Wright No 2 went to Ogilvie, but on 16 October Short-Wright No 3 was delivered to McClean, and he set about learning to fly it. Here he was at disadvantage compared

with Rolls and Alec Ogilvie, the owners of Short-Wrights Nos 1 and 2 respectively, as they had both acquired Wright-type gliders on which to gain some advance experience of the control system. McClean managed a straight flight after a launch on 2 November (his own notes record 'four runs on Wright machine' that day), and more on the following day ('First crash on Wright machine'). He made further runs on the 5th, but on the 6th he crashed again after a 150-yard flight. In its 16 November issue *The Aero* reported:

. . . after three trips along the starting rail merely to get used to the balance, Mr Mc-Clean, at the fourth attempt, turned his elevator upwards to rise at the end of the rail, but, lifting too much, lost the way of the machine [i.e. stalled], swung round sideways, and landed broadside on, with the result that he pulled the skids from under the machine, which sat down on the rear of the wings. It speaks well for the construction of the machine that nothing else was damaged, except for a broken wire or two, although the propeller blades were forced nearly a foot into the ground. They had to be dug out, because any misplaced effort in attempting to lift the machine bodily would probably have broken one or other of them, or would, at any rate, have bent the propeller shafts. The machine flew about seventy yards before it landed, and, short as the flight was, it was quite instructive to watch.

The reporter added that the aircraft was ready for use the next morning.

This accident was also reported in the *Sheerness Times and General Advertiser* for Saturday 13 November 1909, the newspaper's account making the damage appear greater than it evidently was:

On Saturday last . . . Mr McClean made some practice with his Wright biplane. Leaving the rail, he flew just off the ground for a distance of 150 yards, and his machine then went up perpendicularly and fell to the ground with a smash. The aviator fortunately escaped injury, but the machine was extensively damaged. The aeronaut, calmly smoking a cigar, watched the removal of the damaged biplane to Messrs. Short's factory.

The differing estimates of the distance travelled are noteworthy.

By the end of the month, however, he was gaining experience, and it was reported that he had accomplished 'several short flights up to about a quarter of a mile in length'. McClean later recalled:

It must be remembered that there was no one to teach; that one's only experience had been as a passenger with Wilbur Wright for some six minutes; and that the machine was without stability, depending entirely on its controls to keep it in any position. Also, one had to learn quickly, as the only way to get past a tree was to go round it.

When *The Aero*'s reporter visited the ground he had found it 'practically under water', and

McClean flying Short-Wright No 3 in December 1910. He has just left the rail, and, as he recounted in 1931, the picture was obtained 'by getting a photographer to lay on the ground just in front of him and, by the Grace of God, he just missed the photographer, who thus got a beautiful photograph'. This print, inscribed by McClean, was sent to someone as a Christmas and New Year greetings card in 1910. (AUTHOR)

the site was clearly unsuited to year-round use. Moreover, the number of dykes intersecting the site made it impractical. Horace and Eustace Short, finding that their Leysdown aerodrome was rapidly becoming inaccessible owing to the bad state of the roads, traversed the whole of the Isle of Sheppey in an ancient 7hp Panhard car, 'whose distinctive feature was its ability to negotiate dykes and marshes', in search of a more suitable site. They eventually discovered a large flat tract of unbroken country about three miles from Shellbeach. Hearing of this, McClean bought the 205-acre site, Stonepitts Farm, Eastchurch, in November, and gave free use of it and the buildings to members in return for a fixed rent of one shilling per year from the Club. Initially described as the Aero Club's 'auxiliary flying ground', the site was 'very level and free from ditches', and a great improvement on the earlier site. The Leysdown pioneers quickly migrated to the new location, which was soon to replace Shellbeach altogether, most of the sheds at Leysdown being dismantled and re-erected there. McClean had a shed erected to house his aircraft, and took over a small bungalow named 'Stonepitts'.

He later wrote:

The actual agreement between McClean and Aero Proprietary [the limited company that ran the RAeC] for the tenancy of Eastchurch flying-ground did not commence until 1st January, 1911, but from the end of 1909 it was being run by the Aero Club. The first lease was for six years, but later this was altered to 21 years.

On 20 November Rolls flew his Short-Wright to the new aerodrome, having to make an unscheduled stop *en route* to adjust his elevator.

He was the first person to land there. McClean moved his Short-Wright there the same day, but elected to transport it 'in pieces' by road, probably because he had insufficient flying experience to attempt a cross-country flight. By early December he was making 'good flights' of up to about a quarter of a mile. On 5 December Maurice Egerton saw him make a 'flight' of about 400 yards, observing: 'He attempted to turn, but was not high enough for the rising ground, so touched a wing, and stopped. I notice that he elevates very slightly, and so does not get clean away but touches 2 or 3 times before rising. He seems to run his engine slower than I do.' On the 6th McClean broke some wires when trying unsuccessfully to make a turn, and Egerton noted: 'M'Clean [*sic*] tells me he used to be quite fagged after a dozen runs down the rail.' The following day, having heard that Egerton had also suffered a smash on the 6th, he told him that 'it was no good going on, and that he wasn't feeling very fit, and went off home in a hurry'. This spell of pessimism was brief; Egerton recorded that, on the 9th, McClean had broken up his skids 'trying that right-hand turn of his'. His persistence then began to pay. He recorded a 'circuit' on the 16th (Egerton described it as a 'circular mile'), managed a three-mile flight on the 17th according to Egerton, and on the 21st he flew several circuits of the new aerodrome.

On 30 December McClean rounded off the year by flying Short-Wright No 3 from Eastchurch, rounding Short Brothers' works at Leysdown and heading back to Eastchurch. 'A slight mishap' on the way back, when a connecting rod punched a hole in the engine's crankcase, 'caused a hasty descent' near Capel Creek, which he accomplished 'without difficulty'. He had flown seven miles.

CHAPTER 3

1910: An Accomplished Pilot

Although flying continued at Eastchurch, McClean was absent. A few days after the Leysdown flight he sailed from England on an expedition he had organised to Port Davey, Tasmania, to witness and report on a solar eclipse that was due to occur on 9 May 1910. (Thanks to rain and heavy cloud he 'saw nothing', though he did produce a report.)

In his absence, work progressed apace on preparing the Eastchurch Flying Ground, and by the end of January *Flight* was able to report that all of the ditches would be filled and the necessary draining completed 'in the course of the next few weeks'. Eight RAeC members already had sheds erected on the site.

By 1 February the French-made Bollée engine of McClean's Short-Wright was in the workshop having its crankcase patched. *The Aero* reported on the 'temporary loss' of McClean in its issue of 15 February (the day that the prefix 'Royal' was granted to the Aero Club), saying that he was 'a man who objects strenuously to having his doings made public, but, as he is not now here to resent it, we may say that he acquired a command over his Short-Wright machine just before he left which put him right in the front rank of fliers'. The magazine then described the Leysdown flight more fully. 'The very day he left England he flew two or three times round the Eastchurch ground, then right across to Shelness, round the ground there right out to the sea wall, and half way back to Eastchurch, where unhappily engine trouble forced him to come down, thus spoiling what would have been one of the finest flights yet done in this country. As it was, the distance covered was between twelve and fifteen miles, which is a flight well worthy of note.' The writer then said: 'Mr McClean has unlimited nerve and pluck, and he really understands his machine, so we look forward to some fine performances on his return'.

The reporter saw the dismantled errant engine from McClean's aircraft in the Shorts' factory at Leysdown. 'It is quite clear,' he wrote, 'that the seizing of the big ends was caused simply through lack of proper oil channels in the bearing brasses.' These French-built Wright engines had many faults, and required much rectification even before the aeroplanes in which they were mounted had flown. Egerton had noted that: 'None of the bearings have any oil grooves, except the straight ones opposite the oil-outlet in the shaft, nor are the two halves of the bearings backed off at the join, hence the oil cannot travel along the bearings, being a good fit, consequently after 10 minutes or so at high speed a seize is inevitable.' A remedy was being incorporated in all future engines.

In its issue for 5 February *Flight* published an article by Griffith Brewer entitled 'Aeronautics for the Navy'. In it, Brewer wrote of operating aeroplanes from ships under way, and discussed the value of aeroplane scouts to the fleet. 'Above all,' he added, '. . . should the naval authorities give some favoured young officers a chance to see what can be done, let us hope they will not disdain to take advantage of the work already accomplished by others. Thousands of pounds have been spent by the Aero Club and its members, and all knowledge and facilities thus acquired are at the disposal of the services when the authorities realise that the air is an element already invaded by man.' As we shall see, McClean was to play a leading role in introducing the navy to aviation. A step in this direction was taken that same month, when Commander Curtis and the officers of the Royal Naval Depot at Sheerness intimated that the members of the Aero Club could consider themselves honorary members of their mess.

A mystery machine

Short No 3 (also designated S.III) was much longer in building than its forebears. A real 'mystery machine', in previous accounts of the company's pre-First World War work it has become confused with another Short product. The aircraft initially identified as Short No 3 was a small biplane with a 35hp Green engine that was exhibited at the second Olympia Aero Show, held from 11 to 19 March 1910, and the customer was said to be the Hon. C S Rolls. In the 1970s, however, this attribution was challenged when Short Brothers regained possession of the company's early aircraft order book, which shows that Frank McClean ordered 'One aeroplane (Shorts No 3)' on 3 August 1909 (as mentioned earlier). In addition, the word 'delivered' has been appended to the original entry for the order. It was therefore thought that this was the machine displayed at Olympia, but more recently a letter from Shorts to the Wrights, dated 8 March 1910, has been found in the Wright archive in the Library of Congress in Washington, D.C., which shows beyond dispute that Rolls was the customer for the Olympia aeroplane, and that it was the small biplane delivered to him on 16 March 1910 as the 'RPG IV' (Rolls Powered

Glider No IV). Drawing numbers show that the Short No 3 and the RPG IV were under construction concurrently.

This leaves the problem of identifying McClean's Short No 3, as there is no known general-arrangement drawing or photograph of it. However, surviving component drawings dated between 7 August 1909 and 23 May 1910 do exist, and reveal that its wings spanned 30ft 0in and had a chord of about 5ft 10in, that the ribs were pitched at 15in intervals, the canard elevator spanned 8ft 11in and the tailplane 4ft 10in. Moreover, an undated entry between 30 July and September 1910 in the order book records 'repairs etc' to this aircraft, so it seems that McClean (or someone else) might have attempted to fly it, but there is no record of its fate. In truth, the mysterious Short No 3 was almost certainly rendered obsolete even before it was completed by the advent of the far better Short-Sommer, as recounted below, and was probably quickly abandoned. Unfortunately its configuration, powerplant installation and control system remain unknown.

Although the Rolls machine displayed on Shorts' Olympia stand was described as being 'of special light design', Horace Short seems to have found it hard to reconcile the strength and lightness that were equally essential if an aeroplane was to be capable of flight, choosing to err on the side of strength and sacrifice lightness. Shortly after the Olympia Aero Show the *Daily Mail*'s aviation reporter, Harry Harper, visited the company's works. In the newspaper's 4 April 1910 issue he reported:

Out in an almost deserted corner of the Isle of Sheppey, with nothing but flat grassland around them, intersected with broad dykes, stand several queer buildings, from which, by the removal of a couple of planks, all access may speedily be cut off when privacy is desired – as it often is.

Over the major portion of these buildings, where much secret work is now afoot, I have just had the privilege of being conducted by an extraordinarily interesting man. The buildings are part of a well-organised factory for the building of aeroplanes; the man is Mr Horace Short, now an enthusiastic designer of British-built aeroplanes, but until little more than a year ago one of the right-hand men of the Hon. Charles Parsons in the construction of steam turbines and in experimental work.

I saw a hundred specially trained men hard at work building aeroplanes. Amid the clatter of hammers, the clang of metals, and the swishing sound of planes passing up and down long rods of wood, a big biplane was growing – a queer medley of wood and wire and thin steel tubing, all seemingly ridiculously heavy when one remembered that it was designed to fly through the air.

"A thousand pounds is the weight of a soundly built biplane, with engine in it and the aviator in his seat," explained the maker of flying machines. "When you see a man 1,000 feet high, his life dependent upon the wood and metal and fabric you have given him, it makes you determine not to stint the weight where it is possible to make an aeroplane strong. As a matter of fact, the fashion – there are already fashions in aeroplanes – is to fit heavier and therefore more reliable engines than was first the case, and to put stronger wood and wire into the machine's construction. An aeroplane swoops to the ground at forty miles an hour on landing; flimsy wheels or skids crumple up like paper. There must be strength."

And then we passed through test rooms where every length of wire destined for use in an aeroplane was being subjected to enormous strains, where sections of wooden rods were being examined with microscopes to detect flaws, where nuts and bolts and connecting levers were undergoing a merciless scrutiny.

As my guide was leading me to the part of the factory where propellers are made, we heard a curious penetrating hum from without. We stopped and gazed through a window. It was a quiet evening, with the clear faint light that heralds the dusk. From out of the wide expanse of land which forms the aerodrome of the Royal Aero Club came an aeroplane on the wing. It wheeled superbly not far from our window. Then it darted off again and was lost to view. Mr Short smiled. The aeroplane which flew off so splendidly into the dusk was a creation of his own brain, with a British pilot at its controlling levers.

"In a year's time," he declared with emphasis, "England will not only have made up her lost ground in aviation, but will be leading the whole world." Then we entered a long, airy workroom. Everywhere there were long wooden aeroplane propellers in all stages of construction – some crude, shapeless forms of wood, others half-turned to the requisite curve to thrust upon the air, others again quite finished and being coated with a dull, lead-coloured paint. Each propeller is built up from three sections of wood, which are glued and pressed together; each section of wood is critically examined. Even with this care propellers crack and break under the enormous strain.

"If I am very lucky," said Mr Short, "I get a 60 per cent efficiency with an aeroplane propeller. [The Wright brothers had already exceeded this by a substantial amount, achieving 66 per cent efficiency with the propellers of their first Flyer of 1903, and attain-

Rolls in his Gnome-engined Sommer biplane at Eastchurch at end of April 1910. His enthusiasm for this design led to its adoption by Shorts in place of the Wright biplane. (AUTHOR)

Short Brothers' works in 1910, after their removal to Eastchurch. (AUTHOR)

ing an extraordinary 81.5 per cent with the propellers of the Flyer III of 1905.] What we are straining every nerve to do now is to make the aeroplane propeller as efficient in the air as the marine propeller is in the water. With propellers doing more efficient work, we can give the over-driven engine a respite, with the result that they will run longer without breakdowns. And, apart from propeller efficiency, aviation engines are improving to an extent that is astounding when one remembers what is asked of them."

In the assembling shops we came to a bi-plane practically complete. There was no weight stinted in it. A big engine sat in a metal framework in the centre of it. There were landing skids with broad, strong timbers in them. The craze to weaken struts and stays by tapering them in order to lessen resistance to the wind had been completely ignored. The aeroplane looked so big and strong that it seemed scarcely credible that it should raise itself in the air and carry a man.

"Strength and weight – both are beginning to enter more and more into the construction of a flying machine," said Mr Short. "The

Like several other owners and pilots of early Wright biplanes, McClean later had a wheeled undercarriage added to his Short-Wright No 3, doing away with the need for a take-off rail, plus a rear elevator behind the twin rudders. The protective upward-curved 'horn' on the lower wingtip leading edge was a distinctive feature of Short-built Wrights. (AUTHOR)

weight of the aeroplanes of the future, and the speed at which they will fly, will give them the power to remain in the air when high winds are blowing."

During McClean's absence several interesting developments took place. Early in 1910 Rolls bought a French-built Sommer biplane, a pusher type very similar to the Henry Farman biplane, with monoplane tailplane and forward elevator and powered by the ingenious and light 50hp seven-cylinder Gnome air-cooled rotary engine. He exhibited his new acquisition in the RAeC's section at the Olympia show. Impressed by the engine's reliability and simplicity, Rolls exulted over the freedom from the cumbersome ground handling and catapult

Charles Rolls prepares to take off from Dover on 2 June 1910 for his successful non-stop cross-Channel return flight. For this exploit he used his French-built Wright biplane, fitted with a fixed tailplane aft of the rudders and flotation bags as a precaution in the event of a ditching. Just over a month later he was dead. (AUTHOR)

45

launching of the Wright machine, with the need to move the launch rail when the wind shifted.

Evidently impressed by the Sommer, Horace Short seems to have seen the light, as he now designed a new machine on similar lines. The first example to be completed was the Short-Sommer No 1/Short S.27, ordered by another Short customer, the Irish-American Cecil Grace, on 8 April. In May Short Bros moved from Shellbeach into a newly-built factory at Eastchurch. Late that same month the S.27, powered by a water-cooled eight-cylinder ENV engine, was rolled out and flown by Grace. Also during May, McClean's Short-Wright was fitted with a fixed tailplane and wheeled undercarriage, among other modifications.

The Short-Wright and Short pilots, Rolls, Moore-Brabazon, Ogilvie and Grace, all became competent pilots, making increasingly longer flights and venturing cross-country. Tragically, at Bournemouth on 12 July Charles Rolls met with a fatal accident when his French-built Wright biplane suffered an in-flight structural failure during a spot-landing competition.

Back in the air

When Frank McClean arrived back in England late in June he was clearly itching to get back into aviation. He attended the Bournemouth meeting on 13–17 July, not as a participant, but possibly to help sort out the sad aftermath of the Rolls tragedy, and was at the Blackpool meeting from 29 July to 2 August, but again not as a flyer. On 3 August he moved into 'Stonepitts', so that he was now living on the flying ground. In its issue of 10 September *Flight* reported that, on Wednesday 31 August, 'Mr Frank McClean was . . . out for a short trial along the ground on the new Short biplane

constructed for him. This machine is the first of Messrs. Short Bros' design to be fitted with a Gnome engine.' The description of the aircraft as 'new' and having been built for McClean is misleading. In fact this was Short-Sommer No 2 (c/n S.28), initially powered by a 60hp ENV engine, which had been built for J T C Moore-Brabazon, who had flown it once or twice at Eastchurch and then entered it for the Bournemouth 1910 meeting, but had not flown at that event. Following Charles Rolls's death, Brabazon's pregnant wife had asked him to give up flying, and, as he wrote in his autobiography *The Brabazon Story* (Heinemann, London, 1956): 'I acquiesced, for, quite apart from our sadness at Charlie's death, I was beginning to think flying a sort of circus in which the private man had no place – firms were producing planes and paying professionals to fly them'. Brabazon had expressed his feelings on the matter in a letter published in the 13 August 1910 issue of *Flight*, when he wrote:

There seems to be an impression that I have definitely given up aviation, owing to its dangers or what I do not know, so that if you will grant me a few lines of your paper for an explanation of my apparent cessation of experiments, you would do me a favour.

First of all, *re* the danger of aeroplaning. This, to my mind, is diminishing every day – granted, owing to there being many more aviators, there are, consequently, more accidents; but nothing will persuade me that aviation is not getting safer every day, engines are more reliable, machines more stable, engineers more conversant than formerly with the construction of machines.

It seems, therefore, to me hardly fair, either to Mr Cockburn [a fellow aviator] or myself, to assume that we are giving up aviation because it is, or has become, dangerous. If it is dangerous now, it was *more* dangerous a year or more ago, before most of the present-day cracks [i.e. crack pilots] had learnt to handle a machine.

What has happened is that Mr Cockburn, as also myself, have realised the small chance and impossible position the real amateur has at public meetings. He has to compete, not against men of similar means with machines of their own, but against firms with a great deal of capital at their back, and with the idea of advertisement before them accruing from winning certain prizes, a situation entirely similar to what occurred in early motor-racing days.

An engine misfires! No one thinks of putting it right. Another engine is slipped on to the machine. A wheel buckles. Another machine is brought out, while half-a-dozen mechanics from the "maison" repair the disarranged parts.

Were I a millionaire, I possibly could compete against such organisation, but unfortunately I am not, and therefore I believe it best to let it alone as far as appearing in public is concerned. In the very early days, private men with time and money were wanted, and I think, perhaps, did a lot to help the movement on, but now the private man is the unfortunate individual the cracks wish to sell machines to.

Do not let it be supposed I think ill of the professional with a firm at his back. On the contrary, I think he is doing a lot of good, more than the private man now could; but do not let us confuse the two individuals, the private individual and the firm's professional.

The day of the private investigator is over, and I for one very much regret it, but it is for the good of the movement that it is so, and consequently we must welcome it.

Flying in public, or at meetings, I certainly have given up, under present conditions, but

that in no way is the same as abandoning flying altogether. To abandon aviation at the present time would be similar to abandoning motoring after the Paris-Bordeaux race, when the automobile movement was in its infancy.

When I took up aviation nearly four years ago, I looked upon it as a scientific investigation with a vast future before it. In that future I still believe, but whether the best interests of aviation are being studied by turning a highly complex mechanical problem into a travelling form of entertainment, I very much question.

That Mr Rolls' death was *directly due* to this form of gymkhana I emphatically believe, and, on this account alone, you will forgive me if the tone of this letter is somewhat bitter against aviation meetings of any kind.

Consequently Brabazon sold S.28 to McClean. (It was subsequently misidentified as S.26, which at that time still belonged to G C Colmore.) He also placed a classified advertisement in the 20 August issue of *Flight*, seeking a buyer for the 'Short Wright biplane' (actually Short No 2), in which he had won the £1,000 *Daily Mail* prize for the first closed-circuit one-mile flight by a British pilot in an all-British aeroplane, and the British Michelin Cup and £500 for the longest flight made by an all-British machine before 31 March 1910. Describing the aircraft as 'being used for exhibition', he offered it for 'Immediate disposal, without Engine £200; or near offer'. Apparently there were no takers, as another classified advertisement appeared in the magazine's 3 September issue that simply read: 'Biplane, winner of "Daily Mail" £1,000 Prize, Michelin Trophy, etc., fine condition, has been used for exhibition; best cash offer gets it by September 10th . . .', and in the 24 September and 1 October issues the advertisement said, in

Frank McClean's first Short-Sommer, No 2/S.28, was acquired from Moore-Brabazon. This photograph was taken by William J Lockyer, who was given his first flight as an aeroplane passenger in this machine by McClean at Eastchurch on 22 October 1910. (AUTHOR)

part: '. . . splendid condition; accept £100, or best first offer; material worth double'. In truth it was already an outmoded design, and the airframe would only have been of use as a potential source of materials and components. At this early stage its significance in the early development of British aviation was probably not fully appreciated, and this historic aeroplane, which should have been preserved for posterity, did not survive.

By this time some of the owners of Short-Wright and early Short aircraft had been trying to sell them. Over some months Grace, Moore-Brabazon and Rolls had all been placing classified advertisements in *Flight*, offering various

machines for sale. Grace was not only trying to sell his Short-Wright No 5 and his Antoinette monoplane, but also his 'Short Farman' (i.e. Short-Sommer; probably S.27, later acquired by McClean). Ogilvie, however, remained a staunch adherent of the Wright aeroplanes, and continued to fly and modify them.

On 2 September McClean made 'several long hops' in S.28, then circled the ground two or three times at a height of about 20ft. 'This,'

Even when others had changed over to the Sommer-type biplanes, Alec Ogilvie maintained his allegiance to the Wright type. Here he is flying his Short-Wright No 2 after fitting it with a wheeled undercarriage. (AUTHOR)

Frank McClean's Royal Aero Club aviator's certificate, No 21, dated 20 September 1910. He had made the qualifying flight and performed the required evolutions at Eastchurch on the previous day. (FLEET AIR ARM MUSEUM)

McClean's Fédération Aéronautique Internationale (FAI) aviator's certificate, No 21, also dated 20 September 1910. (FLEET AIR ARM MUSEUM)

said *Flight*, 'at only the third attempt, and with the engine not yet adjusted to give off its full power, was undoubtedly a promising performance.' In this aeroplane, at Eastchurch on 19 September, McClean, now aged 34, set out to complete the tests for his aviator's certificate,

and 'after negotiating the course several times in greatly improved style, he successfully accomplished the necessary circuits at an altitude of some 20ft'. At an RAeC committee meeting on the following day he was awarded Aviator's Certificate No 21.

Although these pictures are said to show Frank McClean flying Short-Sommer No 3 (S.26) at Eastchurch on 5 November 1910, this is probably wrong, as that machine still belonged to Colmore at that time. It is almost certainly S.28/Short-Sommer No 2, ex-Moore-Brabazon. (AUTHOR)

The late awarding of his certificate always remained something of a sore point with McClean. In *Fellowship of the Air: The Jubilee Book of the Royal Aero Club 1901-1951* (Iliffe, London, 1951) the author, B J Hurren, writes: '. . . Sir Frank McClean recalls that he, although obviously in the very front rank of the pioneers, was abroad when the first British certificates were mooted and then issued. It was therefore with some degree of annoyance that he found himself omitted from a most justifiable pride of seniority, and through the post was eventually awarded certificate No. 21.' While it was certainly unfortunate that McClean's absence deprived him of an earlier certificate to which he might have been entitled by merit, he seems to have forgotten that he did actually take the required tests that had been introduced by the RAeC in February 1910, while he was abroad.

On the 22nd he made several flights, includ-

Frank McClean prepares to take his friend Dr William Lockyer for a flight in the S.28 at 10.40am on 6 November 1910. Lockyer was the first passenger to be taken up by McClean. (Fleet Air Arm Museum)

ing two trips to Shellbeach, and in the afternoon of the 23rd Cecil Grace flew McClean's Gnome-powered S.28 for 20min. On Friday 30 September McClean made several circuits over Eastchurch and then flew along the coast to Shellbeach, turned, and flew back to the Swale. Just before crossing the river he lost height in a 'rather sharp turn' and dropped lower still as he crossed the water. He just cleared the bank on the opposite side, but before he could gain height he was confronted by a dyke. Although he jumped it, the tail scraped the bank as he landed on rough ground and the rest of the aircraft ended up in a ditch. Although the tail and skid were damaged, McClean was unhurt, and *Flight* said that it was 'one of Mr McClean's best performances, and it is a great pity this accident occurred to mar the finish'.

Following Rolls's death, McClean bought his Eastchurch sheds from the executors for £275. They were later used to house the two aircraft loaned to the Admiralty in 1911. Also in September McClean ordered a monoplane that was destined never to be built, and his own Short-Sommer, No 6/S.33, which he planned to use to compete for the £4,000 Baron de Forest prize. First announced in July 1909, this was to be awarded to the British aviator who, from a point fixed upon by himself, and approved by the RAeC, flew the longest distance non-stop from England to the Continent in an all-British aeroplane during 1910.

At an RAeC committee meeting on Tuesday 27 September McClean was one of nine members asked to join a special committee to deal with cases of club members or certificated aviators making unnecessary flights over towns or thickly populated areas.

In its issue of 15 October *Flight* reported that he had been making good flights, and that on 4 and 5 October he 'made half-a-dozen trips of some 20min each at an average height of about 100ft'. 'His machine behaved splendidly,' the account continued, 'and Mr McClean appears quite at ease in her now that he has accustomed himself to the Gnome engine.' The magazine added that he spent a total of nearly six hours in the air on the following Sunday (the 9th), in flights averaging half an hour in duration. 'The feature of his flying this week,' it concluded, 'has been some very creditable exhibitions of planing [gliding with the engine off].'

On Saturday 15 and Sunday 16 October a 'large number' of naval officers from Sheerness and Chatham visited Eastchurch and witnessed some flights by McClean. On 22 October he made some more good solo flights, and also made several short ones carrying a passenger for the first time, the gentleman in question being his friend and fellow astronomer Dr W J S Lockyer. Early in the week ending 29 October he made more good flights, but then his aircraft dropped several feet after a *vol plane* [engine-off glide] and suffered considerable damage to its undercarriage. 'It speaks well for the machine,' said *The Aero*, 'that it was not completely broken up.'

Recalling this aircraft (which he described as being 'of Farman type') in the late 1930s, McClean wrote:

The pilot sat on the leading edge with his feet in space and a strut to hold on to with one hand while the other did the work. The passenger (if any) sat behind him and also held on, but in moments of nervous breakdown was liable to grip the pilot with his or her knees, thereby making the manipulation of the controls more erratic.

. . . These machines did not necessarily fly when they first left the Works, but if after charging the largest bumps on Eastchurch Aerodrome they refused to stay in the air, extra lengths were added to the wing tips and success thereby achieved, even though the speed was reduced from some thirty-five miles an hour to a possible thirty.

November saw McClean making numerous flights. In its issue for the 19th *Flight* reported:

On Wednesday, the 9th inst, he brought out [his Gnome-engined Short biplane], and despite a stiffish breeze immediately rose to about 100ft. He was content, on this occasion, to remain within the immediate vicinity of the grounds, flying in circles and figure eights and executing several successful *vols plane*, at which . . . he is becoming quite an adept. One of these exhibitions was particularly clean, the machine approaching to within 15-20ft of the ground before the engine was re-started. Later in the day Mr McClean was again seen to advantage, on this occasion making several short trips carrying a lady passenger.

On Thursday, the 10th, Mr McClean . . . made a splendid flight of over an hour's duration [*The Aero* put it at 67 minutes]. He frequently passed over Harty and the surrounding country, returning each time along the coast line, and ultimately effecting a good landing from a steady *vol plane* of some 150ft.

Friday was an impossible day, but on Saturday Mr McClean beat all his previous performances by remaining aloft for well over an hour and a quarter. His journeyings on this occasion extended over Harty and Shellbeach on the one side, and Queenborough and Sheerness on the other.

Mr McClean's performances this season have been consistently good, and his total mileage since July now stands at well over 600. His machine has behaved splendidly, and has not given the slightest trouble since leaving the works.

In contradiction of the *Flight* report, *The Aero* said that he had made a 'beautiful flight lasting for forty minutes at about 100ft high' on the Friday, covering the course nineteen times, and that he flew both in the morning and afternoon on the Saturday, taking a passenger on the second occasion.

Another aeroplane

Flight's report went on to say that, on Tuesday the 15th, McClean brought out his latest Short biplane, 'on the lines of the Farman, but [embodying] all the original features of Short Bros' productions'. The report continued:

The machine was only completed on Monday, but after devoting about half-an-hour to the tuning up of its Gnome engine, Mr McClean essayed a short trial. She rose at the first attempt in about 100yd or so, and flying at about 50ft Mr McClean completed several circuits before bringing her down. After lunch Mr McClean was quickly off the mark, rising sharply to a height of some 150ft. Keeping at this altitude he completed eight or nine circuits of the ground in good time, when he landed for a few further adjustments to the engine. Shortly afterwards he made a further flight, and this time gave a good exhibition of 'planing'. These three flights represented a total of some three minutes short of the hour – not bad for the first spin. The machine rides the wind beautifully, answers to the helm readily, and from all appearances will develop a good turn of speed when the engine is thoroughly tuned up.

This was Short-Sommer No 6/S.33, powered by a 50hp Gnome, which, according to Short's order book, was delivered to McClean on 12 November. It was this machine which McClean intended to use for his attempt for the de Forest Prize, but in its original form, powered by a French engine, it was ineligible. Competitors were required to produce a certificate from the aircraft manufacturer certifying that both the machine and its motor were of British manufacture. Nonetheless, McClean used it to gain experience of long flights. Following a brief 15-minute flight at dusk on the 16th, at 3.20 on the afternoon of the 21st, the next day when the weather was suitable, he ascended to 300–400ft, circled the Eastchurch course twice, then made a wide detour round Stanford Hill and headed for Eastchurch. Skirting the village, he made for Leysdown, then passed over the Swale and circled over Whitstable. As he returned via Harty he 'experienced an adverse current which caused the aircraft to drop some 100ft', but ascended again to between 300 and 400ft. After 40 minutes in the air he glided in from about 150ft to land outside his shed at 4pm. He then took up his mechanic as a passenger for some half-a-dozen circuits of the ground at 50–80ft. McClean was reported to be 'strongly fancied' among the Baron de Forest Prize competitors, and intended to start from Dover on his attempt.

On the morning of the 23rd McClean flew circles and figure eights for 35 minutes, finishing with a *vol plane* from 200ft. At 2.30pm he went up again, making a half-hour circling flight at about 400ft and 'giving a good exposition of gliding', and then took a passenger up for a 10-minute flight. Two days later he made another 30-minute flight. At midday on Saturday the 26th he 'gave a sound exhibition flight of about half an hour, turning and planing in excellent style', and then spent 15 minutes making passenger-carrying flights. After that, McClean in the S.28 and Grace in McClean's S.33 set off together, the former at about 400ft and the latter at over 1,000ft, passing over

Sheerness and returning to give 'a brilliant exhibition' over the grounds before landing.

It could well have been during this period that a rather alarming event occurred, though the actual date seems not to have been recorded. McClean often treated ladies to flights, and Major C C Turner, in his book *The Old Flying Days* (Sampson, Low, Marston, London, 193?), relates:

One morning when Mr McClean was preparing to make a flight an unknown lady approached and begged to be taken up as a passenger. The pilot was not too eager to do this, but as another passenger had just been landed he had no ready excuse for refusal. He was on the point of assenting when Mr Oswald Short took him aside and remarked in a low voice: "That woman is carrying a long knife in her stocking."

The idea of taking her into the air became even more distasteful and the pilot was preparing to refuse when Horace Short came up, and while the lady was gazing at the aeroplane, and giving a glance from time to time to the three men, he learned about this extraordinary affair, refraining from laughing only with difficulty.

"Well, Short," said Mr McClean addressing Horace, "if you will get the knife away from her I'll take her up."

"All right," said Horace; and to their amazement he approached the lady and began to converse with her, strolling away from the machine towards the Club House.

In two minutes they returned, and he carelessly rejoined his brother and Mr McClean, and without being observed by the lady showed them a long and formidable knife.

With no great enthusiasm the pilot now fulfilled his part of the bargain; the lady was given a flight. Shortly afterwards they learned that she had been readmitted to a nursing home for mental cases!

Horace Short never revealed the cajolery by which he had disarmed this dangerous aeroplane passenger.

Creating naval aviators

In the 3 December issue of *Flight* it was announced that the Committee of the RAeC had offered to place two aeroplanes at the disposal of the Admiralty for the use of naval officers based at Sheerness and Chatham, at the Club's flying ground at Eastchurch. The aircraft were reported to be Gnome-engined landplanes, and several Club pilots had promised to assist in giving practical instruction to the officers. The Admiralty thanked the Club for the offer, which was made known officially on 6 December in a general order issued by Admiral Sir C C Drury, C-in-C at the Nore. The aircraft were to be available 'at all times, free of charge, but naval officers piloting them were to be asked to make good any damage done', and to conform with the rules they had to become members of the RAeC. The number of officers who accepted the offer was to be limited to four. Towards the end of the month the Admiralty announced in a General Fleet Order that Colonel H S Massey of The Aerial League of the British Empire would be delivering a lecture on aviation to Vice Admiral Sir George Neville (commanding the Third and Fourth Divisions of the Home Fleet) and the officers of the Fleet and Dockyard at Sheerness in January 1911, and that officers who decided to volunteer for an 'aviation course' were to give their names to the admiral after the lecture. It was also stated that junior officers from other fleets and depots could volunteer, and that the course would last about six months and cost £20, but that the Admiralty might see fit to pay the fee for the selected officers.

At about 12.30pm on Sunday 4 December McClean and Grace brought out their Short biplanes and flew circuits in a stiff breeze for some time. Then, on the afternoon of Monday the 5th, Grace was again flying S.33, and had flown to Sheerness at 600ft and then right back across the island to Leysdown, again in a stiff breeze, when he found that the engine 'was not running properly'. Cutting the engine at about 1,000ft, Grace 'thanks to his nerve and judgement . . . landed perfectly on the nearest available piece of flat land without so much as straining a wire', an account in the 4 January 1911 issue of *The Aero* states. 'However,' the account continues, 'that piece of ground was miles from the hangars, and the machine had to be lifted bodily over many fences, and planked over many dykes, but, because the machine was Frank McClean's and not his own, Grace refused to leave it out in the rain, so he and his men laboured far into the night [towing the aircraft back across the marshes to Eastchurch by car from 3pm to 10pm] to get it home. Next day the men had a holiday. Grace merely turned to other work as calmly as if he had not had a hair's-breadth escape with his life, followed by six hours strenuous work in the wet and cold and dark only the day before. Of such stuff are heroes made.' It was initially reported that he found that a piston ring had failed, but it was subsequently stated that a connecting rod had broken, 'practically wrecking the inside of the engine'.

An entry in Short's order book for 10 December records alterations 'to No 33 Machine (60 job)'. It has to be assumed that this refers to the fitting of a British engine in S.33, both to replace the broken Gnome and make the aircraft eligible for McClean's attempt for the de Forest Prize. The engine was probably a 60hp Green. This was quickly done, as *The Aero* reported that McClean had his 'Green driven

This picture is believed to depict S.28 after McClean's landing accident on 11 December 1910, when a strong wind blew the aircraft over on to a wingtip and broke the main spars of the lower wing and a forward-elevator support boom. (FLEET AIR ARM MUSEUM)

Short biplane . . . which he intends using for the de Forest flight' out on the afternoon of the 11th. Unfortunately, after flying a few circuits he broke a skid 'owing to a rough landing'. Undeterred, McClean then brought out his 'Gnome Short' (S.28), but after making a few circuits 'had to descend'. As he came in to land, the strong wind that was blowing at the time tilted the aircraft on to a wing, breaking the main spar of the lower plane and a strut.

In mid-December, at the suggestion of Claude Grahame-White, the RAeC Committee again took up 'with considerable activity' the question of bringing about the formation of an Aeronautical Reserve Corps, which it hoped would form the nucleus of a very wide movement throughout the whole of Great Britain. Needless to say, McClean was on the eight-man Special Committee formed to formulate a detailed plan of action.

Another tragic loss

On 18 December McClean took the opportunity of a break in the week's rainy weather to fly a few circuits in his 'Short Green-engined biplane' (the re-engined S.33), despite a gusty wind. *Flight* reported that 'it was obvious that the machine was not up to the mark, and the engine not turning up to speed'. It transpired that this was caused by the radiator being choked with scale and sediment. On the same day Grace flew his ENV-engined Short (almost certainly S.32) from Sheppey to Swingate Downs, Dover, in readiness for an attempt for the de Forest Prize. The fifth Short-Sommer pusher biplane, S.32 had been delivered to Grace on 7 July 1910. Later in the year it was allotted for conversion to a tractor biplane for Grace (it was initially intended to use S.27 for this), but this work was not begun before he took it Dover.

Shortly thereafter the manufacturer carried out 'work on 33 at Dover' on Cecil Grace's account, which suggests that McClean had lent the aircraft to Grace for the latter's attempt for the de Forest Prize. This is quite possible as, according to *The Aero* of 4 January 1911, both McClean and G C Colmore, who had his repaired S.26 at Dover in readiness for an attempt on the prize, '. . . wisely recognising the risks involved, and knowing the capabilities of their machines, decided not to start . . .'. The reason for Grace's change of mounts is undetermined, but he was certainly familiar with S.33, having flown it several times.

At about 9am on the morning of 22 December Grace left Dover and flew to France, but landed at Les Baraques, near Calais, as the weather militated against his chances of beating the 169 miles flown by Tom Sopwith from Eastchurch to Thirimont in Belgium on 18 December. He decided to fly back to Dover to be ready for a fresh attempt, and arranged with the captain of the mail boat *Pas de Calais* to

One of the last photographs taken of Cecil Grace on 22 December 1910, before he left Dover on McClean's Short S.33 (Short-Sommer No 6) to fly to mainland Europe in a last-minute attempt to win the Baron de Forest prize. After abandoning the attempt in France, Grace disappeared over the Channel on the return flight. (AUTHOR)

Cecil Grace prepares to take off from Dover in S.33 on 22 December 1910. Just why he chose to use McClean's aeroplane rather than his own S.32 is not known. (AUTHOR)

take off some time after the vessel's departure and follow its course from its smoke. Unfortunately the ship was some 10 minutes late leaving Calais, and Grace flew out to sea before it sailed, apparently becoming engulfed in the bad sea fog. He was heard passing over the North Goodwins Lightship and seen by a fishing boat near the East Goodwins, but then vanished without trace. A fortnight later his cap and goggles were found on the beach at Mariakerke, Belgium. A terse entry in the Short's order book against the S.33 records the aircraft as being 'Lost at Sea'.

In its issue for 4 January 1911, *The Aero*'s reporter wrote: 'On Thursday, December 22nd, I saw him [Grace] leave the Swingate Downs. . . . His machine was the new type of Short biplane, far lighter and speedier than anything produced before by Mr Horace Short. It was driven by a 60-80 hp ENV engine, and had the Short patent wheel and skid landing device.' The Short's order book quite clearly states that McClean's S.33 was the aircraft lost. In January 1913 a petrol tank believed to be from S.33 was washed up on the shore at Ostend.

Another contender for the de Forest prize was G C Colmore, the owner of Short S.26, who eventually withdrew. He left his aeroplane at Dover, and it was later bought by McClean. (AUTHOR)

CHAPTER 4

1911: Teaching the Navy and Army to Fly; Multiple-engine Aeroplanes

In the first half of 1911 McClean went on a Government solar eclipse expedition to the Vava'u Group in the Tonga Islands as a representative of the Norman Lockyer Observatory, of which he was a joint founder. Sir Norman Lockyer was in charge of the party, which sailed on 31 January in the cruiser HMS *Encounter* and was due to return in late June/early July after recording the eclipse on 29 April.

From the outset Eastchurch had been frequented by naval officers and ratings who, McClean said, 'wished to see what was going on and possibly get a joy-ride'. So before his departure McClean offered the loan of two machines to the Royal Navy and left a set of instructions with Horace Short, stating that the ex-Colmore S.26 and his own S.28, plus a new Short machine 'similar to the Grace "de Forest" machine' should be provided for navy use (this emerged as S.34, delivered on 8 March), and that three Gnome engines be provided for these aircraft. He also included an instruction to build a 'possible (and entirely at Mr Short's discretion) new Multiple Plant Machine. This latter either for the Navy or other Pilots', also Gnome powered, for use upon his return in July 1911. McClean stated that this machine could be sold provided that 'the latest type of similar machine will be ready for me on my return . . .'. In addition he instructed that the twin sheds formerly belonging to Rolls be put at the navy's disposal to house these aircraft, adding that the Club was to

make arrangements for housing the new machine when it was ready. McClean advanced £1,000 to cover the employment of a 'first class competent mechanic' to attend to the navy machines and the cost of the two new aircraft and the necessary Gnome engines. His cottage was to be made available rent-free for members of the RAeC Committee and the Secretary, and also for 'persons teaching Naval Officers, and for Naval Officers', though the users would have to pay their living expenses.

Short S.26, a Short-Sommer built for G C Colmore, had started life as Short 'Job No 18', a duplicate of Short 13, a Wolseley powered Short biplane for Maurice Egerton. Begun on 27 January 1910, it was modified during construction to emerge as Green-engined Short-Sommer No 3/S.26, and was delivered to Colmore on 2 June. He used it to win his pilot's certificate on 19/20 June, and continued to fly it until 13 August, when, during the Scottish International Flight Meeting at Lanark, he came down into clump of trees, smashing his propeller and wrecking the lower wing. The repaired S.26 was acquired by McClean when it was derelict at Dover after Colmore had abandoned his attempt for the de Forest prize in December 1910.

The 'multiple plant' machine, which was eventually to emerge as the S.39 Triple Twin, was a direct result of McClean's realisation that a single-engine aeroplane was not sufficiently safe or reliable for long over-water flights, a fact tragically confirmed by Grace's disappearance.

On Saturday 14 January 1911 McClean flight-tested his Gnome-engined Short before handing it over for use by the navy. After a solo trial flight in the morning he made a five-minute flight with Mr George Deverish (or Devenish) of Mitcham as his passenger. After lunch he gave the same gentleman another, longer flight, going round Leysdown and over Capel Hill, some three miles away, at a height of 700ft, and then circling the ground two or three times before planing to the ground opposite his shed. He then took up fellow Eastchurch pioneer J L Travers for a short flight, their combined weight being nearly 26 stone. This was followed by a solo cross-country, overflying Minster at 1,000ft and then passing over Neat's Court, near Queenborough. He then steered to the Sheerness golf links, where Vice Admiral Sir G Neville of the Home Fleet and other naval officers were playing golf. 'He brought the machine to within 100ft of the ground,' reported *The Aero*, 'and then returned in good style to Eastchurch.' After landing, McClean said that the fog was so thick high up that he lost sight of the ground and had to make repeated downward glides before he could determine his whereabouts.

On Sunday 22 January McClean took his sister Anna for a flight over 'Harty Road Station, Capel Hill, etc', and then made a second trip over the marshes with Mr Morris Bidder.

Credit where credit is due

In its 'Editorial Notes' in the issue of 25 January 1911, *The Aero* took the national press to task for reporting that, in referring to the government's lethargy in matter of aerial defence, Colonel H S Massey had stated that 'all the Admiralty could do was place two second-hand

hired aeroplanes at the disposal of the Navy'. The journal pointed out that this 'did not give credit where credit is due', and actually made 'an extremely patriotic action into a very ordinary commercial deal'.

The writer continued:

The basis of the statement is that, through the Royal Aero Club, two exceptionally fine aeroplanes built by Short Bros. at Sheppey have been placed at the disposal of naval officers absolutely free of all cost, with the very simple conditions attached that officers using them must pay for breakages . . . and that the said officers shall become members of the Royal Aero Club, so as to have the right of *entrée* to the Club grounds at Eastchurch.

No charge is to be made for the housing of the machines, and, further, instruction in their use will be given by members of the Club who are thoroughly competent to do so.

Though the ownership of these machines has been hitherto kept more or less secret among the members of the Royal Aero Club out of respect for the wishes of the donor, it is undoubtedly, under the circumstances which have arisen, one's duty to state definitely that the machines are the personal private property of Mr F.K. McClean, and, further, that owing to the loss of one of the machines originally intended for this purpose, the machine being that driven by poor Cecil Grace, Mr McClean has ordered from Mr Short another machine to replace it.

Unfortunately, Mr McClean is leaving this country in the course of a few weeks on an astronomical expedition to Tasmania [actually the Solar Eclipse Expedition to the Vava'u Group in the Tonga Islands in the South Pacific], to observe an eclipse on April 29, 1911 (Eastern date), but in the meantime he is himself giving his services as an instructor, and during his absence various other members of the Club who are competent pilots of standard type biplanes will take up his duties.

Mr McClean's action is surely as thoroughly patriotic as anything that has been done, and it is only to be hoped that when, in the future, we shall have in this country an adequate system of aerial defence in connection with the navy, Mr McClean's name will go down in history as the founder of our British Naval Air Fleet.

Mr McClean's name is nothing like so well known in the world of aviation as it should be, considering his ability as an aviator, and many a man has attained international fame without having done half as many good flights, or one-tenth as much hard work as Mr McClean has done.

It is necessary to appreciate this fact in order to realise the true modesty which has hitherto insisted on hiding the name of the man who had practically given two first-class aeroplanes to the British Admiralty; for, though the pupils who learn on these machines may pay for breakages, the fact remains that by the time Mr McClean returns from Tasmania [sic] they will probably have been so broken up and repaired that he will have to have a new machine for his own driving.

Under any properly organised system a Government Department of National Defence would feel ashamed to accept weapons of war – for such aeroplanes are today – from a private individual, and certainly it would feel ashamed to think that the men who were to operate such weapons were to receive their training from mere civilians. All these facts, taken into consideration, merely accentuate the part which Mr McClean is playing in the affairs of the nation, and it is only to be

hoped that in due time his action may be properly recognised.

More than 200 officers had volunteered for the course of flying training at Eastchurch. From these, four (three naval and one marine) were selected for a six-month course of instruction commencing on 1 March. They were Lieutenants Gregory, Samson and Longmore, RN, and Lieutenant Wildman-Lushington, RMS. In McClean's absence Mr G B Cockburn, an RAeC member and certificated pilot who had already been giving free instruction to army officers on Salisbury Plain, consented to give flying instruction. The officers were also to be given a course on aircraft construction by Short Brothers. Wildman-Lushington was taken ill just before the course started, his place being taken by Lieutenant E L Gerrard of the Royal Marine Light Infantry.

The four officers were given confidential instructions direct from Admiral Drury that their task was to become instructors in their own right; that the main point to be kept in view was the 'adaptability' of aeroplanes for ship work, but that they were to keep from Shorts their views on working aeroplanes from ships lest Shorts gained a commercial advantage; and that Shorts were not led to believe that the Admiralty were bound in any way to buy their machines. The officers were not to fly on Sundays, and they were to make at least three flights as passengers before going solo. In particular they were to have experience as a passenger in a 'strong wind' before going solo in a wind in excess of 4mph, the local flying area and arrangements for medical assistance were to be clearly defined, and, even after obtaining their certificates, they were to have 'considerable experience' before flying over ships or towns. 'Sensational vol plané' and flights at 'unnecessary heights' were forbidden. Samson was

The Royal Aero Club sheds and Shorts Brothers' works at Eastchurch in 1911. (AUTHOR)

appointed senior officer with responsibility for inspecting the aeroplanes, and made weekly reports to Admiral Drury.

Instruction began in March, and Samson and Longmore were granted Aviators' Certificates Nos 71 and 72, respectively, on 25 April, and Gregory and Gerrard were awarded certificates 75 and 76 on 2 May. They quickly became competent pilots, and all four made flights in the presence of Admiral HRH Prince Louis of Battenberg, the Second Sea Lord (First Sea Lord 1912–14) when he visited Eastchurch on 11 May and 10 June.

Wreck and replace

McClean had given Egerton permission to try out the new S.34, which was fitted with a nacelle ('canoe') to protect the occupants, before it was handed over to the navy. It was completed at about 5pm on 8 March, and Egerton immediately took it for a run along the ground. He 'Started about 3/4 downwind with the in-

An improved S.27-type with a nacelle for the pilot outside the Eastchurch sheds in 1911. (AUTHOR)

The Short S.34/Short-Sommer No 7, a copy of S.33, was built for McClean to be used to train Royal Navy pilots. Although it initially had a nacelle for its occupants, this was removed. It was eventually bought by the navy and became T.1. (AUTHOR)

tention of coming back against it', but found the aircraft 'very difficult to handle' on the ground after his big machine, and could not steer it at all because it kept getting its head to wind and the lifting tail was troublesome. He made one or two sharp turns and buckled the axle, and the back-rest broke which prevented him from getting any purchase on the rudder bar. After stopping the engine at the top end of the ground he had to be guided back. The repairs were quickly effected. Egerton flew S.34 on 9 and 10 March, and made a 20-minute flight on the 12th. On the 16th Cockburn flew it for the first time and gave Samson a few lessons.

On 1 May Egerton was asked to test the repaired S.28, which had also been fitted with a nacelle. He had 'just got it over the trees with the tail down' when it 'suddenly swung round and down', and he was unable to correct it. Ac-

cording to McClean's captions on photographs of the wreck, it 'fell from about 80 feet' and suffered major damage. Although Egerton had noted that 'about 3 new spars [were] required, a fairly extensive smash up', Samson faced a choice of repairing the wreck at a cost of £100 or spending £260 on a new machine incorporating the nacelle and engine salvaged from S.28. He recommended the second option in a letter to Admiral Drury dated 1 May, arguing that S.28 had been so badly damaged that its safety would always be doubtful after repair.

The aircraft was therefore deemed unrepairable, and the Admiralty, in accordance with

Two views of the newly repaired S.28, now fitted with a nacelle for the pilot, after Egerton's accident of 1 May 1911, while he was testing it in McClean's absence. Although Egerton thought it repairable, the Admiralty disagreed and it was written off, the engine and nacelle being incorporated in its replacement, the S.38. (AUTHOR)

its agreement with McClean, ordered a new machine to replace it. Things moved quickly, and on Wednesday 24 May Samson took up the 'new' Short biplane, S.38 (Short-Sommer No 9) which had been ordered to replace S.28 and was 'just out of the workshops'. (The order book identifies 'F. McClean (Navy)' as the customer, and gives the delivery date as 23 May.) Known as the 'improved S.27', this machine had a nacelle, upper wing extensions and ailerons on upper and lower surfaces. To improve structural rigidity kingposts had been added above the spars in the inner bays and below the spars in the centre bay, and the whole wing truss had been strengthened by the addition of solid compression ribs below the lower surface of the upper wing, between the top sockets of the interplane struts. After a 'trial

Lieutenant Gerrard, left, and Frank McClean try out the nacelle devised for the Short S.27-type biplanes. For obvious reasons this accommodation was initially dubbed the 'canoe', but the name did not stick. Worthy of note are the pilot's instrument panel, the large control column, the map board worn on the pilot's back for use by the occupant of the rear seat, and the large petrol tank immediately behind that seat. Although these nacelles appeared to be an improvement, providing the occupants with a degree of protection from the elements, they evidently proved unpopular and were soon removed, perhaps because they impeded accessibility. Nacelles reappeared on later Short pusher biplanes. (AUTHOR)

trip' of 45 minutes, during which he found 'everything in perfect working order', Samson made a 65-minute flight, landing in fading light and mist. By this time the naval pilots were also using S.32, which had passed into McClean's ownership along with S.27 (Short-Sommer No 1; Grace's first of the type) after Grace's disappearance on McClean's S.33. In addition, they had frequent use of McClean's other aircraft and of Maurice Egerton's S.35. The old S.26, which had deteriorated as a result of a series of crashes and had proved sluggish, had been relegated to preliminary taxiing lessons, being nicknamed 'the Dud' and 'Th' owd Bitch' by the naval pilots. Early in June the nacelles were removed from both S.34 and S.38.

Meanwhile, the creation of S.39 was apparently causing some problems for Horace Short. Having patented a variety of configurations in January 1911, he began its design, and 'drawings' of a twin-engine machine, described as 'really lovely', were displayed on Short's stand at the Olympia Aero Show in March. However, according to E Travers, author of the book *Cross Country* (Hothersall & Travers, 1989), although Horace had great 'brainpower and intelligence', his designs to date had

The Short S.27, alias Short-Sommer No.1, was powered by a 60hp ENV engine and built for Cecil Grace. McClean acquired it in 1911, and after he had unsuccessfully put it up for sale it was converted into the Tandem Twin. (AUTHOR)

LEFT
In June 1911 Horace Short employed engineer/pilot J L Travers as his assistant and designer. The new recruit was immediately put to work on the S.39, which was to have two engines and had been posing some problems for Horace. (AUTHOR)

been based largely on other people's aeroplanes. He was not a trained engineer, and despite his engineering background and practical experience he struggled unsuccessfully for some months to bring McClean's 'multiple plant' machine into being.

Finally, early in June, Horace took on the trained engineer and early Eastchurch pioneer J L (Jim) Travers as his assistant and designer. Travers tackled his new task energetically and, though the extent of his input into the S.39 is unclear, many alterations were made. On 18 June he wrote to his parents: 'I have been very busy today hurrying on the new twin-engine machine which should be finished in about a month.' As it was to transpire, even this forecast was over-optimistic.

The aviator Claude Grahame-White and aviation journalist Harry Harper had evidently persuaded McClean to indulge in the precarious pursuit of prophecy, and in their book *The Aeroplane: Past, Present, and Future*, published in 1911, McClean was one of several prominent aviators who contributed to the final chapter, 'The Future of Flying'. As might be expected at such an early stage in the aeroplane's development, his comments were a mixture of cautiously vague forecasts and sage advice regarding safety:

From the point of view of freight carrying, the prospect of success with the aeroplane is undoubtedly still very distant.

For carrying 'mails,' there is a good possibility of use in certain cases, but only where there is considerable difficulty in land or water transport.

For carrying up to half a dozen passengers of ordinary weight, this is possible at any time, but is hardly to be considered a commercial undertaking, as the expense would be very great.

For rivalling trains or steamers, in carrying capacity, the prospect of the aeroplane is unlikely.

The aeroplane of 1911 will certainly be as easily manipulated and as safe as a motor-car, provided that continuous care is taken, and only well-tried machines are used.

This must, however, be qualified by the restriction that the machine is only used in reasonable weather. No motor-car is expected to stand a cross-country run at 40 to 50 miles an hour.

A large factor of safety must always be employed, to stand any uncalculated stresses due to wind gusts tending to damage the planes, or due to an uneven landing and starting ground, which will injure the under-carriage. The latter is as important as the former both from the point of view of actual danger and from the consideration of large repair bills.

Also incessant care is absolutely necessary to see that no bolts or split pins or wires are in a dangerous condition. All controls should be doubled.

Forced landings, due to engine troubles, would be eliminated by the use of two engines running entirely separate, which will probably be in common use at an early date. Even if one engine alone is insufficient to keep the machine flying – it would so increase the landing radius that danger would be minimised.

During their return from the eclipse expedition McClean and Lockyer stopped over in the USA, and on 24 and 25 June they visited and dined with the Wrights in the family home at Hawthorn Hill, Dayton, Ohio. Bishop Milton Wright, father of Wilbur and Orville, recorded the visit in his diary, noting: 'McClean is six feet high and well built.'

At 1.45am on 11 July McClean arrived at Paddington Station in London. Unfortunately, as J L Travers recorded, '. . . he was far from well and suffered spasmodic bouts of sciatica well into September'. In *The Aeroplane* for 7 September 1911 the editor, C G Grey, remarked that McClean 'has been laid up with sciatica practically ever since he came back from eclipse-hunting in the South Seas'. This undoubtedly accounts for the hiatus before his first post-expedition flights at Eastchurch.

His first flight appears to have been made on Saturday 29 July, *Flight* for 5 August reporting that he 'demonstrated that he had lost none of his skill, for although the Short biplane which he piloted on this occasion was somewhat different to what he had previously been using, he made several good flights over Leysdown and Eastchurch during the evening'. This was probably S.38. The proceedings were rudely interrupted towards 8pm when a thunderstorm broke 'with alarming suddenness' and the wind speed rose from a dead calm to 30mph, reaching 60 or 70mph at 500–600ft and forcing McClean, Samson and Gregory to return in haste to the aerodrome, where they all landed safely. McClean was flying again on the Sunday and Monday.

On the evening of Monday the 31st the flying ground at Eastchurch was visited by Their Royal Highnesses Prince and Princess Louise of Battenberg, Princess Henry of Prussia, and party, 'who witnessed some splendid flying during their two hours' stay', as *The Aeroplane* reported in its 3 August issue. Between 6 and 8 o'clock McClean, Samson, Longmore, Gregory

and Gerrard gave exhibition flights on Short biplanes, as did Ogilvie on his 'Baby' Wright (modified Short-Wright No 6). Several ladies of the royal party were given passenger flights by naval officers.

Also in its 5 August issue, *Flight* reported on the aerostatic and aeronautical activities of the London Balloon Company of the Royal Engineer Territorials, recounting flights given to the NCOs and men by Geoffrey de Havilland on 28 July. The article concluded: '. . . a good, strong and reliable aeroplane is just the thing needed by the Company, and would make a very welcome present to the London Balloon Company, RE Territorials. Will somebody assist them to their desires?'

Early in August McClean acquired his only non-Short aeroplane when he bought the Universal Aviation Birdling monoplane, a Blériot

In August 1911 McClean acquired his only non-Short prewar aeroplane when he bought this Universal Aviation Company Birdling monoplane, a Blériot XI copy, from H J D Astley, who is seen in it here during the 1911 Circuit of Britain Race. (DAVID BROWNING)

XI copy, flown by H J D Astley in the Circuit of Britain from 22–26 July. On the 26th Astley withdrew owing to inferior castor oil lubricant causing engine problems, and he finally arrived back at Brooklands on the 31st. McClean's purchase was announced in the 10 August issue of *The Aeroplane*, and the Birdling was quickly made available to the navy pilots. By early September, however, it was in pieces at Eastchurch, 'having been the victim of some stray sheep which wandered across Lieutenant Samson's path when he was landing'. 'Not being used to the machine, on which he was making his first monoplane flight,' *The Aeroplane* later reported, 'he reached for his switch alongside, as it is placed on the Short, and forgot it was on the control wheel in front, a very natural mistake. Unfortunately, the short delay brought him too close to the sheep, and to avoid running into them he tried to jump over them, but, the throttle not being full open, the machine pancaked just beyond and smashed itself fairly completely.' The Naval Flying School subsequently used the Birdling from November 1911 to 20 July 1912, when it was again damaged, repaired by Shorts and put back to work. It was still being used in early November 1912. In December 1913 McClean lent it to the Science Museum in London for a temporary aeronautical exhibition opened on 14 February 1914. It was apparently retained by the museum.

McClean himself did a fair bit of flying in the first week of August. *Flight* reported that he was flying 'his favourite Short biplane, . . . on which he has done an aggregate of nearly 1,000 miles without any more serious breakage than a broken stay-wire'.

At the end of the month the six-month agreement for the use of McClean's aircraft to train navy pilots expired. The four airmen had done a considerable amount of flying, Lieutenant Gerrard claiming the world's record for cross-country flying with a passenger and Lieutenant Samson establishing a British duration record. Their favourite Short biplane, affectionately known as 'Little Willy' (believed to be the S.28), had flown over 4,000 miles, and S.34 and S.38 had logged 3,000 and 2,000 miles respectively. C G Grey was told by 'those who ought to know best' that the total cost of breakages in that 9,000 miles of flying 'would be covered by about £25'.

Twin-engine aeroplanes

Meanwhile, Shorts had been working on two more machines for McClean. The first was the tractor biplane which Horace had designed in conjunction with the late Cecil Grace (S.36) and which Travers had redesigned, and the second was the twin-engine S.39.

The S.39, described by *The Aero* as 'a daring and original departure, devoid of freakishness', was 'very nearly completed' by late August. Larger than the standard biplanes hitherto produced by the company, it was a sturdy 45ft-long, 34ft-span three-bay biplane with double-surfaced wings, powered by a pair of 50hp Gnomes mounted at the front and rear of the covered nacelle positioned on the lower wing centre section and driving three propellers. The front engine drove a pair of tractor propellers mounted 24ft apart on the central front struts on each side via long chain drives running in tubular guides *à la* Wright, the chain on the port side being crossed so that the propellers counter-rotated to eliminate torque. The gear reduction was 2:1. The rear engine had an ungeared 'high-speed' pusher propeller attached directly to its driveshaft. The pilot and passenger were seated side-by-side between the engines, the pilot, to starboard, being provided with a pivoted control column topped by a

wheel. Turning the wheel operated the ailerons, and fore-and-aft movement of the column worked the elevators attached to the outrigger booms projecting ahead of the wing cellule and to the monoplane tailplane. Rocking foot-pedals worked the triple rudders; there was no fin. Duplicate controls were provided for the passenger. Two cylindrical fuel tanks were carried, each one being fitted between the first pair of interplane struts on each side.

Although it was intended that the engines would be run simultaneously, giving the aircraft a speed of about 55mph, the S.39 was designed so that it could sustain flight on either engine at a speed of about 36mph. The provision of two completely independent powerplants and systems was expected to obviate the risks of an engine failure almost entirely, enabling the pilot to 'leisurely choose a suitable landing place, where he may descend to make any adjustments to his temporarily disabled engine'.

The Aero said that the initial experiments would be carried out with 50hp Gnomes, but

The first multiple-engine aeroplane built for McClean was the S.39, dubbed the 'Triple Twin' because its two Gnome engines drove three propellers, one attached directly as a pusher to the rear engine, and two driven by chain drives from the engine mounted on the front of the nacelle. This picture was taken at Eastchurch in late September 1911, at the time of the S.39's first trials, and McClean is at the controls, 'just ready to start'. (AUTHOR)

that 'for experimental purposes' it was expected that one or both of them would give way to a 70hp unit. The magazine added: 'Messrs. Short Brothers and Mr Frank Maclean [*sic*] must be congratulated upon their enterprise in bringing into being the machine which, although admittedly experimental, indicates that all British constructors are not mere copyists, but can be original without producing freaks.'

The S.39 was delivered to McClean on Monday 18 September, and he piloted it on its first trial flights that same day. *Flight* reported that they proved 'very successful . . . the machine

Three-quarter-front and -rear close-ups of the S.39 during its early flights, showing the front and rear engines and propellers. McClean is at the controls and Lieutenant Charles Rumney Samson is in the passenger's seat. (Author)

answering fully the expectations of its constructors'. McClean first made a short, straight solo flight 'in which the machine showed great buoyancy, rising rapidly into the air in spite of the preliminary run being uphill'. He then flew eight laps of the ground with Samson as his passenger, frequently throttling down either engine. 'A strong feature of the tactics,' said *Flight*, 'was the large margin of power exhibited by the machine . . . , it being possible to vary the speed considerably, by throttling down either or both engines without causing a descent.' The report added: 'Mr McClean stated afterwards that he found the warping control very effective and the biplane very steady in flight; it also showed a very flat gliding angle when the engines were cut off . . .' In 1938 McClean recalled that the S.39 was 'a perfect lady, without vices and rather slow'.

The trials continued, and on Thursday the 21st McClean took up several naval officers as passengers, making a tour of the island at 600ft. *The Aeroplane* and *Flight* reported that he was 'particularly pleased with the climbing qualities of his new mount; it seems to have unlimited powers in this direction'. In the afternoon of the following day he made flights of more than two hours, making sharp right- and left-hand turns and occasionally flying with both engines throttled down, reducing the aircraft's speed considerably. On Sunday the 24th McClean in S.39 followed Egerton on a long cross-country flight by way of Sheerness, and on return to Eastchurch made a faultless landing with both engines stopped. In mid-October he flew it from Eastchurch over Capel Hill to Leysdown, along the Swale to King's Ferry and then skirted Queenborough and Sheerness before returning to Eastchurch. 'There was a stiff breeze,' reported *Flight*, 'but with the new control system the minor air currents scarcely affected the machine'. The magazine added

that Shorts were now building another, similar biplane, and that the company 'will shortly commence another biplane embodying one or two new features, and fitted with two 100hp engines driving four propellers'.

At Shorts, Horace Short and Travers had indeed been hard at work producing a second twin-engine machine for McClean. Horace was not happy with the effect on lateral control of the outboard slipstream created by the S.39's tractor propellers, so he decided to investigate the effect of co-axial counter-rotation on stability. Travers was not keen on the chain transmission. However, instead of building a completely new machine they modified the ex-Grace S.27 airframe. An additional 50hp Gnome was mounted in front of the nacelle, with the pilot and passenger sandwiched side-by-side between the two engines, with dual controls, as in the S.39. This time the front engine drove a single propeller attached directly to its driveshaft. As the engines turned in opposite directions, gyroscopic action and torque were cancelled out. Other modifications included extensions to the upper wing, a beefed-up undercarriage and the addition of two extra rudders above the tailplane.

Work on the twin-engine S.27 began on 25 September, and McClean took it up for its first flights on 29 October. *Flight* and *The Aeroplane* reported that he '. . . did not attempt any preliminary ground rolling, but took the machine straight into the air and made a lap of the aerodrome at a height of about 100ft. On descending he expressed great satisfaction at the behaviour of the machine, which flew extremely well and at great speed'. That afternoon he made several extended flights, taking up Lieutenant Samson, Lieutenant H V Gerrard (brother of the aviator Captain Gerrard) and J L Travers. Travers, who had also become a competent pilot by now, was somewhat dis-

appointed, writing to his father: 'I was originally told that I was to fly it but when it came
to the point Maclean [*sic*], (who after all was
paying for it) couldn't resist taking it up himself. I have done an awful lot of work on the
machine, drawing, scheming and hurrying the
job through.'

Unhappy with certain aspects of the S.39's design,
Horace Short and J L Travers modified the S.27 to
create the 'Tandem Twin', with two Gnomes driving
tractor and pusher propellers at the front and rear of
the nacelle. It first flew in late October 1911.
According to McClean's later accounts this was not a
very pleasant machine to fly, though contemporary
reports suggested otherwise. (AUTHOR)

Frank McClean at the
controls of the S.27
Tandem Twin in 1911.
For obvious reasons
the machine was
familiarly known as the
'Gnome sandwich', the
'filling' comprising the
pilot and passenger!
(AUTHOR)

For the final flight of the day McClean took Lieutenant Gregory on a long tour of the island at an altitude of about 600ft, passing over Queenborough and Sheerness. 'The machine exhibited splendid climbing powers,' the journals reported, 'rising with unusual rapidity.'

These glowing accounts of the twin-engine S.27's performance are at odds with McClean's later recollections of it. In 1931 he said 'it flew very well indeed, but, unfortunately, [I] could never make it fly level; you either had to climb and subsequently slide back into the ground with your tail or dive straight away with your nose into the ground'. In 1938 he wrote: 'She was a disgraceful machine without stability either laterally or fore and aft. She would not fly level but hunted up and down and her landings were promiscuous. The rear air screw was ten inches behind the pilot's head and his feet were against the front engine.' He also recalled that it was known as the 'Vacuum Cleaner' owing to the draught in the seats between the propellers, alleged to be able to pull the hairs out of a fur coat. This was largely attributable to an open hole in the cockpit floor, the sole means of access.

There was again reference to plans to build a four-propeller aircraft. This machine, designed by Horace, was to have a central pair of 120hp engines driving four propellers arranged in tandem pairs between the biplane wings, with independent chain gears for the front and rear engines. It was never built.

Shortly afterwards, McClean visited C G Grey at *The Aeroplane* office in Piccadilly, London, and 'expressed himself as being greatly pleased' with his latest aeroplane. He said that it flew quite well on either engine, and could attain about 55mph with both working. One peculiarity the S.27 shared with the S.39 was that it did not bank itself naturally 'going round a corner', but when banked by use of the ailerons it manoeuvred very easily. 'Mr McClean . . . is quite enthusiastic about the possibilities of machines with two engines,' the magazine reported. McClean and navy pilots continued flying the twin-engine S.27 during November, McClean making a good many passenger flights. On 1 November he took Egerton for a 20-minute flight. This was Egerton's first flight as a passenger, and he noted: 'Not very comfortable, and too much wind and oil.'

On the afternoon of Tuesday 21 November a race was arranged between Captain Gerrard on the 'tandem-twin' S.27 (also informally dubbed the 'Gnome sandwich') and Lieutenant Longmore on the triple-propeller twin-engine S.39, the 'triple-twin' (these names appearing in print for the first time in the reports of this event in the 2 December issue of *Flight*). The aim was to test the relative speeds of the aircraft over a course to Leysdown and back to the aerodrome, but the result was not quite conclusive because Gerrard rounded a different point to Longmore. The S.39 had a slight edge, completing the run at a little over 50mph.

Later that afternoon the advantage of having two engines was dramatically demonstrated. Samson was flying S.39 at 600ft over Brambledown, some four miles from Eastchurch, when the rear engine's magneto came loose and worked out of gear, upsetting the tuning and causing the engine to stop suddenly. Accustomed to single-engine flight, Samson prepared to make a *vol plane*, scanning the ground for a suitable place to land. This proved unnecessary, however, as the aircraft continued to fly well on the good engine, descending at a very gentle angle. Samson landed safely on the aerodrome, 'having plenty of room for a turn in order to alight close to the shed'.

In London that day a meeting of a large

number of aircraft manufacturers, pilots and RAeC Committee members took place with the aim of considering what action should be taken with regard to the Government's planned Military Aeroplane Competition for 1912, and the 'attitude of the War Office toward British constructors'. Horace and Eustace Short and McClean were among them. A resolution stated, in part, that '. . . the Under Secretary for War [Colonel Seeley] should be requested . . . to consider the advantages to the Government, as well as to the British industry as a whole, of placing conditional orders, with such British firms as are willing to accept them, for an aeroplane or aeroplanes to fulfil the requirements of the War Office; the conditions being that delivery will not be accepted unless the planes carry out the specified tests'. A committee was then appointed to deal with the question of a deputation to Colonel Seeley; it included McClean and Horace Short.

Helping the Terriers fly

That same week it was announced that The London Balloon Company and the Territorial Force had been offered the use of two Short biplanes at the RAeC grounds at Eastchurch 'for the purpose of instructing members in aviation'. The lender, described as 'a prominent member of the club', was of course McClean, who had undertaken to see to the aircrafts' hangarage and maintenance. Fourteen of the company's sixty-two members had already volunteered for a course of training towards gaining the Club's higher aviator's certificate, and the first pupil was due to start in a few days. 'Those who cannot afford the time,' reported the *Morning Post*, 'will be taken down to Eastchurch at week-ends to be trained in the handling and care of aeroplanes and their motors.' 'Is Mr McClean qualifying

for the post of First Lord of the Admiralty?' asked *The Aeroplane*.

Travers, who was to undertake the training of the Territorials, adapted S.32 by replacing its ENV engine with a 70hp Gnome and fitting it with side-by-side seats and dual controls. *Flight* reported that, on Sunday 26 November, Travers was 'out testing the new [*sic*] 70hp Gnome-engined Short biplane which has been specially prepared for [the Territorials'] instruction'. Officers, NCOs and men under the command of Captain M M Bidder went to Eastchurch and, acting on the authority received from the County Association, a shed was taken by them. As previously announced, in addition to those who were able to go to the aerodrome during the week for individual training, weekend parties of eight to ten were organised under authority from the GOC 1st Division for ground work and repairs to machines and engines. On Monday 4 and Tuesday 5 December Mr S P Cockerell and Mr A V Barrington-Kennett of the Territorial Balloon Company began their training under Travers on the S.32. Cockerell was already a qualified aviator, but Barrington-Kennett had his first experience of piloting from S.32's passenger seat, using the dual controls. He flew his first solo the following week. Other Territorials were soon sampling the delights of aviation.

Another 'biplane Type 38' was ordered for McClean on 8 December. This aircraft, S.40/Short-Sommer No 10, was to have a particularly interesting career.

The S.27 and S.39 continued to be flown by navy pilots. Shorts' order book records a series of repair jobs from January 1912 onward, charged to the navy's account (the RN doing the 'right thing' by McClean). A Committee of Imperial Defence subcommittee report in February 1912 recommended the purchase of 'One twin engine biplane (now in use) from Messrs

Later, the Triple Twin was fitted with extensions to its upper wing, as seen here. It was purchased by the Admiralty early in 1912. (AUTHOR)

In its ultimate form the S.39 had four fuel tanks beneath the upper wing centre section. In this picture, taken on 6 December 1911, Commander Samson and Captain Gerrard are aboard. The S.39 was serialled B3, T3 and 3 in naval service, and in June 1913 it was rebuilt as S.78, an S.58-Type pusher biplane. (AUTHOR)

Short Brothers' for £1,400. This was the S.39; the S.27 Tandem Twin remained McClean's property, though he loaned it to the Naval Flying School free of charge.

The naval aviators expressed their gratitude in the concert room of the Crooked Billet Inn at Eastchurch on the evening of 16 December, when they gave a dinner to the employees of Messrs Short Brothers, and treated them to an 'impromptu entertainment'. Several toasts were drunk, 'none with more enthusiasm than that

of Mr Frank K. McClean, who, all regretted, was absent . . .'.

Promising new biplane

Upon McClean's return from Tonga Horace Short had shown him a design for a two-seat tractor biplane powered by a 70hp Gnome, developed from an earlier design drafted to meet a requirement outlined by the late Cecil Grace. McClean ordered one for his private use, and late in 1911 this machine, S.36, was completed. Although it was initially built as a landplane, it was designed to incorporate a float undercarriage devised by J L Travers, with a large single central float and lateral stabilising air-bag floats towards the lower wingtips.

The S.36 represented a marked change from the company's pusher biplanes. It had two-bay wings with strut-braced upper-wing extensions and ailerons on the upper wing only. The fuselage was a simple wire-braced girder structure,

initially left uncovered apart from the aluminium panels enclosing the tanks and the overhung engine mounting, and the plywood panels alongside the tandem cockpits. It was attached to the middle bay struts in mid-gap, and the lower wing centre section was left uncovered. Its land undercarriage comprised a twin-skid chassis attached to the two lower longerons and carrying two wheels on a rubber-sprung cross-axle. There was a sprung tailskid. A non-lifting tailplane carried divided elevators, and a partly balanced rectangular rudder was hinged on a vertical sternpost. It was a handsome and promising machine.

School for navy pilots

At an RAeC Committee meeting on 21 November McClean had made proposals resulting from discussions with Admiralty officers. These were that the navy be granted permission to use the flying ground at Eastchurch for the instruction of officers and petty officers, who need not necessarily be members of the Club, and that a charge be made to the navy for these facilities. No time was wasted, and at a meeting on 28 November it was agreed that

The S.36 tractor biplane, built for Frank McClean, in January 1912, shortly after completion, with its rear fuselage as yet uncovered. It marked a step change in Short Brothers' aeroplane design. (FLEET AIR ARM MUSEUM)

the navy would have use of Eastchurch for the flat sum of £150 per annum; that it would use not more than ten machines at any one time; and that no more than two uncertificated RN officers or men would be in the air at any one time. On 25 December the Admiralty entered into an agreement with the RAeC, McClean and Short Brothers Ltd, whereby for £150 it rented from them ten acres of ground near the RAeC's aerodrome, with the proviso that the ground might be bought for £16 per acre as from 25 December 1918 if the Admiralty so desired. Thus England's first naval flying school was established.

Consequently, in a report dated 27 February 1912, the Technical Sub-Committee of the Standing Sub-Committee of the Committee of Imperial Defence recommended that:

The Naval Wing of the Flying Corps should be established for the present at the Naval Flying School at Eastchurch. For the immediate present its energies will be devoted mainly to elementary training in flying, so as to provide a nucleus of fliers for the first requirements of the Navy, pending the establishment of the Central Flying School, and to experimental work in the development of aeronautics for the Navy.

These plans were confirmed in a *Memorandum on Naval and Military Aviation* issued by the War Office on 11 April 1912, and, as mentioned later, a formal Indenture was signed on 1 May 1913.

For administrative purposes only the school at Eastchurch was to be under the orders of the captain of HMS *Actaeon*, a torpedo school-ship in Sheerness Dockyard, and all of its officers and men were to be borne on *Actaeon*'s books. This meant that the officers could live at Eastchurch. The Technical Sub-Committee

produced a final list of twenty-two types of aeroplanes and hydro-aeroplanes recommended for purchase abroad or order in Britain at an estimated cost of £35,308, plus six large sheds and three portable canvas sheds to house them, at a cost of £3,800. The Sub-Committee was satisfied that Eastchurch Aerodrome, which was held by the RAeC on a long lease, was 'quite suitable for a Naval Flying School of moderate dimensions', and its use was granted to the Royal Navy on favourable terms. However, it was considered advisable for the government to enquire into the possibility of securing the freehold of the ground.

The desire for independence had also been expressed by Rear Admiral E C T Troubridge, Chief of Staff, Admiralty, in a paper dated 23 January 1912 and entitled 'The development of Naval Aeroplanes and Airships'. In a section headed 'Royal Aero Club and Private Firms', Troubridge stated:

While every advantage should be taken of private assistance, the Navy should not lean unduly for help on any one private firm or the Royal Aero Club's Aeronautical Engineers for Naval aeroplane development. If this is done, too much of a water-tight compartment is made, and the machines will be restricted in their development.

At the present moment, Messrs Short's machines have never done anything of very great importance to the aeronautical world. Therefore the Navy must not be unduly tied to them.

It seems that McClean was made aware of Troubridge's somewhat pointed remarks, for in the coming months he was to make several demonstrations of the naval potential of aeroplanes, using machines built by Short Brothers.

CHAPTER 5

1912: Waterwings

Despite unsettled weather and gusty winds, both naval pilots and Territorials continued their training at Eastchurch in January 1912. A significant event occurred on Wednesday the 10th, when Lieutenant C R Samson, in command of the Naval Flying Establishment at Eastchurch and one of the three naval officers then training there, made the first aeroplane flight from a British warship. At 12.30pm he flew S.38, fitted with three flotation bags in case of an unscheduled descent on the water, from Eastchurch to Sheerness, alighting on the marshland behind the sea wall off Cockleshell Hard, on the Isle of Grain. A party of bluejackets then hauled the aircraft across the sea wall and beach to No 126 coaling lighter, and at 1.50pm the biplane was brought alongside the battleship HMS *Africa*. By means of a derrick the aeroplane was placed on planks extending from the fore turrets to the bows and projecting a few feet over the ship's stem. Then, at 2.20pm, Samson gave the signal to 'let go' and the S.38 ran down the staging, passed the bows and rose to a height of about 100ft. He then flew over the destroyer *Cherwell* and then encircled *Africa* 'at a height of several yards below her topmasts'. Gradually rising to 300ft, Samson then passed up the Medway,

The wrecked S.28 was quickly replaced by S.38/Short-Sommer No 9, which was ordered from Shorts by Samson on McClean's behalf. Used to train naval pilots in 1911, it was subsequently fitted with floats, as seen here, and used by Longmore for float experiments and by Samson for pioneering take-offs from ships. (AUTHOR)

crossed overland at West Minster, and flew back to Eastchurch.

January 10th was also a memorable day for McClean, for that was the day he made the first flight of his new S.36 tractor biplane. It was a resounding success. *Flight* and *The Aeroplane* reported:

> On Wednesday, the 10th inst., Frank Mc-Clean tried his new Short tractor biplane, which was just out of the factory. After running the engine for a short time, McClean took the machine up for its first flight, and was so satisfied with its behaviour that he had no hesitation in continuing to fly for the remainder of the afternoon. The machine showed itself to be very swift in the air, and in the opinion of the aviators watching the trials, must have been doing something like 55 to 60 miles per hour. A distinctive feature of the test was the perfect way in which Mc-Clean made his landings, and the very flat gliding angle of the machine, which owing to its small head resistance and general design, is very efficient in this respect.

Frank McClean prepares to take his sister, Anna, for a flight in the S.36, which quickly became a favoured machine. By this time, May 1912, the rear fuselage had been covered. (FLEET AIR ARM MUSEUM)

In a postcard to his mother, J L Travers, whose workload had been lightened by the addition of two draughtsmen to Short Brothers' staff, reported 'Tractor Biplane a great success'. McClean flew S.36 again the following day, and then lent it to the Naval Flying School and departed for Switzerland in late January. On Monday the 15th Samson, now promoted acting commander, and Captain E L Gerrard, RMLI, were out early on the aircraft and tested its speed during the day; it 'slightly exceeded' 56mph. They found it had excellent controllability, and Gerrard, who took it up to 700ft with a passenger, said it climbed remarkably well. 'When the fuselage . . . is covered in,' reported *Flight*, 'she will be really quite fast for a biplane, although she was not designed particularly for speed.' Lieutenant Arthur Longmore also flew it.

On Sunday 28 January Barrington-Kennett smashed S.32 and it had to go for repair. Both the Tandem Twin and Triple Twin continued to be flown by naval pilots. Early in the morning of Monday 29 January the temperature was some degrees below freezing but weather conditions were good for flying, so Samson and Lieutenant Gregory made two excellent flights. Samson remained aloft in the Tandem Twin for more than two hours with Engineer-Lieutenant Randell RN as his passenger, and Gregory, with Lieutenant C J L'Estrange-Malone RN as his passenger, stayed up for over three hours in the Triple Twin. During these flights the wind rose considerably, and Gregory, flying at about 1,000ft, found conditions 'very choppy', especially when nearing the coastline and meeting the incoming currents from the sea. Upon landing he remarked on the Triple Twin's great stability under such conditions.

Grounding the Terriers

On 5 February a Minute was sent from the War Office, presumably to the Officer Commanding London Troops, Royal Engineers, stating:

I am commanded by the Army Council to inform you that the question of organisation of an Aviation Service for the Territorial Forces is now under consideration and pending a decision being arrived at in this regard it has been decided that the personnel of the London Balloon Company should not be trained in aeroplane work. It is therefore regretted that travelling grants for the Detachment of the Company carrying out training at the Flying Ground, Eastchurch, Sheppey, cannot be authorised.

Even so, the following Territorials 'took their tickets': S P Cockerell (before going to Eastchurch), H D Cutler, A V Barrington-Kennett and C W Meredith. T O'B Hubbard and R H Kershaw qualified immediately after they had left Eastchurch. Although this suspended the official activities, the Territorials continued to train 'in their private capacities', with Jim Travers often instructing, frequently using the side-by-side dual-control trainer.

McClean was back at Eastchurch on Saturday 10 February, when he flew the Triple Twin 'in his usual skilful manner'. That same day Longmore crashed the S.36 and it went back to Shorts for repair at the navy's expense. On the 11th McClean took Mr Fowler as a passenger in the Tandem Twin, flying 'with great steadiness in what was undoubtedly a choppy wind'. *Flight* commented that 'This machine, which is fitted with huge petrol tanks, showed herself to be very fast in the air even against the strong wind blowing'.

Tragedy struck on 17 February when Douglas Graham Gilmour, one of the foremost English pilots, was killed when his Martin-Handasyde monoplane suffered a structural failure and crashed in the Old Deer Park at Richmond, Surrey, during a cross-country flight from Brooklands. McClean was among the group who examined the wreckage on the 20th as part of an accident enquiry instigated by the RAeC. At Eastchurch on that same day Lieutenant Longmore flew the S.36 with Lieutenant Spencer Grey as his passenger, and the latter was reported to be 'much impressed with the speed and stability of the new machine'.

On Wednesday 21 February Longmore, again with Lieutenant Spencer Grey as passenger, made an attempt for the Mortimer Singer Prize on the S.36. The prize, put up by Mr A Mortimer Singer early in 1911, offered £500 each to army and navy commissioned officers who, accompanied by a passenger also in the Regular Service (combined net weight to be not less than 20 stone), and starting from any recognised flying ground, or other starting point sanctioned by the RAeC, made the longest out-and-back cross-country flight in the British Isles on an aeroplane between 1 April 1911 and 31 March 1912. Longmore took off at 9am with sufficient fuel for eight hours, but after he had flown 100 miles 'in excellent style' the Gnome began misfiring badly when he was about 1,000ft up and a mile from the aerodrome. By cleverly judging his glide he managed to land within the aerodrome boundary with the engine stopped.

On Saturday 24 February Sergeant Cutler of the Territorials took his certificate in a fine flight, with McClean acting as the RAeC's official observer. On that day McClean, 'to whose generosity and energy the whole of the present forward state and activity at Eastchurch may be traced', reported *Flight* and *The Aeroplane*, also flew his S.36 again, 'which looked very fast when flying with other machines'. On the previous day Shorts had completed a new Blériot-type monoplane with a 50hp Gnome, 'to which the well-known Short chassis has been adapted', one of two ordered as S.42 for Mc-

Clean but then taken over by the navy. Samson took it for its official test on the 24th by making a one-hour flight. It was allotted the temporary naval serial M2.

On 27 February the London Balloon Company's commanding officer, Captain Bidder, sent a letter to the Officer Commanding London Troops, RE. After reporting the progress made in aviation work, he continued:

The cost of these weekend trainings to the War Office amounted to only about £5 per week, and for this expenditure men were being trained both as pilots and also in the ground-staff work. Should we be allowed to continue on these lines, I have no doubt but that by the Summer we would be able to put in the field at least half a dozen pilots and three squads of men trained in ground-staff

First flown on 24 February 1912, only one Short S.42 Blériot-type monoplane was built. Initially two had been ordered by McClean on 11 August 1911, but the second was uncompleted. This one was purchased by the Admiralty and allocated the serial M2; apparently McClean never flew it. (AUTHOR)

The end of the Tandem Twin? Although the Admiralty declined to buy it, McClean lent it to the Naval Flying School at Eastchurch free of charge, and it was crashed while being flown by Samson on 11 March 1912 in an attempt to win the Mortimer Singer prize. (FLEET AIR ARM MUSEUM)

work. Mr McClean has further promised that, should no army machines be available for the Summer training, he would be prepared to lend us two for that period . . .

It would appear that for any scheme in contemplation trained men must be an advantage; and for this reason may I therefore ask whether there is any chance for the decision arrived at being altered, and the training on these lines allowed to proceed.

Sadly his appeal fell upon deaf ears, and the training was not resumed. In 1950 McClean commented with hindsight:

A horrible suspicion is roused that if £5 a week had been given to the Balloon Company (or, in other words, if the War Office had been saved that enormous sum of public money) the training might have continued with the results looked forward to by Bidder.

But flying in those days was beyond the comprehension of many who should have known better.

The 29 February issue of *The Aeroplane* contained a long report by C G Grey on 'Busy Eastchurch', which he described as 'one of the busiest, most workmanlike, and cheerful places in this country'. It now had twenty-eight sheds, 'all with authentic aeroplanes in them', 'various cosy bungalows', 'a manufacturing establishment where the Short Brothers can really turn out machines in quantities', and 'on a moderately fine day half a dozen or more machines in the air at a time'. Shorts was in the throes of completing a new and considerably bigger workshop that would at least double the factory's capabilities.

Short-Sommer S.40, which McClean had ordered in December 1911, was active by early March, and it appears that McClean had made it available to the Territorials at this period. On 7 March McClean ordered Shorts to fit it with a 'speed indicator' and new tyres and wheels, and on the following day he instructed Shorts to 'fix extra rudder off Biplane No 36' to it, all of this work being completed on the 9th. The additional rudder might have been a preparatory modification in readiness to have the aircraft fitted with floats, as shall be seen.

Sunday 10 March again saw McClean out on S.36, 'his favourite machine', taking Samson on a tour of the island by way of Sheerness. On the following day Longmore made another attempt for the Royal Navy Mortimer Singer prize in S.36, and covered 172 (*Flight*) or 180 (*The Aeroplane*) miles. Samson also made an attempt that day, flying the S.27 Tandem Twin, but crashed, damaging the engines. Bad weather then intervened for the last week before the time limit for the competition expired, and, as his distance had not been bettered, Longmore won the £500.

The birth of accident investigation

In *Flight* for 16 March it was announced that the RAeC had appointed a Special Committee, chaired by Colonel H C L Holden, to enquire into the causes of aviation accidents. The ASGB was invited to nominate representatives to serve on the committee, which, as the Public Safety and Accidents Committee, issued its first accident report in May 1912. One of the initial committee members was Frank McClean, who was also appointed one of the three RAeC representatives, along with Ogilvie and Samson, to enquire and report on all accidents at Eastchurch. This committee was the forerunner of the UK's present-day Air Accidents Investigation Branch.

On Wednesday 20 March Jim Travers travelled to London to tell McClean that Mr Bar-ton, a pupil with the Territorials, had crashed school machine S.32 the previous day. McClean and Captain Bidder, a friend of McClean's as well as a pupil of Jim's, had to decide whether the pupils might use a newer machine. Jim's aunt, Emmie, wrote: 'They said of course Jim might but that is not the point. Maclean [*sic*] is an awfully decent man and very good natured but disgusted with the Government and cannot keep the territorials going for ever.' Jim Travers seems to have left Shorts in April 1912.

On 29 March Shorts began repairing S.40 after it had been smashed by Sergeant Cutler on Sunday 24 March. It must have been quite badly damaged, as the job was not signed off as completed until 28 May. During this work, on 13 April, McClean instructed Shorts to supply a float undercarriage for the aircraft.

A tragic accident occurred at Eastchurch late in May, when Seaman Pullen went inside the tail booms of the Triple Twin to remove the wheel chocks in readiness for take-off and ran into the rear propeller. He was killed when a blade fractured his skull.

At the 11th Annual General Meeting of the RAeC on 21 March the chairman, Mr Roger W Wallace, 'had the pleasure of acknowledging the generosity of a member of the Club who had placed aeroplanes at the disposal of the Admiralty for the instruction of naval officers and who had also lent machines to the Territorial Forces'.

On 31 March McClean placed an order with Shorts for '1 Hydro Monoplane fitted tandem fashion with 2 70hp "Gnome" engines'. This was designated S.48, but was cancelled and never built. However, an apparently similar machine, the S.46, was built for the Admiralty, though a photograph of it has yet to be found (see box 'The 'Double Dirty", page 104.)

On the afternoon of Saturday 6 April, during

the Easter Holidays, McClean was aloft in the S.36 in 'very unsettled' weather, and he had 'a particularly rough time when flying near Harty Ferry on Sunday afternoon'. On the following Tuesday evening he was again out on S.36, 'flying in a considerable wind' said to be 22mph on the ground. By 7pm, however, the wind had dropped to a calm, and he took up two passengers, Miss Marion Spicer and Mr Lancelot Spicer, 'giving them a fine flight round the aerodrome at an altitude of about 200ft'.

McClean records that he was 'Gliding with Ogilvie' on 20 April. Ogilvie had altered his old Wright-type glider, built by T W K Clarke, by doing away with the front elevator and fitting an 'elevator tail', and it was probably on this that McClean enjoyed a bit of unpowered flying.

On 13 April the Royal Flying Corps (RFC) was constituted by Royal Warrant, and the structure of the Air Battalion of the Corps of Royal Engineers, which had preceded it, was officially absorbed into the new body in May. The RFC was to comprise a Military Wing, a Naval Wing, a Central Flying School and a Reserve. The Reserve was seen as a way to make use of the growing number of qualified civilian aviators who might be called upon to come to the aid of their country in the event of war, by bringing the squadrons' strengths up to war establishment. Initially the Reserve was to be divided into two classes, and a War Office memorandum of 12 April specified that '. . . the officers of the First Reserve should be required to produce on the first day of each quarter satisfactory evidence that they have performed during the previous quarter flights amounting to an aggregate of nine hours in the air, and including one cross-country flight of not less than one hour's duration'. 'Flyers of the First Reserve,' it added, ' should be given facilities for their obligatory flights every quarter at one of the naval or military establishments, or if this is impossible, at a private aerodrome.' It was specified that 'no aeroplanes should be purchased for the Reserve of the Royal Flying Corps at this stage', but that 'the Commandant of the Central Flying School should keep a register of privately owned aeroplanes, which might usefully be purchased for the use of the Royal Flying Corps in case of emergency'. It was suggested that 'Members of the Royal Flying Corps who own aeroplanes should be encouraged to bring these to the Central Flying School, when they undergo their training there, and to naval and military manoeuvres.' 'The Government believe,' the memorandum continued, 'that a considerable proportion of the qualified flying men in this country can be attracted to this Reserve, which will then be of real value, being available in any part of the world and for either service.' Announcement of the creation of the Special Reserve, as it eventually became, brought a large response, and one of the foremost among the qualified pilots who volunteered their services was Frank McClean. Effectively, however, he was already making a substantial contribution at Eastchurch.

Flight for 27 April reported that the naval authorities proposed to erect at Eastchurch 'a structure resembling the deck of a battleship on which tests of alighting and starting by aeroplane may be practised'. In its issue of 2 May *The Aeroplane* reported: 'Eastchurch is getting busier and busier, and the Short Brothers' premises are rapidly evolving from a workshop into a regular factory.' There was plenty of work in hand, a great deal of it 'purely for Government purposes' and therefore of a secret nature (doubtless including the S.46 and S.47, of which more later). However, the magazine reported that 'those critics who are so fond of de-

The temporary encampment at Lodmore early in May 1912, in readiness for the Naval Review at Weymouth. A Nieuport monoplane and a Deperdussin monoplane with flotation bags are in the foreground, and a Short biplane, also fitted with flotation bags, is behind them. (AUTHOR)

On 18 May 1912, shortly after the Weymouth review, Lieutenant (Acting Commander) Charles Rumney Samson was appointed Commandant of the RFC's Naval Wing. Many years later Samson stated that McClean's generosity 'started the Navy flying'. (AUTHOR)

crying British design and ability are likely to receive something of a shock when some of the latest Short products "take the air," or the water, as the case may be'.

Early in May one Short biplane, a Short monoplane, a Deperdussin monoplane and a Nieuport monoplane were temporarily encamped at Lodmore, and a Short tractor biplane at Portland, in preparation for the Naval Review at Weymouth. The battleship HMS *Hibernia* had been fitted with a scaffolding arrangement extending from the top of the forward turret to the bow, from which an aeroplane was to be launched. The structure took the form of two parallel troughs in which the aeroplane's wheels ran. As *The Aeroplane* pointed out, this was hardly a practical fitting for war purposes, as it effectively put the two 12in guns in the forward turret out of action and reduced the arc of fire of the two forward 9.2in guns by half. But the arrangement was intended purely for demonstration purposes. *Hibernia* arrived at Portland with four aircraft aboard and three were offloaded on Friday 3 May, whereupon Commander Samson immediately tested 'HMS "Amphibian"', alias the Short S.41 100hp tractor biplane recently built for the navy, fitted with three torpedo-shaped floats to make it into a 'hydro-biplane'. He entered the water from the boat-slip in front of the hangar at Portland, circled the Fleet at anchor and returned to his starting point. He made three trips on the following day, and on Monday flew twelve miles out to sea to meet the incoming fleet and escort them in. Despite fog, various flights were conducted on the 8th, including bomb-dropping demonstrations. In the evening of Thursday 9 May Samson flew the float-equipped S.38 pusher biplane from *Hibernia*'s launching platform and flew round the bay before landing at Lodmore.

On 18 May it was announced that Lieutenant (Acting Commander) C R Samson, who 'has been in charge of the naval aviators at Eastchurch for some time', had been appointed Commandant of the RFC's Naval Wing. In its issue of 30 May *The Aeroplane* reported that land had been purchased adjoining the RAeC ground at Eastchurch on which sheds and workshops for the Naval Wing of the RFC were to be erected, one large building being almost complete. It was also reported that McClean was flying on 25 May and on S.36 in the evening of the 26th.

The repaired S.40 had its new float undercar-

The S.38 (left) and S.41 stowed on the makeshift launching platform erected on HMS *Hibernia* for the Naval Review at Weymouth in May 1912. (AUTHOR)

After brief initial use as a trainer for the Territorials, S.40/Short-Sommer No 10 went back to the manufacturer for conversion to a twin-float seaplane, re-emerging in this form at Harty Ferry at the end of May 1912. (AUTHOR)

Three small snapshots of S.40 at Harty Ferry during Frank McClean's early trials. (AUTHOR)

riage installed by Shorts at Harty Ferry on 28 May, this final part of the job being signed off as completed on the 30th. Also on the 28th, Shorts received an order from McClean for 'one pair of planes' for S.36. On Thursday and Friday the 30th and 31st McClean was testing his 'hydro-aeroplane' (S.40) at Harty. In addition, on the 30th he took off from Eastchurch in S.36, carrying a passenger, and flew to Dover, circled Dover Castle and the National Harbour at about 2,000ft and returned to Eastchurch after a flight lasting an hour and a half. One of his passengers at this time was his sister Anna. He carried several passengers in S.36 on 8 June, including Captain Bidder, Mrs Bidder, Miss G Brown and Captain W S Stafford. Each was given a trip round the island, attaining a height of about 500ft. Then, on the following day, he was flying S.40 at Harty Ferry, again carrying passengers. Captain and Mrs Bidder had further flights, and also Alec Ogilvie, the aircraft 'behaving in a highly satisfactory manner'. Later Ogilvie flew over Harty Ferry with F B Fowler, the owner of Eastbourne Aerodrome, as his passenger to watch the hydro-aeroplane experiments. McClean was flying S.36 again at Eastchurch on 10 June, after which the weather turned bad.

Reverting to his test-pilot role, at Eastchurch in early June McClean tested the S.43 and S.44 'Ordinary Type' biplanes ordered by the War Office on 5 March for the Central Flying School. They were delivered to Upavon in July.

Aerial marine photography

The demonstrations of naval flying at Weymouth led to assertions that the submarine's days were numbered, as it could easily be discovered by scouting aeroplanes. To determine the truth of this claim, Hugh Spottiswoode, chairman of *The Sphere*, a glossy weekly illustrated broadsheet newspaper, set about 'organising an initial experiment which should give some idea of the penetrability of water above a sunken vessel'. The magazine professed that it 'did not hold a brief either for the submarine or the air scout. It does not favour one arm of our national defence more than another, but it feels that this is a question into which it is highly desirable to impart some quantity of definite fact.' Although the newspaper implied that the experiment was its own idea, *The Aeroplane*, in its issue of 20 June, had suggested that the project was McClean's, and that he was being 'assisted by some of the cleverest Press photographers on the staff of one of the big illustrated papers'.

To this end *The Sphere* arranged for an aeroplane flown by McClean to carry a photographer to take aerial photographs of the liner *Oceana*, which had sunk seven miles off Eastbourne in March after colliding with the barque *Pisagua*. The *Oceana* lay on grey mud with some 40ft of water above her decks, the approximate diving depth of a submarine. 'The vessel was therefore a conveniently fixed objective which ought to give the air scout a fair chance of proving his contention,' the newspaper stated. 'The decks are certainly no longer white but are covered with green slime.'

Initially the weather conditions were entirely in the submarine's favour, surface winds on and near the shore being 'very troublesome', and for ten days no aeroplane could set out from Eastbourne with any degree of safety. 'During this period,' said *The Sphere*, 'submarines could have been patrolling or investigating the coast without hindrance from any airman.' Meanwhile, on 13 June, McClean had Shorts fit S.36 with 'floats' and cut a hole in the fuselage underside 'for photographic work'. This work was completed the following day, and on the 17th, with his chief mechanic as passenger and also carrying some luggage, he set off in S.36 for Eastbourne Aerodrome, which had been kindly made available as a base for the experiment by its owner Mr Fowler. The aircraft was sighted over Pevensey shortly after 6am, and landed at Eastbourne after a splendid *vol plane* from about 500ft, McClean thus completing his longest direct cross-country journey to date, covering over 60 miles and lasting 1 hour 17 minutes. On the way he had made a detour to fly over his home at Tonbridge 'to wake up the establishment'. In fact the S.36 had not been fitted with floats to make it a seaplane, but had been fitted with a pair of flotation bags to keep it afloat in the event of ditching. Curiously, these were attached to the outer sides of the innermost pair of interplane struts, low down in the gap between the upper and lower wings, so that, had the machine descended on the water, the lower wings would have been sub-

merged. It can only be presumed that this was done to avoid any top-heaviness that might cause the aeroplane to capsize in choppy water.

Towards the end of the third week in June the weather turned, and on the 21st McClean saw his opportunity. With *Sphere* photographer Charles Cusden in the rear cockpit with his 'special camera and fast plates', he took off from Eastbourne. The plan was to fly out to *Oceana* and circle the liner three times at different heights. Cusden was to watch through his trap in the cockpit floor and take a photograph each time they passed over the ship.

After take-off, McClean climbed to 300ft, and as he rose to 500ft over part of the beach at 10am the radiation under a very hot sun created some very disturbing air currents. The going was better once he was over the sea, but at 1,000ft a cloud hid everything from view. He descended to 900ft, and then made his three circles over the *Oceana*, with the salvage steamer *Ranger* across its stern, Cusden taking his three photographs in bright light and a stiff breeze at 900ft, 500ft and 300ft. The return flight was made through 'very stiff and troublesome wind', but 'a fine vol-plane brought the aviator and passenger safely to earth'.

In mid-June the S.36, fitted with inter-wing emergency flotation bags, was used by McClean to take aerial photographs of the sunken P & O liner *Oceana*. The aircraft is seen here at Eastbourne Aerodrome, from where McClean took off for the site off Beachy Head where the submerged liner lay. (AUTHOR)

Cusden's photographs were published in the 6 July issue of *The Sphere*. The outline of the submerged liner was not as clear as might have been hoped, but the magazine said that, at 900ft, despite the green slime on its decks and the intervention of 'much thick chalky water', the outline of the vessel 'was looming through the water'. At the lower altitudes the *Oceana*'s outline was harder to distinguish owing to a great deal of reflection from the broken-wave surface of the sea, but the magazine claimed that 'with a calmer sea there is no doubt that a very much clearer result would have been obtained'.

In assessing the results of its experiment, *The Sphere* said:

It is evident that at 900ft altitude the form of the submerged vessel was becoming visible, and this under the conditions of a choppy sea with broken light-reflecting surfaces and thick water full of chalk solution from the neighbouring cliffs. Had the clouds permitted photographs would have been taken at 1,000ft and 1,200ft altitude, and it seems reasonable to believe that at these heights the vessel would have appeared with increasing clearness. Height appears to render the local movements on the water less disturbing to general form of the submerged object.

On the other hand, it was pointed out that:

It is evident that weather conditions will often shield the submarine from the unwelcome attentions of the air scout and that the thick water which swashes backward and forward far out into the channel from the chalk cliffs will be a welcome covering from sharp eyes poised overhead. The gusty, dangerous airs off the cliffs would in the present state of aviation prove too much for the air scout,

leaving a free unchallenged field for the submarine. The heated air rising from the shore was found to set up the most undesirable movements from the aviator's point of view.

McClean set out from Eastbourne on 2 July to fly back to Eastchurch, but encountered rain and fog. He therefore landed at his family home in Tunbridge Wells, and S.36 was dismantled by Shorts on the 4th and returned to Eastchurch by road. During his 300ft pass over *Oceana* he had encountered blown spray, and the engine had to be overhauled, the fuselage re-covered, and the wings were found to be waterlogged and had to be replaced.

Also on 2 July, McClean ordered from Shorts 'One twin 70h.p. Tractor Biplane', which Shorts designated S.53. The project seems to have been abandoned very quickly, as no more was heard of it.

Taken to court

In June 1912 McClean was elected an Associate Fellow of the ASGB. However, his flight from Eastchurch to Eastbourne on 17 June had angered Thomas Partridge of 'The Merry Harriers' at Cowbeach, Sussex, who subsequently brought an action for damages against him. It was alleged that 'the defendant did so unskilfully and negligently fly over Spratts Farm that a valuable mare was frightened', and the alleged negligence also included 'driving an aeroplane too near the ground' and 'failing to comply with the Motor Car (Use and Construction) Order of 1904 with regard to silencing exhaust gases'. In addition, as an alternative charge, Partridge claimed damages for 'entering upon the property of Spratts Farm', and two further alternatives, that the aeroplane had rendered the house unsafe to live in, and 'that the defendant drove through the air a dangerous machine, the said aeroplane, so as to be dangerous to persons and property on the ground'. Partridge assessed the depreciation of his mare at £30, and with the addition of veterinary fees and other charges McClean faced a bill for £45. Because an important principle was at issue, affecting all aviators, the RAeC paid for counsel's opinion on the matter from Mr Clavell Salter, KC, and Mr James Scarlett.

Five questions were put to counsel: (1) Is an aviator in flight trespassing over property below? (2) Does the Roman law *'Cujus est solum ejus est usque ad coelum'* ('Whoever owns the soil, it is theirs up to Heaven') apply, and is not the air the property of all and not the special property of any particular persons? (3) Is it an act of negligence to fly over property and frighten livestock? (4) Would such negligence apply to property adjacent, even on the highway, over which he was not actually flying, but was flying near to? (5) Can an aeroplane or airship be called a nuisance by reason of its noise in flight? The counsel expressed the opinion that an aeroplane passing over property did infringe a proprietary right, but that any action of trespass might come under another legal maxim: *'De minimis non curat lex'* ('The law has no concern with trifles'). It was thought that an injunction might be granted against a trespasser, and that at least an undertaking would have to be given that the offence would not be repeated. Counsel said that negligence was always a question of fact. The question was one of whether the aviator used all proper care and skill, and the jury would decide.

Next, the extent of 'dedication of any highway' was a question of fact. There was no evidence of any intention to give the public right of passage through the air over the land dedicated any more than through the soil under the surface. Therefore, an aviator over a highway has no more rights than when flying over enclosed lands. Action could only be taken if the aeroplane were a nuisance: and a nuisance involved 'a sensible interference with the comfort and safety of others'. An aeroplane could certainly not be called a nuisance as a matter of law. It was a question of fact in each case whether the particular aeroplane used constituted a nuisance to the person complaining.

McClean's S.40, after floats had replaced its wheel undercarriage, at Westgate in 1912. (FLEET AIR ARM MUSEUM)

The action brought by Partridge was eventually settled out of court by making a payment to him of £25. As Hurren comments in *Fellowship of the Air*, 'It was the easy way out, as undoubtedly McClean had been flying low; but the case aroused great interest among aviators (who could never believe that they were not popular with earthbound people who regarded the flying machine as an abomination).'

While S.36 was under repair McClean apparently did little or no flying at Eastchurch, but on 9 July at Harty Ferry S.40 was fitted with the 50hp propeller from S.32, and from 16 to 22 July it was fitted with 8ft upper wing extensions with 'flaps' (single-acting ailerons), which suggests that a little extra lift was needed.

On 21 July McClean was back in the air at Eastchurch in S.36, now fitted with new wings since its 'Eastbourne wettings'. He then took up Mr Marshall as a passenger.

Yet another new Short machine made its first appearance at Eastchurch on the evening of Tuesday 23 July. This was the S.47, described as a 'new naval triple twin Short tractor'. Ordered by the Admiralty on 25 March as a 'Triple Tractor Biplane', it was powered by two 50hp Gnomes mounted in tandem, the front one driving a direct-coupled propeller and the

One of the more unusual aeroplanes flown by McClean in his 'honorary' role as Short's test pilot was the S.47 'Triple Tractor', built for the Admiralty, which he took for its official test flight on 24 July 1912. This ungainly machine had three tractor propellers driven by two 50hp Gnomes housed beneath a 16ft cowling, and the heat generated by this installation earned the aircraft the nickname 'Field Kitchen'. (AUTHOR)

rearwards-facing rear engine driving wing-mounted counter-rotating tractor propellers through Wright-type chains and sprockets. It was fitted with double-acting ailerons that worked both above and below the 48ft-span wings, which was said to have made the lateral control far more sensitive. This indicates that the aircraft had already made its maiden flight, probably with McClean at the helm, though Shorts' order book gives the 'Date Completed' as 24 July. On the 24th McClean flew the S.47 on its one-hour test with Lieutenant Malone as passenger, successfully completing the test despite having to fly the last 15 minutes in a thunderstorm. Malone flew it himself on the 25th, handling it 'very well'. It had a tendency to generate heat beneath its 16ft-long metal engine cowling, and was consequently nicknamed 'Field Kitchen'. Malone frequently piloted the S.47 at Eastchurch on subsequent occasions,

The Shorts works and Royal Aero Club sheds at Eastchurch, photographed by Dr W J S Lockyer from Frank McClean's 70hp Short tractor biplane on 27 July 1912. (AUTHOR)

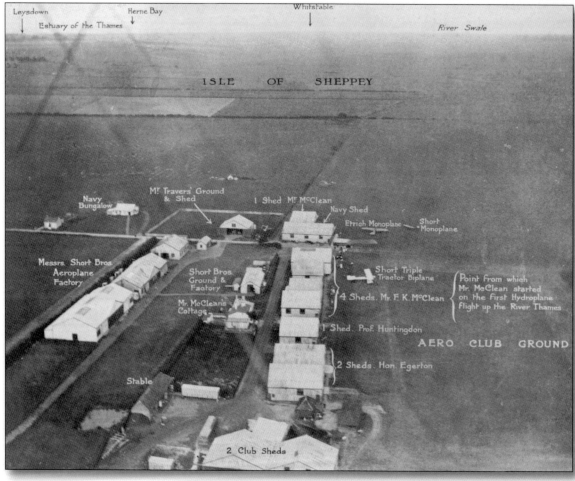

Leysdown

Estuary of the Thames

Herne Bay

Whitstable

River Swale

ISLE OF SHEPPEY

Navy Bungalow

Mr Travers' Ground & Shed

1 Shed Mr McClean

Navy Shed

Etrich Monoplane — Short Monoplane

Messrs. Short Bros. Aeroplane Factory

Short Bros. Ground & Factory

Mr McCleans Cottage

Short Triple Tractor Biplane

4 Sheds. Mr F.K. McClean

Point from which Mr. McClean started on the first Hydroplane flight up the River Thames

1 Shed. Prof. Huntingdon

AERO CLUB GROUND

2 Sheds. Hon. Egerton

Stable

2 Club Sheds

his handling of the aircraft being described as 'excellent'. It was given the naval identity T4.

At Eastchurch parish church on Friday 26 July McClean was present for the unveiling of a memorial window to the late Hon. Charles Rolls and Mr Cecil Grace by the Archbishop of Canterbury. McClean flew S.36 again that evening and in the evening of the following day. On Sunday the 28th he had planned 'some hydro work' with S.40, but a strong wind all day ruled out any flying.

Up the Thames and under the bridges

On Friday 26 July *Lieutenant de Vaisseau* de Conneau (alias 'André Beaumont') of the French Navy, who was also managing director of the Donnet-Lévèque company, set off from Juvisy in one of the company's single-engine biplane flying boats, intending to fly from Paris to London. He followed the Seine to Berons, where he alighted after covering thirty-six miles. His plan was to continue along the river to Havre, cross the Channel, go round the English coast and up the Thames to Westminster. Unfortunately bad weather intervened and forced him to bide his time, but he was able to resume his flight on 9 August, setting course along the Seine for Havre. After alighting briefly at Quillebouef for replenishment, Conneau continued to Havre, where he alighted in front of the casino. The aircraft was slightly damaged when it collided with the shore, but he was able to make a non-stop run to Boulogne after lunch. There, enthusiastic but overzealous fishermen damaged a float in their efforts to assist, halting progress for that day. After overnight repairs Conneau took off on the afternoon of the 10th for the cross-Channel flight, but the aircraft was considerably buffeted by the wind and he quickly had to put the flying boat back on to the very choppy water.

Suddenly a very strong squall caught the aeroplane, and it was overturned. Conneau swam clear and oversaw the towing of the wreck back to the shore. It was intended to make another attempt to fly to London once the aircraft was repaired.

In England, the *Daily Mail* newspaper had loudly proclaimed Conneau's anticipated arrival, saying he would become the first aviator to fly up the course of the Thames through the City of London, and that a reception at Carmelite House, the newspaper's head office, had been arranged. Lord Northcliffe, the newspaper's owner, had obtained special permission for the flight, and on the 10th reporters and photographers were strategically positioned to record the event, unaware of the happenings across the Channel.

McClean later recalled: 'This roused the fighting spirit at Eastchurch, and the night before [Conneau] was due to arrive, my cottage was invaded by all and sundry, demanding that I, being the possessor of a machine with floats (prehistorically known as a Hydro-Aeroplane), should start not later than 8 o'clock next morning, and so get there first.'

The apparent spontaneity of the subsequent event is open to question, as *The Sphere*, which now seemed to regard McClean and his aeroplane as its own, and even described his adventure as '*The Sphere* flight', stated in its issue for 17 August 1912:

After the completion of *The Sphere* marine aviation experiments in the English Channel the attention of this journal has been turned more particularly to the development of the hydro-aeroplane. It is felt that in view of our insular position as a nation the hydro-aeroplane must rapidly assert its pre-eminence over the flying machine pure and simple. The length of our coast-line seems to point in-

The overturning of Lt de Vaisseau de Conneau's Donnet-Lévèque flying boat in a squall prevented him from making his heralded flight up the Thames on August 10 1912, and McClean took the opportunity to upstage the Frenchman. (AUTHOR)

evitably to increasing uses for the hydro-aeroplane with its combined usefulness on sea and land.

With this leading idea in view *The Sphere* has been organising, in collaboration with Mr F.K. McClean of the Eastchurch Aviation Ground, a number of experiments by which the present state of the hydro-aeroplane's efficiency can be demonstrated to the general public. A flight up the Thames to London was projected in the belief that by this means thousands who had never seen a hydro-aeroplane would witness its wonderful capacities.

After considering all the widths of the river bridges the aviator came to the conclusion that the flight was possible. Then M 'Beaumont,' the well-known French aviator, announced his intention of flying up the Thames. Bad luck, however, prevented the accomplishment of his journey and the lau-

rels fell to Mr McClean, who successfully reached London on Saturday morning.

The Sphere's account of the flight reads as follows:

. . . Mr F.K. McClean left the Royal Aero Club ground on the Isle of Sheppey at 6.30am on Saturday morning. At first there was a short journey across land; then the aviator began travelling up the waters of the Thames. In the initial stage the height maintained was about 400ft, but this varied according to circumstance, and when some thick, murky air was encountered the hydro-aeroplane dropped to 50ft. The course of the river was followed throughout; no corners were cut off at the bends as the flight was to be a strictly river one. The machine which Mr McClean selected for the journey was a large Short biplane fitted with two hydroplane floats shaped so as to act in the same way as the body of a hydroplane boat. The machine was 62ft broad from wing-tip to wing-tip and stood from 13ft to 14ft above the water. This great width gave the hydro-aeroplane splendid lifting capacity, but at the same time it increased the difficulties of negotiating the arches of the river bridges. The machine,

however, is an extremely steady one, and Mr McClean was able to fly straight and sure through the Tower Bridge; that is, the space enclosed between the upper footways and the roadway bascules. From this point he saw that all was well for passing beneath the other bridges. The machine dropped gracefully towards the water and skimmed through the succession of bridges . . . , just touching the water at one or two points. The bridges and the Embankment were lined with enthusiastic crowds waiting to see M Beaumont, and great cheers arose when Mr McClean drew up off Westminster Pier and threw out his anchor, which gripped the bottom of the river.

McClean's flight up the Thames to the Houses of Parliament in S.40 on 10 August 1912, passing between the footbridge and road spans of Tower Bridge, as seen here, and under several other bridges, made national headlines. (AUTHOR)

The journey was over. London had been reached, and throughout the remainder of Saturday and part of Sunday morning throngs of people gazed their full on the white-winged water-skimmer which for the first time rested under the shadow of the Clock Tower. On Sunday Mr McClean started on the return journey to Eastchurch. He did not attempt to rise from the water till all the bridges had been passed. . . . More crowds were out to see the white-winged ap-

parition as it floated past barge, wharf and steamer . . . . Gaining Shadwell Reach the aviator turned in order to rise from the water with the advantage of the wind, which was then blowing downstream. Rising easily from the surface the machine turned in the air to resume its homeward course, but unfortunately a side-blast of air deflected against the machine by some tall buildings tilted it in such a way that the right-hand float struck the water too smartly. No barge or other object was struck, and the damage done to the machine was very slight, but unfortunately it prevented the completion of the homeward journey by river. The wings were unshipped and the biplane returned to its hangar by train.

This spread from the 17 August 1912 issue of *The Sphere* charts McClean's Thames flight. Note the illustration at bottom left, showing the aircraft after suffering damage in the attempt to take off after taxying back down to Shadwell Basin. (AUTHOR)

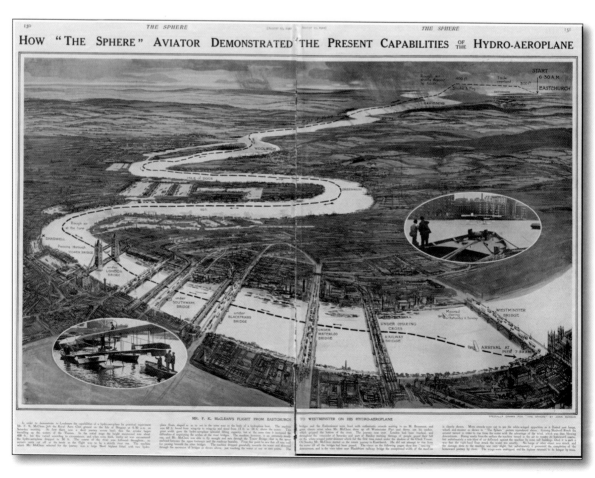

HOW "THE SPHERE" AVIATOR DEMONSTRATED THE PRESENT CAPABILITIES OF THE HYDRO-AEROPLANE

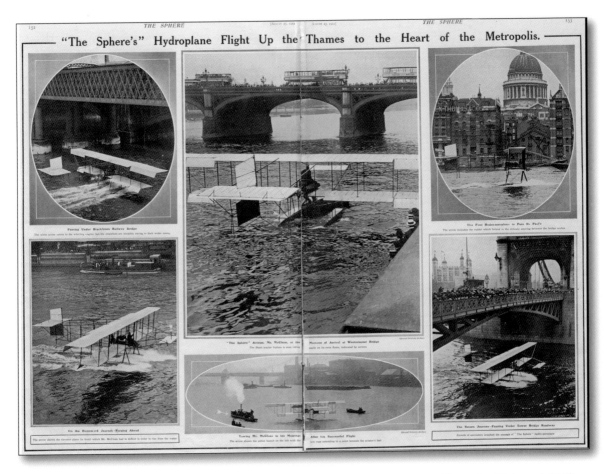

"The Sphere's" Hydroplane Flight Up the Thames to the Heart of the Metropolis.

Flight's account of the event included a rather weak attempt to offer an excuse for McClean's flight:

Another imposing spread from the 17 August 1912 issue of *The Sphere* follows McClean's progress through London along the Thames. It will be noticed that he actually taxied, rather than flew, beneath some of the bridges. (AUTHOR)

Although London was deprived . . . of the sight of M. Beaumont piloting his hydro-aeroplane up the Thames, the visit of Mr F.K. McClean more than compensated for the loss. Remembering an appointment in town on Saturday morning, Mr McClean thought it would be a good idea to come up on his Short machine [S.40], and so at 6am he had it brought out of its shed at Harty Ferry, in the Isle of Sheppey, and after seeing everything in order he started off. Following the coast round Leysdown, Warden Point to Sheerness, he continued over the Thames. At

Gravesend the smoke of the various factories rather troubled the aviator but he made good progress. Approaching London Mr McClean brought his machine lower down and negotiated the Tower Bridge between the lower and upper spans, but the remaining bridges to Westminster he flew underneath, the water being just touched at Blackfriars and Waterloo bridges. He reached Westminster about 8.30 and was taken ashore to Westminster Pier on a Port of London launch.

The return journey on Sunday afternoon

Frank McClean examines the S.40's seven-cylinder Gnome engine at the time of the Thames flight. (AUTHOR)

was not so successful owing to restrictions as to rising from the water which had been imposed by the police. The bridges had all been safely negotiated, and when near Shadwell Basin Mr McClean started to manoeuvre to get into the air at the point designated by the river authorities. He had made one circuit when the machine side-slipped, and either through hitting a barge or by sudden contact with the water one of the floats was damaged. The machine was then towed into Shadwell Dock, this operation being superintended by Mr McClean from the driving seat, and dismantled for its return by road to Eastchurch.

The S.40 moored on the Thames at the end of its sensational flight. McClean was later congratulated by King George V for this adventure. (AUTHOR)

After he had gone ashore at Westminster McClean went to lunch at Hatchett's, and during the meal he was approached by a nervous head

waiter and told that the police were looking for him. Taking the bull by the horns, McClean asked for an interview with the Commissioner of the Metropolitan Police, Sir Edward Henry. During the interview he was reprimanded and told that no action would be taken if he took his aeroplane away, provided he did not leave the water until he had passed all the bridges. In his own brief account of the flight, written in 1938, McClean wrote:

It was a dreary dawn as the enthusiasts pushed me and the machine down the slip-way into the Swale, but the engine did its job, and at a steady thirty miles an hour or so the river slipped past below until the Tower Bridge loomed ahead.

Then temptation took a hand in the game, and instead of going over the top, I put the machine through the opening. There was room and to spare, although the bus horses crossing the bridge had other ideas.

London Bridge was not so commodious. I had, however, lost too much height to make it advisable to cross above the roadway. When I reached the farther side, I knew that there was sufficient room for the machine, but the remaining bridges to Westminster were negotiated on the water.

An invitation to visit Scotland Yard followed, and a promise not to repeat the offence gave me freedom. But the subsequent return journey ended abruptly when I discovered, too late, that there was not enough space among the shipping below the bridges in which to manoeuvre in the air, and the home-coming with the debris was by road.

The Aeroplane's account, almost certainly the work of C G Grey, its patriotic, opinionated and pugnacious editor, was longer and rather more entertaining, though inaccurate in places:

Quite one of the neatest sells for which aviation has as yet been responsible was that perpetrated by Mr Frank McClean and his Short hydro-biplane on the British public on Saturday last. When all London, or at any rate all that section of it which reads the *Daily Mail*, was anxiously awaiting the much boomed arrival of Lieut. de Conneau, of the French Navy, on his French aero-hydroplane, a mere British aviator, Mr F.K. McClean, on a mere British hydro-aeroplane, calmly flew up the Thames, and after passing by the elaborate arrangements made for Lieut. de Conneau's reception at Carmelite Street, alighted by the new County Council building opposite Westminster.

Evidently the *Daily Mail*'s 'Special Correspondent' was somewhat chagrined that British enterprise should have got in front of France for once in a way, for he opens his description of the arrival by saying, 'The crowd that gathered on the Victoria Embankment, London, on Saturday morning in the hope of seeing M. Beaumont arrive were fortunate enough not to go away *entirely disappointed*. While the French airman was kept at Boulogne by the tardiness of his mechanics in arriving from Paris an English flier *stole his thunder*.' Incidentally, it may be well to point out that Mr McClean is Irish rather than English, and that the italics are ours.

Mr McClean started out from the Isle of Sheppey at about 6.30am and alighted at about eight o'clock. Strangely enough, he adopted the course of flying under all the bridges instead of over them, which certainly added to the risk so far as he was concerned, as there can have been very little room to spare under some of the older bridges. The machine he used is one of the ordinary type Short biplanes with front elevator and monoplane tail.

Mr McClean said that on his way up the river he had a good journey as far as Plumstead, where he got among London smoke and so had to come down low, and when approaching the Tower Bridge, where the river becomes much narrower, he found that air currents from the various buildings made it advisable to fly as low as possible.

To those who have followed aviation from its beginning in this country, it is peculiarly gratifying that Mr McClean and his Short biplane should have achieved the distinction of being the first water-fliers to arrive in London, for not only was Mr McClean one of the first men in this country to take up aviation, but he has from the commencement flown Short machines, and of course the Short Brothers were the very first firm to equip a proper aeroplane factory in England.

Mr McClean has long been recognised as one of the soundest and most capable fliers in this country, but he has never brought himself before the public, for he has never had any desire for personal publicity. Recently his name became known to the outside Press, because for purely scientific purposes he made flights over the wreck of the SS *Oceana* to test the possibilities of submarine photography. It will, however, be remembered by those more closely in touch with aviation that it was he who lent two Short biplanes to the Admiralty, in 1910, for the purpose of training the officers who are now the senior pilots of the Naval Wing of the Royal Flying Corps, the actual training of these officers being undertaken by Mr G.B. Cockburn during Mr McClean's absence in the Pacific on an astronomical expedition.

Knowing Mr McClean's objection to personal advertising, the writer has no hesitation in saying that this flight could only have been undertaken by him in a thoroughly sporting

patriotic spirit, to show that, after all, there are British pilots who can do good flights without being on the advertisement staff of a halfpenny paper.

On behalf of British sportsmen *The Aeroplane* congratulates Mr McClean and the Brothers Short on the success of a thoroughly sporting undertaking.

As a sign of the times, it is worth recording that about mid-day, when Mr McClean's machine had been sitting in the river for a few hours, the police rang up the offices of *The Aeroplane* and asked whether the staff could give them any clue to Mr McClean's whereabouts, as they wanted to know what he was going to do about leaving his machine in the river unattended. The inquiry was made just in the same way as an inquiry might be made about a car left in a street without a driver.

About noon on Sunday Mr McClean started on his return journey and kept on the surface of the water under all the bridges, but when he had passed the Tower Bridge Mr McClean turned round so as to rise against the wind, and rose to about 50ft. In turning down stream again, the machine was caught by a gust and side-slipped into the water, apparently narrowly missing some barges and a boat. On hitting the water one of the floats collapsed, so the machine was towed into one of the docks and taken to pieces for transport to Sheppey.

Shorts set about repairing S.40 on 14 August and the job was completed on the 17th. In *Flight* for that date it was reported that the Committee of the RAeC, of which McClean was a member, was considering the desirability of flights over the Thames through London, and had decided, pending a conference with the authorities, to forbid such flights. (In 1911 the RAeC had suspended D Graham Gilmour's

Dismantling the damaged S.40 in Shadwell Dock after its attempted take-off from Shadwell Reach on 11 August 1912. Frank McClean, on the left, looks decidedly disgruntled. (Fleet Air Arm Museum)

aviator's certificate for a month after he flew over Henley when the Regatta was in progress on 7 July that year, ruling that his flying was 'dangerous to the public safety'.) In the Editorial of the following issue it was announced that 'A conference is to be held at which the police, the Home Office, the Army and Navy and the Club itself are to be represented to consider the whole question of flights over the Thames and, if they are to be allowed at all, under what restrictions'. The magazine remarked:

... whatever their value, it cannot be denied that there is an element of danger in them which we do not think should be unduly encouraged at the present moment. Under proper regulation, the worst of that danger would disappear, and, we take it, it is just this element of regulation which the proposed conference may be looked to to supply. As it is, it would seem to be open to everyone owning any jurisdiction at all over the river to make whatever regulations he likes – it appears to us it was really because of the restrictions suddenly enforced by someone in authority that Mr McClean came to grief on his return journey – and the sooner that is all changed the better.

The 'Double-Dirty'

One of the most mysterious of all Short aeroplanes made its debut at Eastchurch on Saturday 21 September 1912. Allotted type number S.46, it had been ordered by the Admiralty on 25 March, the same day as S.47 was ordered, and was described as 'One Hydro Monoplane H2 fitted tandem fashion with 2 70 h.p. Gnome Engines. Machine No 46.' In its 26 September issue *The Aeroplane* reported, 'The new twin 70-h.p. engine Short monoplane made its appearance but did not essay a flight on account of heavy wind. The two 70-h.p. engines are fore and aft of the pilot and passenger, who sit side by side. The lateral control is by means of ailerons. She has been built for water work only.' Despite this last remark the S.46 was destined only to be flown as a landplane. In its issue for 12 October *Flight* reported: 'The twin-engine system has recently been installed on a monoplane built by Messrs. Short Bros., and during tests made by Commander Samson at Eastchurch, the machine, which has two 70 h.p. Gnome engines, performed very satisfactorily.' The Gnomes were mounted at the front and rear of a short nacelle, driving one tractor and one pusher propeller, and the tail surfaces were carried on open braced booms as with conventional pusher machines. The undercarriage carried streamlined pneumatic flotation bags which would not have enabled the machine to take off from the sea, so it seems that it was meant for launch from a shipborne runway. As the occupants were subjected to a fierce slipstream laden with castor oil lubricant, the S.46, given the Admiralty serial number 12, was soon nicknamed the 'Double-Dirty'. When C G Grey of *The Aeroplane* visited Eastchurch early in October, the 'great 140 h.p. experimental monoplane' S.46 'was having some repairs and alterations made'. On October 21 the machine was 'again

out at Eastchurch with Commander Samson', and on the afternoon of the 23rd Samson flew it twice, taking Engineer-Lieutenant Briggs, RN, as a passenger on the second flight. The next day Samson flew the monoplane from Eastchurch to the navy's new and yet-to-be-commissioned hydro-aeroplane station on the Isle of Grain, opposite Sheerness, with Briggs in the passenger seat. He was back at Eastchurch flying S.38 in the afternoon, apparently having suffered a mishap with the S.46 at Grain, as there is record of a landing accident, with the aircraft being 'towed to Grain' on that day.

An entry in the Short's order book, dated 24 October, records: 'To repair Twin 70 h.p. Monoplane No 12 after damage at the Isle of Grain'. It was repaired by the following day, and in its issue for 2 November *Flight* reported that 'Last week . . . the new Short 140 h.p. double-engined monoplane' was 'being tested over the River Medway in the neighbourhood of Sheerness'. But it was evidently damaged again at the end of the month, as an order book entry for 30 October records: 'Monoplane No 12. To repair the above Machine at the Isle of Grain'.

On the morning of 6 November Samson, with Seaman Twelvetrees as his passenger, flew S.38 to the Isle of Grain and then flew back solo in S.46, while Lieutenant Hewlett brought Twelvetrees back in S.38. Samson flew the monoplane again on the afternoon of 8 November, and on the afternoon of the 9th he made 'several flights' in it. On 23 November Shorts supplied 'one manganese steel shock absorber band' for No 12, and on the 26th the company provided '14 complete inlet valves, new pattern' for its Gnome engines. After that the S.46 vanishes from the record until it is recorded as being dismantled in the week ending 2 August 1913. No drawings or photographs of it have ever been found.

On Sunday the 18th McClean put in a good 30-minute flight on S.36 at Eastchurch, but he may have had a rough landing, as on the 19th it was at Shorts, having a new tailskid and a spare wheel fitted. McClean appears to have done no flying in September, and on the 9th S.36 was back at Shorts to have its wings doped with Cellon and then given a coat of varnish. This was completed on the 14th.

In *Flight* for 7 September and *The Aeroplane* for 12 September it was reported that the Home Secretary had informed the RAeC that he proposed to call a conference at the Home Office, about the middle of October, to discuss the question of the control of aviation over London and up the Thames, and had invited the Club to send representatives to the conference. It was hardly surprising that McClean was one of the four appointed representatives.

There were several fatal accidents during August/September 1912, and McClean was involved in some of the subsequent investigations by the RAeC's Public Safety and Accidents Investigation Committee. One victim was H J D Astley, from whom McClean had bought the Universal Birdling Blériot-type monoplane in 1911, who crashed at Belfast on Saturday 21 September. McClean attended Astley's funeral on 26 September.

At Harty Ferry from 1 to 3 October Short Brothers' staff removed the floats from S.40 and replaced them with a wheel undercarriage. Then, at the factory on the 4th, work started on dismantling the aircraft and reconstructing it 'as instructed' by McClean. It was to undergo a dramatic transformation.

On the 7th S.36 went into the works for repair work to its petrol tank and other components, this work being completed on the 12th. The following day, Sunday 13 October, McClean took two lady passengers in turns on S.36, and on the afternoon of Saturday the 19th he gave his sister Anna a flight in the same machine. His passenger on the morning of the 21st was Miss Greg, and he also made a 30-minute flight in the afternoon. The machine then went into Shorts' factory to have a new axle fitted and to have its tail altered 'as instructed'. This was completed on the 24th, and a 20-minute flight in S.36 was made by McClean on 25 October. On 7 November he took Staff-Surgeon Wells, RN, for a flight in the afternoon. He was aloft again with a passenger on the afternoon of the 9th.

On 29 October McClean attended an RAeC Committee meeting at which the following notice was directed to be issued to all aviators:

The Royal Aero Club, being the sole authority under the provisions of the Fédération Aéronautique Internationale for regulating all matters relating to aeronautics and aviation in the British Empire, hereby issues the following notices and regulations to aviators of all nationalities within its jurisdiction.

(1)   Flying, to the danger of the public is hereby prohibited. This shall be taken to include:

(a)   Unnecessary flights over towns or thickly populated areas or over places where crowds are temporarily assembled.

(b)   Flying over River Regattas, Race Meetings, Meetings for public games, and sports, except flights specifically arranged for in writing with the promoters of such Regattas, Meetings, &c.

(2)   Any disregard of the above notices and regulations will render the aviator liable to censure, suspension of certificate and removal from the Competitors' Register.

Changed beyond recognition

The reconstruction of S.40 was completed on 15 November, and when it re-emerged it was so different that had been renumbered S.58. Unfortunately both *Flight* and *The Aeroplane* ceased reporting on activities at Eastchurch at the end of 1912, so progress with this machine is not recorded, apart from a brief reference in the 28 November issue of *The Aeroplane*, stating:

Messrs. Short Bros. are to be congratulated on the success of their new biplane built on the lines of the 'S.38,' described recently in this paper. This machine has the pilot and passenger well out in front of the lower plane and the planes themselves are swept back further than in the 'S.38'. With a 70 hp Gnome engine, the machine, piloted by Lieut. Parke, RN, who was accompanied by two passengers, rose to 1,000 feet in 9 minutes without actually being forced up, and it is said to be exceptionally handy and stable.

By this time the ancient S.38 had undergone several repairs and a major rebuild, and it no

After it was wrecked on 9 July 1912, S.38 was rebuilt. It emerged in much-altered form, with a long nacelle, reduced gap, extended wings, revised tail surfaces and shortened booms carrying the forward elevator. It carries its naval serial number, 2, on its rudder. (AUTHOR)

longer looked like the Short-Sommer biplane of its original form. On 22 July Shorts had started a thorough overhaul and repair, including the fitting of 9ft extensions to the upper wingtips and the installation of a compass and aneroid, this being completed on 5 September. Further modifications were then immediately instructed by Lieutenant Parke, and on 6 September Shorts began 'Alterations to tail outrigger etc & controls', these taking until 18 October to complete. In fact the rebuilt S.38 was flying before that date, as C G Grey of *The Aeroplane* saw it in the air, piloted by Lieutenant Seddon, when he visited Eastchurch in the week preceding the issue of the magazine dated 17 October, in which he described it.

In its new form the extended sections of the upper plane have a pronounced dihedral angle, and taper sharply backwards. The gap between the planes has been reduced. The chassis is lower. The engine and its bearers are considerably above the lower plane, and are fixed to a raised body or fuselage, in which the pilot sits a good way in front of the leading edge. The passenger is slightly in front of the leading edge, and has an excellent

By January 1913 the S.38's nacelle and undercarriage had undergone further changes, as seen here. The aircraft formed the prototype of a small batch of similar machines, these having the forward elevator carried on small supports extending from the nacelle. (AUTHOR)

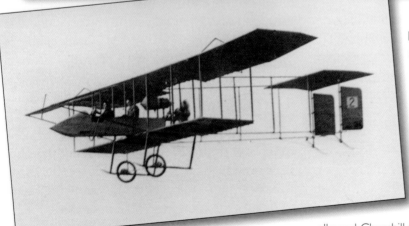

In its ultimate form the S.38 soldiered on for some time. These shots of it in flight at Eastchurch were taken on 10 October 1912, when Lieutenant L'Estrange Malone was carrying Lieutenant Clark-Hall as a passenger. On 29 November 1913 Winston Churchill, then First Lord of the Admiralty, was given a flight in this machine by Lieutenant G.V. Wildman-Lushington, RMA, who allowed Churchill to take the controls. Churchill thus became the first Cabinet Minister in the world to control his own aircraft. (AUTHOR)

view below and on each side. His seat is on the same level as the pilot's, so that he is comfortably protected from the weather, and he has plenty of leg-room in which to stow drawing tackle, maps and instruments. The front elevator is very small and practically flat, and it is placed only a few feet in front of the pilot; in fact it seems to be there to keep him company more than for any other reason. As a matter of fact, it has quite a lot of effect, for the machine is very quick on her controls, though practically automatically stable when once in the air and going ahead, as was shown by the fact that the machine was scarcely moving when the others were pitching and rolling badly.

Even when landing and catching the wind off the sheds she just gave a slight kick and came back at once. Her performance may have been due to Mr Seddon's fine flying, but it would have been impossible on anything but a very good machine. Also, it must be remembered that she does not owe any of her stability to her speed, for she is a very big machine with only a 50hp Gnome, and consequently she is one of the slowest machines in the Service, for her power goes in lifting efficiency and stability.

So the S.58 was very like the rebuilt S.38 as described by Grey, but with an extra 20hp. The old Farman-type forward elevator carried on booms extending well ahead of the mainplanes was done away with, the elevator being carried on much shorter struts extending only a short distance from the nacelle housing the occupants. The 70hp Gnome attached to the rear of the nacelle drove a two-blade pusher propeller. Three-bay wings of 70ft 6in span, with large overhangs on the upper surface, replaced

the original two-bay units. Four booms from the upper and lower trailing edges carried a high-set monoplane tailplane and elevator, beneath which were twin rudders. Although S.58 initially flew as a landplane, it was soon fitted with floats. On 17 December Shorts strengthened the seating of 'hydro aeroplane S.58' and supplied and fitted an aneroid, this work being completed two days later.

Frank McClean had a motive for this drastic rebuild. He and the explorer John Herbert Spottiswoode were planning a seaplane expedition up the River Nile, to see the Aswan Dam and investigate the cataracts between there and Khartoum. McClean later wrote that the scheme came about because, in the early years, when aeroplanes had 'poor or non-existent instruments and unsheltered seating', the British climate 'brought about continual inactivity during the winter months'. The S.58, with its high power and low wing loading, essential requirements to enable it to take off in a hot climate, was to be the chosen vehicle.

By now McClean was finding the role of test pilot to Short Brothers too exacting to continue on an honorary basis. The company's order book testifies to the fact that work for the Admiralty, building, maintaining, repairing and modifying machines, had increased steadily through 1912. Consequently it was announced in the 5 December issue of *The Aeroplane* that 'Mr Gordon Bell, who has probably flown more different makes of machines than any pilot in the world, has signed on as chief pilot with Messrs. Short Bros., of Eastchurch, and will pilot the Machines they are building to naval and military orders when undergoing their official tests'. Bell retained his status as a freelance pilot, however, and would continue to fly other manufacturers' aeroplanes as well.

CHAPTER 6

1913: Successful Negotiations; Unsuccessful Aeroplanes

Frank McClean's friend Griffith Brewer, who acted as UK patent agent for the Wright brothers, had become concerned that no action had been taken to restrain infringement of the patents in the UK. At the time of Wilbur's death in 1912 the foreign patents had yielded no income, and Brewer was worried that the fourteen-year monopoly for the 1903 patent would expire on 23 March 1917 with nothing having been done. When he visited Orville in November 1912, therefore, Brewer said that if Orville would be unable to take any 'vigorous action' he would be glad to form a company amongst the Wrights' British friends, with the aim of enforcing recognition of the invention in England, and especially gaining recognition from the British Government. Orville expressed his willingness for Brewer to do this, so Brewer returned home and immediately enlisted the support of Alec Ogilvie, Frank McClean, Percy Grace and Maurice Egerton, 'all of whom were anxious to see that the Wrights were treated better in England than they had been up to that time on the Continent'.

Brewer outlined a company of £6,000 capital with these friends of the Wrights as his associates. They were to put up £3,000 to take half the shares, and give the other £3,000-worth of shares to Orville in exchange for his British patent. Brewer recalled:

The company proposed to approach the British Government and endeavour to exact royalty in recognition of the validity of the Wrights' claim. Seeing that the Crown cannot be sued for infringement of a patent granted by the Crown and that an action to force such a claim was unprecedented, we had little hope of obtaining a settlement and still less of succeeding in any action which it might be possible to bring. We were out in the true crusader's spirit and were prepared to risk our £3,000 to twist the lion's tail.

Orville approved of this scheme, and on 31 January 1913 the British Wright Co Ltd was registered as a private company with a capital of £6,000 in £1 shares, 'to carry on the business of constructors of aeroplanes and other aircraft, etc., and to acquire certain patents in the names of Orville and Wilbur Wright'. Its first directors were O Wright (chairman), G Brewer, A Ogilvie, G N Ogilvie and T P Searight. Each shareholder paid cash for the face value of the shares and no company promotion expenses or commission was paid to anyone. While they were in England in February 1913, Orville and Katharine Wright met with McClean on the 18th and 19th, and Orville attended a meeting of the directors on the 21st.

A formal application was then made for compensation for the British Government's infringements, but after a year there was no sign of a reasonable settlement being reached. Brewer therefore applied for permission to sue the Crown through a nominee, and the Government named Colonel Mervyn O'Gorman, Superintendent of the Royal Aircraft Factory, as the defendant against whom the action could be brought. When the action began, a commission was appointed to go to the USA to take Orville Wright's evidence, Brewer also going.

In August 1914 war broke out and Brewer quickly returned to Britain, where he found that most of his fellow-directors had joined the armed forces. 'It was evident,' he said, 'that we could not reasonably serve our country and at the same time sue it in the action for infringement.' Brewer therefore interviewed General Henderson, who was acting on the War Office's behalf, and secured a lump-sum settlement of £15,000 for the use of the Wright patents for the Forces of the Crown. This did not include civilian use of the invention. The settlement was announced in the 16 October 1914 issue of *Flight*, which commented:

The action by the British Wright Co against Mr Mervyn O'Gorman, the nominee of the War Office, has been proceeding quietly for more than a year past, following several months of earlier discussion, and we understand that the offer to accept £15,000, in settlement of the original claim of £25,000, was made by the British Wright Co in order to relieve the Government from an unnecessary embarrassment during the stress of war.

Both sides are to be congratulated on their good sense in coming to this settlement.

At the war's end Orville decided to wind up the British Wright Company, which had been manufacturing aeronautical instruments, and the shares were liquidated at £1 7s per £1 share.

As a result of the action against the British Government and the wartime manufacture of instruments, a payment of over £24,000 in dividends and share redemption money was made, of which Orville received some £12,000 in recognition of the invention. The shareholders who had backed the action received back four times the amount they had hazarded. As a result the British patent was more profitable than any of the Continental patents, and the friends of the Wrights, who had anticipated losing their money but getting a good run for it, were pleasantly surprised by the reward. In 1916 Orville had decided not to apply for an extension of the British patent. As Brewer pointed out, this amounted to a gift from Orville to the British aircraft industry, and this was warmly applauded by Lord Northcliffe.

Naval activity

On 31 December 1912 the first Naval Air Station had been commissioned. Established on the Isle of Grain at the estuary of the Thames and Medway, it had already seen some use by naval pilots, and on 27 December the Admiralty had announced that Lieutenant John W Seddon, RFC, who had been serving as a flying officer at the Naval Aviation School at Eastchurch, was to take charge of the new station with the rank of Flight Commander. The sheds at Grain, located close to the shore of the Medway, were soon occupied by 'hydro-aeroplanes', many coming from the Short Brothers factory close by. *Flight* reported that it was 'the first of the chain of aviation centres which the Admiralty propose to establish along the coast'. So great was the naval aviation activity in the area that the regular published reports of flying at Eastchurch had ceased to appear, evidently prohibited by the Admiralty. Even the doings of the few civilians still flying from the site were seldom revealed.

In January 1913 the Science Museum at

South Kensington in London put on a temporary exhibition illustrating the history of aeronautics and the research side of the science. One exhibit was the Birdling monoplane lent by McClean.

On Monday 13 January, despite a high wind, five aeroplanes took off from Eastchurch and descended on Dover. About noon, Commander Samson and Lieutenant Spencer Grey started from Eastchurch on 100hp and 70hp Short tractor biplanes respectively, and an hour later they were followed by Frank McClean on his 70hp S.36, Captain Risk in a 100hp twin-engine Short and Sub-Lieutenant Hewlett in a 70hp Henry Farman. All carried a passenger with them. After lunching with Captain Marley of the Dover Aero Club, Samson returned to Eastchurch, but the others decided to remain overnight. In its next issue *Flight* reported: 'It appears that the visits of the naval aviators to Dover have been in the nature of prospecting expeditions, and the Admiralty are now negotiating with the proprietors of the aerodrome with a view to utilising it as a base for the naval wing of the RFC.'

The 1913 International Aero Exhibition was held at Olympia, London, from 14 to 22 February. On the opening day the Exhibition's patron, His Majesty King George V, the 'first visitor', toured the stands. At the stand of Mr Percy Grace, the agent for Short Brothers, where an 80hp tractor hydro-biplane was displayed, Frank McClean was presented to His Majesty, who 'congratulated him most heartily on the magnificent performance he had accomplished in flying from Eastchurch up the River Thames into the very heart of London some months since on a Short hydro-biplane'.

During the early part of 1913 McClean was flying the S.36 and S.58 at Eastchurch when the opportunity arose. By now the S.58 was being operated permanently as a landplane,

and by late February the forward elevator was carried on short curved extensions from the nose of the nacelle, the booms having been done away with.

On Sunday 23 February McClean and Lieutenant Gregory, RN, 'carried out a practical experiment . . . with a view to ascertaining whether a pilot could reasonably find his way without a map or compass'. Setting off from Eastchurch in McClean's 70hp S.58 'hydro-aeroplane' fitted with a wheeled undercarriage, they crossed the Thames at an altitude of 1,500ft and passed over Stanford-le-Hope. They hoped to follow the River Lea, but it was obscured by fog, and consequently they had to descend twice to ask the way. Eventually, after a journey lasting an hour and a quarter, they landed safely at Hendon Aerodrome late in the evening. McClean flew S.58 at Hendon the following day, and on the Tuesday afternoon he was invited to take part in a private race with M. Brindejonc des Moulinais on a Morane-Saulnier monoplane, Mr Valentine on a 70hp tandem Blériot monoplane and Mr Gates in the 'Grahame-White brevet 'bus'. He opted out, preferring to 'do laps alone, his 62ft span [*sic*] not being quite the thing for pylon racing'. Having spent a week away from his home base, McClean left Hendon at 4 o'clock on the afternoon of Sunday 2 March, carrying a passenger, and made the return flight to Eastchurch in 50 minutes.

The 6 March issue of *The Aeroplane* contained a proposal for the formation of a 'Territorial Air Corps', the author pointing out that:

During the last year or eighteen months much has been said, and many hard words have been used over the policy of the War Office with regard to military aviation. The result of it is that there is now a chance of our having a respectable air fleet for the Army,

The S.40 was extensively rebuilt after its Thames flight, re-emerging in November 1912 as the S.58, an S.38-type biplane that bore scant resemblance to its original form. This picture of it was taken on 2 March 1913, as McClean was about to depart from Hendon after a rare visit to the famous London Aerodrome. It was initially intended to operate this aircraft as a seaplane, but its disappointing performance led to it being used only as a landplane. (FLEET AIR ARM MUSEUM)

and possibly for the Navy. Very little, however, has been done until the last six weeks or so with regard to the Territorials. The case for the Terriers stands as follows:- A few officers have taken their aviators' certificates on machines of various makes at their own expense, and a certain well-known aviator, with his usual patriotic generosity, undertook the task of instructing several members of the London Balloon Section in the piloting and general management of aeroplanes.

And that is about all.

As a result of the unusual public exposure occasioned by his appearing at Hendon, McClean was featured in the 15 March issue of *Flight* as that week's personality in the 'Men of Moment in the World of Flight' series. At the time he was serving on three RAeC committees; the Executive Committee, the Public Safety and Accidents Investigation Committee and the Competitions Committee, and had a good attendance record on all of them for the previous year. With regard to his re-election on to the Executive Committee for the coming year, *The Aeroplane* commented in its 13 March issue: 'It will, of course, be universally accepted that everyone must vote for Colonel Holden, and Messrs. McClean and Ogilvie, three of the retiring members who are not only among the hardest workers, but whose knowledge of aviation generally is extensive and practical, the last two being pilots of the best class.'

The sad but valuable work of the Public Safety and Accidents Investigation Committee was typified on 7 March, when McClean was among nine of its members, along with Harold Perrin, the Club's secretary, who went to Larkhill on Salisbury Plain that day to investigate the fatal accident suffered by Geoffrey England, who had crashed in a Bristol monoplane two days previously. Perrin, along with Major Fulton and Major Gerrard, the Club's representatives on Salisbury Plain, had already made a careful inspection of the wrecked aeroplane on the day of the accident, but on the 7th the committee members spent 'a considerable time' examining the wreckage, which had been left untouched pending the investigation. They then held an enquiry at the George Hotel in Amesbury, where they took the evidence of eyewitnesses and discussed matters with representatives of the British and Colonial Aeroplane Co Ltd. The enquiry was then adjourned until 12 March.

The annual RAeC Dinner was held at the Royal Automobile Club on 13 March, and McClean was among the 'distinguished members and guests' who heard a speech by the guest of the evening, Colonel Seely, MP, the Secretary of State for War. *Flight* remarked that Seely's presence 'gave a peculiar interest to the occasion in view of the possibility of a momentous utterance from him on the subject of the aerial defence of the British Isles'. Seely paid a generous appreciation to the members of the Aero Club, to which His Majesty's forces owed so much, and suggested that they should endeavour to secure greater safety for aeroplanes, for not only would that be of incalculable benefit to the Army and Navy but to the industry itself. Replying on behalf of the guests, Mr W Joynson-Hicks made some 'pointed remarks' that, to judge from the enthusiasm aroused among the guests, were greatly appreciated. He described Seely's speech as an excellent essay in 'skating',

adding that, quite outside the realm of party politics, the nation's position in regard to military and naval aviation did not redound to the honour of Great Britain. He hoped that Seely would shortly be able to announce that Britain's aerial forces would be brought up to the level of Germany's within the next twelve months.

Despite McClean's generosity towards the Admiralty, on 18 March he was obliged to ask the RAeC Committee why their Lordships had not yet paid for the last year of rent at Eastchurch, in accordance with the agreement. He was told that the Admiralty had not paid up because it objected to the costs of the Club's solicitors. His reaction was not recorded.

On 26 March Mr Winston Spencer Churchill, the First Lord of the Admiralty, in explaining his memorandum on the Naval Estimates to the House of Commons, provided figures that illustrated the growth of the Naval Wing of the RFC.

The aeroplane service plays a much smaller part relatively in the naval organisation than it does in military affairs, and, of course, in the Navy as well as in the Army, it is in its infancy. This time last year the Navy had five machines and four trained pilots; today it has 40 machines and 60 pilots. The anomaly of our having more pilots than machines is due to the unexpected non-delivery of machines which have been ordered, but, owing to one difficulty and another, have been delayed in delivery. Twenty more machines are expected to be received in the next few weeks, and by the date of the manoeuvres in July we shall have 75 naval machines and 75 pilots. By the end of the new financial year, for which we are now providing, we shall have 100 pilots and considerably over 100 machines in the naval wing . . .

What Churchill did not acknowledge, of course, was the fact that the initial impetus for the development of British naval aviation had been largely provided by a generous gesture by a patriotic civilian and the enthusiasm and commitment of a few civilian pilots and officers from the lower ranks.

A seaplane race round Britain

In its issue of 1 April the *Daily Mail* announced that it was offering two substantial prizes totalling £15,000 to promote the development of waterplanes. The largest was a £10,000 prize for the first waterplane flight across the Atlantic in either direction, open to pilots of all nationalities and machines of both foreign and British construction, and the other was £5,000 for a flight round Great Britain in an all-British-built waterplane. Sir Charles Rose, Chairman of the RAeC, sent a telegram to the newspaper's proprietor, Lord Northcliffe, the same day, stating:

> The announcement in your today's issue of your magnificent offer of prizes for a circuit of Great Britain by hydro-aeroplane and flight across the Atlantic, affords further proof of the patriotism and generosity of the *Daily Mail* in all progressive movements, and especially in the development of aviation, about which the public is so much concerned at the present time in connection with the defensive security of the country. The assistance of the Royal Aero Club will be entirely at your disposal as in the past.

In the following day's *Daily Mail* it was announced that entries for both prizes had already been received. British airman Eric Gordon England and German aircraft manufacturer Edmund Rumpler had announced

their intention to compete for the Atlantic prize, while Messrs Blériot Ltd and 'Colonel Cody' (Samuel Cowdery, who had made the first powered, sustained and controlled flight in Britain on 16 October 1908) had expressed their intention to enter for both competitions. 'The best experts believe,' the paper reported, 'that the British prize may be won this year and the Atlantic prize before the end of 1914.' 'We wish to drive home', the newspaper added, 'the fact that, for an island and a naval Power, the waterplane, or aeroplane that rises from and descends on the sea, is the best of all aerial weapons. The Germans excel in enormous airships, the French in land aeroplanes. Our prizes are intended to produce a sea-going aeroplane for Britain that shall be capable, as we believe it will be, of seeking out and destroying any airship that leaves its country's shores.' Horace Short was quoted in full as saying:

> The Round Britain Circuit presents no difficulties whatever, except weather conditions. It is more than probable it will be won this year.
>
> The Atlantic crossing from the American side to this side is almost feasible now, taking advantage of south-westerly winds. From this side to America it is doubtful for at least eighteen months.

Significantly, a tearsheet of page 5 from the 2 April 1913 issue of the *Daily Mail*, on which these responses are reported, is to be found among the Francis McClean papers in the Fleet Air Arm Museum at Yeovilton. On the same page is printed a photograph of McClean flying through Tower Bridge in S.40 the previous year.

At an RAeC Committee meeting on April 29 McClean was listed as being on the Grounds Inspection Committee, the Club Ground Committee and the Public Safety and Accidents Investigation Committee.

On 1 May 1913 an Indenture was signed between Aero Proprietary Ltd of the first part, Frank McClean of the second part and the Commissioners for executing the office of the Lord High Admiral of the United Kingdom of Great Britain and Ireland of the third part, granting the use of Eastchurch flying ground to the Admiralty 'during the term of 21 years less three days calculated from 25th December, 1911, at a rent of £150 per annum, with right to determine after seven or 14 years'. It was agreed between Frank McClean and the Admiralty that the Admiralty might purchase the land, subject to leases, etc., at £16 per acre if notice was given by them before 24 June 1918.

In fact, Eastchurch Aerodrome was taken over by the Admiralty in December 1914. McClean's cottage, 'Stonepitts', was taken over in June 1917, and the land was purchased according to the agreement in June 1918.

In the 1 May 1913 agreement the Admiralty were bound by the following restrictions:

(a) That the number of flying machines in use at any one time under the liberty hereby granted shall not exceed 10 without the consent in writing of the Lessors which shall not be unreasonably withheld in any case when the Admiralty are willing to pay a reasonable sum by way of additional rent in respect of every machine in excess of 10.

(b) That if more than two flying machines are in use at any one time under the liberty hereby granted each flying machine in excess of that number shall be in charge of an Aviator holding a Certificate recognised by the Royal Aero Club.

In May and June details were released of the *Daily Mail* 1,600-mile round-Britain 72-hour race for seaplanes 'entirely constructed within the confines of the British Empire', including their engines. The race, set to take place from 6am on Saturday 16 August to 6pm on Saturday 30 August at the latest, was to start and finish on Southampton Water, and a passenger had to be carried. Competitors were free to start at any time and date from the earliest stipulated time, provided they completed the circuit by the deadline, and within 72 hours of starting. Both pilot and passenger could be changed during the contest, and there was a £5,000 prize for the winner. As shall be seen, McClean, with his passion for seaplanes, would find the challenge irresistible, though Shorts had apparently initially intended to enter a machine piloted by Gordon Bell, who was now the company's chief pilot and had put the new Short private-venture S.61 tractor seaplane through its trials for the navy.

C G Grey, editor of *The Aeroplane*, devoted his leader in the 29 May issue to 'The Development of the Naval Air Service'. Under a cross-head entitled 'The Extinction of the Naval Wing' he remarked:

Incidentally, it rather looks as if the Naval Wing of the Royal Flying Corps, 'one and indivisible,' was quietly ceasing to exist. Of course, the beautiful scheme for a corps of 'ultra-marines' was – in the words of the theologians – ordained to be damned, but one scarcely expected the Naval Air Service to develop so quickly. One imagines that the dynamic force of the Right Honourable Winston Spencer-Churchill [*sic*] is somewhat responsible. The young man in a hurry may be a danger to himself and everyone else, but if he is efficient, as in this case, he gets things done.

Predicting that the headquarters of the Naval Wing, RFC, at Eastchurch, 'will become simply a huge training establishment for naval aeroplane pilots', Grey said that the station needed to develop enormously. 'Splendid work has been done by the Navy at Eastchurch in the past, and will be done in the future,' he wrote, 'but it is a long way from Whitehall, and must not be neglected if it is to keep pace with the development of the rest of the Naval Air Service as represented by the new waterplane bases and the [HMS] *Hermes* [the recently-commissioned mother ship for naval aeroplanes].'

The entire personnel of the Naval Flying School at Eastchurch had been turned over from HMS *Actaeon* to the *Hermes* and became absolutely independent of any other branch of the Service, dealing directly with the Admiralty through the captain of *Hermes*. Grey declared: 'The aeroplane now assumes its proper position as a definite arm on an equality with the Submarine Service.'

Meanwhile, McClean had not given up ballooning. He made an ascent on 27 May, his first since October 1909, and on Saturday 31 May he took part in the RAeC's Hare and Hounds race, which saw several competitors drifting across London after ascending from the Hurlingham Club. The balloon acting as the 'hare', the *Banshee*, with Mr J D Dunville in charge, set off soon after 3pm, pursued by five others playing the part of the 'hounds'; the one descending closest to the *Banshee* after it had come down would be declared the winner. Unfortunately it was not the *Chili*, piloted by Frank McClean, that alighted nearest the 'hare' when it landed at Sudbury in Suffolk, but the *Dunlop 1*, piloted by Mr James Radley, who put it down within 200 yards of the *Banshee*.

In its 7 June issue *Flight* published a detailed description of S.58 (the reconstructed S.40), but, confusingly, the two photographs reproduced on the first page of the article depicted a different machine. The aircraft shown was S.62, one of two 'Biplanes of the latest pattern S.38 Type' ordered by the War Office on 14 January 1913. These two machines, S.62 and S.63, were to have 50hp Gnomes, dual control and 'double control mechanism'. The order was recorded as being completed on 21 April, but, as the following account shows, S.62 was evidently completed a month earlier.

On Saturday 22 March Gordon Bell, with his mechanic, Chapman, as passenger, had left Eastchurch in S.62 at 2.45pm and flown to Hendon in 'very boisterous weather' to take part in the three-day Easter Meeting. The gusts were so bad that, over Enfield, the toolbag was lifted clean off the floor and came down again upside-down. Bell landed at Hendon at 3.55pm after a 'terrible journey'. Although attempts were made to keep the flying activities going, a violent gust swept across the aerodrome, followed by 'lightning, thunder and copious rain', and the wind rose suddenly to such a force that the mechanics struggled to hold down the aeroplanes and return them to their sheds. Momentarily left unattended, S.62 was 'lifted up sideways, turned completely over, and laid down – none too gently – upon its back', the force being sufficient to embed the propeller 14in into the ground. It suffered considerable damage, chiefly to its tail booms, rudder and ailerons.

This machine, photographed at Hendon shortly before it was smashed, was the one depicted on the opening page of the *Flight* feature, where it was correctly captioned as Gordon Bell's 50hp aircraft. It has more recently been written that the Army had only one S.38-Type biplane, and that this was S.62, which was given the military serial number 446 with the RFC. In the light of the foregoing, however, it seems more likely that 446 was actually the second of the two machines ordered by the War Office, S.63, and that S.62 was never delivered.

The S.38-type biplane S.62, built for the RFC, at Hendon on 22 March 1913, shortly before it was wrecked by a violent storm as it stood on the airfield. This illustration was confusingly used in a description of McClean's very similar S.58, published in the 7 June issue of *Flight*. (AUTHOR)

This also raises the strong possibility that, after the shattered remains of S.62 were returned to Shorts, some components, especially from the relatively undamaged nacelle, were incorporated in a modification of McClean's S.58.

The general-arrangement drawings and detail sketches on the remaining three pages of *Flight*'s article showed McClean's 70hp S.58. The writer stated: 'It is a Short biplane, originally built for Mr Frank McClean for use over water, that forms the subject of our scale drawings and sketches this week, and equally with ourselves our readers are indebted to Mr F.K. McClean for the courtesy in placing this ma-

chine of his at our disposal for the purpose of their preparation.' 'Although this particular aeroplane is not a new model,' the article continued, 'it has the greater advantage of being well tried and a thorough success. Not only was it a good waterplane, but its owner was so favourably impressed with its qualities as a land machine after he had substituted a set of wheels for the floats, that he has since retained it for this purpose, in order to obtain greater enjoyment from its more frequent use over the Royal Aero Club's grounds at Eastchurch, where he has his sheds.' One suspects this was a cover-up for the machine's shortcomings, as it was evidently underpowered and slow, and this, coupled with the limited capacity of its tandem nacelle, rendered it unsuitable for the Nile expedition flight.

In the first annual report of the Air Committee on the Progress of the RFC, dated 7 June 1913, it was stated that the Naval Flying

School at Eastchurch 'has up to date been utilised for training most of the personnel for the Naval Wing, both in elementary and advanced flying', and that the station 'was also used as a depot for the trained pilots, pending their disposal to the various air stations which are being established round the coast'. 'For this purpose', the report added, 'the school is well situated and equipped, and can undertake the training of a larger number than those at present being trained there.' The school had so far trained twenty-four officers and forty-one men, and another officer and eighty men were under training. Five large double aeroplane sheds had been erected there, and some sheds had been rented from private owners as well.

That same month the Admiralty produced a report on 'Aerial Navigation'. Under the section headed 'Aeroplanes and Hydro-aeroplanes' it was stated that: 'In view of the aerial development abroad it is considered that the money allocated for the construction of hydro-aeroplanes and their appurtenances in the 1913-14 Naval Estimates is insufficient to meet the requirements of this rapidly expanding branch of the Navy.' Among proposed expenditure on aviation totalling £350,000 for the financial year 1913/14 it was thought that £50,000 was needed for the purchase of thirty-five additional aircraft, £30,000 for development of the Isle of Grain and Cromarty Air Stations, £20,000 for aircraft sheds, plus £15,000 for the repair of school machines.

McClean took part in another ballooning event at Hurlingham on 28 June, being the first of the five entrants to start in the Long Distance Balloon Race for a cup presented by Mr A Mortimer Singer. He piloted the balloon *Dunlop*, and had Commander C R Samson for company. The winner was Mr C F Pollock in the much-greater-capacity *Planet*, who, with Mr Mortimer Singer as his passenger, crossed

the Channel and alighted about five miles south-west of Rouen. All of the other competitors descended on the south coast of England, between Bexhill and Hastings.

Eastchurch had grown almost beyond recognition in its few years of existence. In the beginning the whole aviation community had been housed in half-a-dozen buildings, but by mid-1913 the naval installations alone comprised the new barracks of the Royal Naval Flying School, including comfortable officers' quarters, some twenty naval aeroplane sheds, a shed for a meteorological balloon, and various subsidiary sheds for stores and other items. The navy's own sewage farm was sited in the middle of the Service's sheds. In addition there were numerous privately owned sheds, occupied by Mr Ogilvie, Mr Jezzi, Professor Huntington, the Hon Maurice Egerton, the Blair Athol Aeroplane Syndicate (whose shed was in the care of C R Fairey, later to found Fairey Aviation), and of course McClean, who in addition to his seaplane experiments at Harty Ferry had his S.58 there. Moreover the Short Brothers' works had expanded enormously. There were two long factory sheds, the machine shop had been extended and the drawing office now accommodated a dozen draughtsmen or more. A new pusher biplane without the front elevator was in production along with many tractor seaplanes.

On the afternoon of Friday 13 June Bell flew a 120hp Martin-Handasyde monoplane from Eastchurch to Brooklands with Lieutenant J R B Kennedy, RN, as his passenger. He then indulged in some dangerously low flying in the vicinity, making very low and steeply banked turns over the airfield which finally resulted in the aeroplane sideslipping into the ground and cartwheeling. Kennedy's neck was broken and he died instantly; Bell fractured the front of his skull and cut his nose badly. He was to be away from test flying for some time, this task being taken on by Sydney Pickles. On 23 June Mc-Clean attended the meeting of the RAeC's Public Safety and Accidents Investigation Committee at which Bell's accident was examined. He had not, however, been among the committee members who had visited Brooklands on the 14th to examine the wrecked aeroplane. In its resulting report the committee concluded that the accident 'was solely due to the handling of the aircraft,' and that 'The pilot, experienced and competent as he was, showed a grave error of judgement in flying as he did over and around the sheds at Brooklands'. Bell was later reprimanded by the chairman at an RAeC Committee meeting.

McClean records that he again went ballooning on 6 July, this time with Brewer and Maurice and Phyllis Bidder in the balloon *North Star*.

Challenging the regulations

The aviation community had been alarmed by regulations issued by the Home Office under the Aerial Navigation Acts 1911 and 1913, which were seen as excessively restrictive and impracticable. As a result of complaints voiced by aviators the Committee of the RAeC appointed a seven-man sub-committee to consider what action the club should take. McClean was one of the seven, and on Tuesday 8 July he was present at a special meeting of the Committee to receive the sub-committee's report. It was found that stringent enforcement of the regulations had prevented British manufacturers from carrying on their manufacture and experiments at various places which were chosen for their fitness but happened to be close to Prohibited Areas; that 'British aviators had been deterred from flying abroad owing to the difficulties of conforming with the requirements of the regulations imposed by the British Government on their return journey';

and that the impracticability of the regulations had prevented the RAeC from organising events in connection with large prizes offered for competition amongst aviators, which 'would have resulted in furthering the progress of the art and manufacture of hydro-aeroplanes and aeroplanes, to the manifest advantage of the Government'.

The Committee therefore forwarded to the Home Office, War Office and Admiralty a document outlining the objections and stating:

In view of these circumstances, and also to modify the feeling expressed abroad that Great Britain is inimical to the advancement of the art of aviation, the Club wishes to place on record its view that the international freedom of aerial navigation is much more to the advantage of this country than of foreign nations, and recommends:

(1) That active measures be taken to protect the interests of aviators and the industry.

(2) That the following alterations in the Regulations be suggested:–

(a) That the Home Office open a register on which shall be entered the names of approved British aviators who shall be exempt from the orders issued under the Regulations, provided that they have commenced their flight in this country and that they report forthwith all details of any flights they have made over any Prohibited Areas. The Committee is of the opinion that regulations for identification can be framed to deal practically with this suggestion.

(b) That approved registered British aviators coming from abroad may pass over any of the prescribed landing areas without alighting, provided previous notice of departure from a foreign country has been given to the Home Office.

(c) That a further portion of the coast line, situated between Archcliffe Fort and Lydd Railway Station, be scheduled as a landing area.

(d) That provision be made for permitting British and foreign hydro-aeroplanes to alight on the water in convenient specified places.

(e) That the existing regulations shall not apply to free spherical balloons taking part in sporting competitions.

In August the government issued a White Paper containing a statement regarding the progress made by the RFC during its first year of existence. With regard to Eastchurch, it was reported that the Naval Flying School 'has been utilised for training most of the personnel for the Naval Wing, both in elementary and advanced flying', and that it was also used as a depot for the trained pilots, 'pending their disposal to the various air stations which are being established round the coast' (namely Calshot, Grain, Harwich, Yarmouth and Rosyth, with other sites under negotiation). The total number trained for all branches of the Naval Wing stood at 184, and another 114 were under training; the staff originally recommended to carry out the training at Eastchurch had been found sufficient. Five large double aeroplane sheds had been erected on the site, and in addition some sheds had been rented from private owners. Permanent residential quarters had also been built at the school.

The race becomes a farce

Gordon Bell's accident ruled out any chance of him flying the Shorts' entry for the *Daily Mail* Waterplane Circuit, but McClean submitted his entry for the event. In its 31 July issue *The Aeroplane* reported that his new machine, the S.68 tractor biplane, was 'well under way' in the factory, and was to be fitted with a six-cylinder in-line water-cooled 100hp Green engine that would give it a speed of 60mph.

As a member of the RAeC's accident investigation committee, McClean had the sad task of studying the wrecks in which many of his fellow pioneer aviators lost their lives. One of his saddest such investigations must have been the trip to Farnborough on 7 August to examine the wreck of S F Cowdery's Waterplane, another of the entrants for the forthcoming *Daily Mail* Circuit of Britain seaplane race, only a few hours after the crash that killed the pioneer.

By mid-August Shorts had completed McClean's entry for this event, set to start from Southampton on Saturday 16 August. Similar to the 100hp Gnome-engined seaplanes that the company was then producing for the navy, the S.68 was supported on two stepless main floats and a small tail float, spanned more than 60ft and had Cellon-doped wings of much narrower chord than usual. It was postulated that McClean might be accompanied by another pilot. On 6 August the machine's Green engine was undergoing a bench test.

The event was beset by troubles. In addition to Cowdery's fatal accident, only one of the three entrants was present at Southampton on the first day. This was Harry Hawker in a Sopwith seaplane, who set off at midday. Upon reaching Yarmouth at 4.38pm he collapsed from sunstroke. Sydney Pickles tried to take his place on Monday, but rough sea and rising wind obliged him to abandon the attempt and the aircraft was dismantled and returned to Cowes for a second try. It was hoped that the competitors would be ready to make another start on Saturday 23 or Monday 25 August.

McClean's absence was due to engine problems with S.68, entry No.4. In a long leader in the 21 August issue of *The Aeroplane* C G

Barely completed in time for the 1913 *Daily Mail* Circuit of Britain seaplane race, the Short S.68 had to be withdrawn when its 100hp Green engine proved troublesome and the aircraft's performance proved inadequate. (AUTHOR)

Grey wrote:

The non-arrival of Mr Mclean's [*sic*] Short in time for the official start was most unfortunate, but considering that the whole machine had to be designed, built and tested inside three weeks, there was sufficient reason for its being late. The task was practically an impossibility, and the Short Brothers came very near achieving the impossible. If the machine is put into flying order this week, it will still be a remarkable feat, for the firm is taking an entirely new departure in fitting a long heavy engine into a type of machine originally designed for a shorter and lighter engine, and the balance will necessarily take some adjusting, apart from the fitting of radiators and other 'gadgets' which are strange to the workmen.

In its 23 August issue *Flight* reported:

. . . Mr Frank McClean and Messrs Short Bros had been working away with solid perseverance to remedy the obstinacy of the engine, the fault being ultimately found to lie in a cracked cylinder. It was no sooner located than its replacement was arranged for by co-operation with Mr Fred May, of the Green Engine Co. Its testing, until Mr May was satisfied with its running, was then started, and at 2am on Thursday the engine was taken over to Grain Island, where the Short machine was comfortably resting, to be installed. All being well by Thursday evening, Mr McClean hoped to make for Southampton by way of the air, and there was the possibility of his making a start during Friday for the race itself.

In its leader the magazine commented: 'That the engine on Mr McClean's Short biplane has not been developing its full power is a matter of regret to all concerned . . .', and added '. . . at the moment of writing it is not even certain that Mr McClean will be able to make a start during the present week.'

The initial trials were indeed disappointing, McClean noting that his attempts to fly S.68 during 14–24 August were a 'failure'. The engine vibrated badly and this caused the radiator to leak. Consequently the water boiled away so quickly that, during one engine run, a piston seized and its cylinder had to be replaced. Although he did eventually manage to fly S.68 for half an hour, it proved too slow and under-powered for racing and McClean was obliged to withdraw from the race at the very last moment, on Saturday the 16th, owing to radiator trouble, even though the start was deferred from 6am to 10.30am in the hope that he would fly over from Grain that morning. In fact there were other problems too. In its 28 August issue *The Aeroplane* described further

modifications made in a desperate effort to get the S.68 up to scratch:

The chief trouble with the Short seems to have been that owing to the brief time available in which to build it, the makers were unable to test thoroughly what amounted to a new combination of engine and machine. The engine appears to have been giving its power all right, but has suffered from radiator trouble, on one occasion the water all running out of the radiator and letting the engine get so hot that it had to be taken to pieces and a piston replaced. Then tests of different propellers had

In a last desperate effort to get the S.68 up to scratch, different propellers were tried and its wings were hastily modified, a considerable amount being added to their leading edges and the lower wings being extended to match the span of the upper wings. In this rare photograph of the modified machine the lower-wing extensions are noticeably lighter in colour than the original surfaces to which they have been added. (AUTHOR)

to be made, and afterwards the surface of the planes themselves was increased, a considerable amount being added to the leading edges of the planes and extensions being put on the lower planes, as, of course, there was no time to fit new planes. As a result Mr McClean withdrew definitely from the competition on Saturday, but he still intends to have the machine put right and do a sufficiently big flight on it to show that if official sanction had been given for the holding of the race in time, he would have been able to put up a good show.

This 'robbed the event of competitive interest', leaving Hawker as the only remaining entrant. When he suffered a bad crash while making a forced descent near Dublin, injuring his passenger and wrecking the machine, the *Daily Mail* made him a £1,000 personal gift in recognition of his skill and courage in covering 1,034 miles out of the full distance of 1,540 miles. The contest was abandoned. In an April 1914 survey of aircraft suitable for military impressment McClean's S.68 was recorded as 'about to be fitted with a different engine', and it is believed it might have become naval aeroplane 182, described as a Short Type 74 dual-control seaplane with a 100hp Gnome.

This débâcle evidently met with the RAeC's displeasure, as a meeting of its Competitions Committee was held on 9 September, and instead of being on the committee as usual, McClean, along with Tom Sopwith, attended at the committee's invitation. The regulations for next year's £5,000 Circuit of Britain were discussed, and 'the Secretary was instructed to place the views of the Committee before the Proprietors of the *Daily Mail*'.

An unusual item appeared in the 6 September issue of *Flight*, in the form of a poem by someone writing under the pseudonym of 'The Governor', and entitled 'To Little Willie'. From its content it is clear that Frank McClean was its subject:

A man who calls a spade a spade,
Who flies for sport and not for trade,
Green-engined Short, all British made.

Two Gordon-Bennetts thou hast sailed,
The trim 'Corona' oft hast trailed
O'er many lands till ballast failed.

The Moon describing its ellipse,
Has drawn thee thrice to an eclipse,
Thy sole reward – dark maiden's lips.

When planes the Navy could not buy,
Who helped the sailor boys to fly
At Eastchurch in the summer sky?

On days when others fume and swear
Seldom dost thou pollute the air,
With language flying men can't bear.

Flying on thine aeroplane
When the sun begins to wane,
Gnomeing round the sheds again.

Gliding gently back to earth,
To the land that gave thee birth.
Smiling in thy merry mirth.

Dreamy eyes so meek and mild
Full of goodness as a child,
Soft as violets growing wild.

Generous beyond compare,
Loved by ladies everywhere,
Both by 'filly' and by *mère*.

May maidens all thy vows believe,
And many may'st ye yet deceive,
Before the day thou hast to leave.

This was no bardic masterpiece, just a simple, light-hearted compliment by someone who evidently knew his subject. What McClean made of it we cannot know, for in his usual reticent manner he did not respond. However, there is no disputing the fact that McClean frequently took ladies aloft and evidently enjoyed their company, and they his. The nickname 'Little Willie' was probably an intimate familiarity used by his fellow pilots, as it does not appear in popular use elsewhere. As noted earlier, this nickname was also applied to one of the Short biplanes loaned by McClean to the navy for training.

Test-pilot troubles continued to hamper Short Brothers. Having put a new Short biplane through its Admiralty acceptance tests on Tuesday 16 September, Sydney Pickles was flying the Champel biplane at Hendon on Saturday 20 September, the day of the second Aerial Derby. While he was taking Mrs De Beauvoir Stocks (herself a pilot) for a passenger flight a spiral dive 'terminated in a sudden dive from about 60ft to the ground'. Pickles suffered a fractured leg and other injuries, and Mrs Stocks suffered concussion and injuries to her back. Both were hospitalised.

That same day the RAeC's grounds at Eastchurch were visited by 120–170 members of the Kent Automobile Club, who inspected the aeroplanes and were shown round the Short Brothers' works. Luncheon was partaken in a hangar placed at their disposal by McClean, and in the afternoon they were treated to exhibition flights by naval officers, and a large number of passengers were taken aloft by Samson and McClean. *Flight* reported, 'Mr McClean and Commander Samson were kept busy taking up members of the fair sex as well as mere man, sometimes at the rate of two per trip'. The visit ended with the guests being 'entertained to tea by the RAeC'. In 1931 McClean, speaking at a dinner given by the Forum Club to some aviation pioneers, recalled an incident that occurred during this event. He said that he took up two old ladies for a joy ride, and that when he had got them firmly fastened in they looked round and said, after due inspection, 'We think, sir, that should it be necessary, we just have room to be sick without inconveniencing you'.

On 22 September the Home Office issued an order in connection with the Aerial Navigation Act, 1911, stating that, 'for the purpose of protecting the public from danger', the navigation of aeroplanes over the area of the County of London within a circle of four miles radius around Charing Cross was prohibited, other than for aeroplanes exempted for special reasons. This was reinforced by a resolution passed by the RAeC Committee on 11 November, which added to the Club's rules a prohibition of 'flying to the danger of the public', particularly 'unnecessary flights over towns or thickly populated areas, or over places where crowds were temporarily assembled, or over public enclosures at aerodromes at such height as to involve danger to the public'. Flying was also prohibited over river regattas, race meetings and meetings for public games and sports, unless the flights were specifically arranged by the promoters of the events.

During the Reims and Gordon-Bennett Trophy Meeting at Bethany in France on 26–29 September a conference was held between the Aero-Club de France and the RAeC, concerning a planned London-to-Paris and return race in the spring of 1914. The RAeC was represented by Messrs. Frank McClean, J H Ledeboer and H E Perrin, the secretary. It was decided to make it an annual event, and to make Paris the starting and finishing point in 1915.

A new Nile machine

The Nile flight was still in the planning, and on 6 September McClean had ordered a new 160hp seaplane designed for the purpose, the S.80. This big twin-boom pusher biplane had an elevator mounted on the front of its wide nacelle, which accommodated two pairs of side-by-side seats and was powered by a 160hp two-row Gnome rotary engine, essentially two 80hp engines joined together, in the rear. Known as the 'Nile Seaplane', it had folding wings that spanned 67ft when spread.

At Eastchurch on 29 September, immediately upon his return from France, McClean was 'flying well at a good height', and on 1, 2 and 3 October he made several flights carrying passengers. On the 6th he flew solo and with passengers, and he was again flying passengers on the 15th and during the following week. Reports of these flights do not specifically identify the aircraft types used, but the S.58 was one of them.

In September and October it was announced that Short Brothers had acquired a site on the River Medway at Rochester, just above Rochester Bridge, and were erecting a subsidiary factory solely for the production of 'waterplanes'. Once launched, new aircraft could be towed into the Medway for testing. The company had also acquired a small area of land at Harty, on the Sheppey bank of the Swale about four miles from Eastchurch, for experimental work.

McClean was present at Eastchurch on 23 October when the First Lord of the Admiralty, Mr Winston Churchill, paid a visit. Churchill first arrived at Sheerness dockyard aboard the Admiralty yacht *Enchantress*, where he watched seaplanes from the Isle of Grain performing evolutions. He then boarded a steam pinnace and was landed on the pier, to be received by Commander Samson, commanding the Eastchurch Naval Aviation School, and Captain-Superintendent Prendergast. Samson then drove his guest to the aerodrome, where Churchill inspected the aeroplanes, 'drawn up in parade order', the hangars and Short Brothers' factory. Churchill was then taken up by Samson in Short biplane No 3 (S.38-type pusher constructor's No S.78, a rebuild of c/n S.39, the Triple Twin) for an extended flight to the Isle of Grain. There the First Lord boarded Naval Airship No 3, the Astra Torres, which cruised over to Eastchurch and performed some 'graceful evolutions' over the aerodrome, then returned to Grain. This was Churchill's first airship flight.

According to his own diary notes, McClean made his first trials of the S.80 Nile seaplane at Eastchurch on 8 November*, it being fitted with a land undercarriage for his initial flights. A *Flight* report on the week's activities at Eastchurch, in the 15 November issue, stated:

> Mr F.K. McClean had his new large 160hp Short machine out during the latter part of the week, several nice flights being satisfactorily accomplished. The machine makes an imposing sight in the air owing to the struts, planes, &c, being white. The machine is fitted with a self-starting arrangement to the engine, and for the preliminary trials land wheels were fitted, the intention being to fly the machine to Mr McClean's hangar at Harty and there affix the floats.

*It has previously been written that the first flight of McClean's S.80 was made by Gordon Bell on 2 October 1913, but from the description of the machine flown by Bell published in the 11 October 1913 issue of *Flight* it is evident that it was not S.80, but the S.65 seaplane for the navy, which had folding upper wing extensions, rather than wings that folded back at the centre section, plus wingtip floats. Bell flew it off to 'Grain Hydroplane Station', and it was given the naval serial number 82. Subsequently S.80 has been confused with S.79, which must have been under construction simultaneously at Eastchurch and was given the naval serial 80.

With its twin pontoon main floats and twin air bags under the lower tailbooms the S.80 showed its weight-carrying capabilities when McClean took four passengers aloft from Harty Ferry on 19 November and flew along the Kent coast, as *Flight* described in its 29 November issue. *The Aeroplane*, in its issue for 27 November, reported:

It has been known for some time that Mr Frank McClean contemplated making a trip up the Nile, accompanied by Mr Alec Ogilvie, on a Short waterplane, this winter. The machine on which the trip is to be made is now packed for transport to Egypt and passed through its trial most satisfactorily last week. The machine is a Short propeller-driven [i.e. pusher] biplane with span of 67 feet, a chord of five feet and a gap of five feet, and is fitted with a Gnome engine of 160hp. There is a small front elevator, which, as Mr McClean explains, is there more for company than for any particular use, as the tail elevator control is quite sufficient. The speed of the machine is about 70mph. The tank capacity is 37 gallons, which is sufficient for 3 hours' flying. The main planes are built so that they can be folded back alongside the tail for convenience in housing or towing, the method employed being that recently patented by the Short Bros.

During these tests on Wednesday last Mr McClean took up with him four passengers, the crew being perhaps the most notable that has ever gone up in one aeroplane. Mr McClean himself has, of course, been flying ever since 1909, and with him on the pilot's thwart was Mr Alec Ogilvie, who is also one of the earliest fliers in this country, and perhaps our leading practical experimenter. In the passengers' seats were Mr Horace Short,

the head of the firm of Short Bros., and Commander Samson, RN, Commandant of the Naval Flying School at Eastchurch, and Captain Courtney, RMLI, one of the chief instructors at the school. With the crew on board and full tanks the machine weighed 3,600lb, yet it got off the water in 22 seconds from the time the engine was opened out, although Mr McClean did not force her up, but simply let her fly off the water. A machine of this type fitted with a gun and wireless apparatus in place of two of the passengers and minus the front elevator is obviously of considerable promise for naval purposes.

On the afternoon of Thursday 4 December McClean was flying at Eastchurch with a passenger, and he was aloft there again on Sunday 7 December. Then, on the morning of Friday 12 December he, Ogilvie and Spottiswoode left England for Cairo, from where they planned to start their seaplane trip down the Nile to Khartoum 'on or about' 1 January 1914. The S.80 and its mechanics had departed some weeks earlier aboard the *Corsican Prince*, and arrived at Alexandria on 27 December. It was claimed to be the first time that a seaplane had been sent to Egypt, and *The Aeroplane* optimistically postulated:

. . . it seems highly probable that waterplanes will be largely used on the great Egyptian waterway as a rapid means of communication between the Egyptian and the Soudanese [sic] capitals, and it is quite possible that there will be a regular air service long before there is a continuous railway from Cairo to Khartoum, which is already becoming a popular winter resort for well-to-do Europeans with whom expense is comparatively little object.

CHAPTER 7

1914: The Nile Expedition and the Last Peacetime Flights

Writing of the Nile flight in the November 1955 issue of *The Journal of the Royal Aeronautical Society*, Alec Ogilvie recalled:

McClean had first asked Commander Samson, RN, to come with him on this 1914 Nile trip but he could not go, and Frank asked me.

As it turned out, McClean would have done better to have taken a really experienced Gnome Engineer, who would have been able to see what was our basic engine trouble, which was overheating. McClean would have avoided a vast amount of trouble and expense, but that was not his way. He wanted his friends with him in his adventures and was prepared to put up with difficulties.

In November 1913 the Nile machine was on trial, first with wheels at Eastchurch and then with floats on the Swale at Harty Ferry.

It was then taken down, crated and sent by ship to Alexandria.

The Dockyard people there gave us every possible assistance and with the help of a couple of Short's own fitters and my mechanic [Graves], we had the machine assembled for trial by 2nd January 1914. In a manner typical of the next three months, the machine with its 160hp engine was carried bodily into the water by a large party of Dockyard hands. I forget what it did weigh but the wings had a span of 60ft [actually 67ft] and the general construction was of the solid Short type. It must have been in the neighbourhood of 3,000lb [3,600lb all-up]. In a calm or steady air condition it flew well and it was very pleasant to sit in front with a fine view, but in gusty weather it was a nightmare to fly and it was as well for all of us that Frank had a strong hand as well as a steady head and plenty of experience. The range of speed was about 55 to 65mph and it could climb at 150ft per minute. We had some 2,000 miles to go. The tanks would only carry supplies for 100 or 120 miles, so a great many fuel depots had to be laid down some in perfectly outlandish places.

Before we started for Egypt the question came up, were we to go around Dongola Bend or across it. It will be remembered that Kitchener in his Mahdi war had a railway built across this stretch and put the job in the hands of Percy Girouard. Frank had not quite made up his mind on this question and so we went to see Sir Percy Girouard in his London home. He strongly advised fitting the machine with wheels at Wadi Halfa and going straight across to Abu Hamed [i.e. across the Nubian Desert]. On this, Frank, who was an obstinate man in some ways, decided to stick to his floats and go round. As long as we were near the railway, supply arrangements were reasonable, but some places entailed camel journeys of five days.

Miss Anna McClean, McClean's sister, was an absolute tower of strength on the 'morale'

A sketch map of the Nile, from Alexandria to Khartoum.

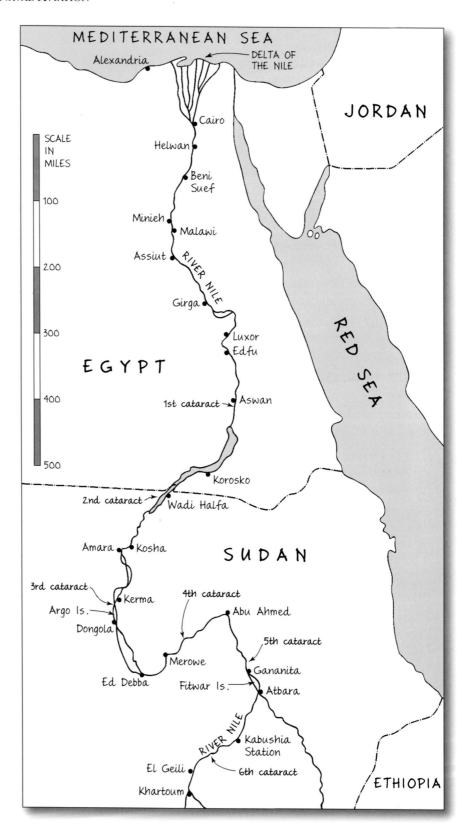

side and we two might have packed up before reaching Khartoum if it had not been impossible to let her down.

In addition to the aircraft's limited fuel capacity, suitable petrol for the Nile flight was available to Alexandria and Cairo, but not beyond, and this was another reason that depots had to be arranged along the route, sometimes by camel. A railway wagon full of spares for the aeroplane accompanied the flight (though it would frequently be many miles away when its contents were required), and, as the machine's weight had to be kept to a minimum, suitcases containing changes of clothing were dotted about the Sudan. All of this 'ground support' was Spottiswoode's responsibility.

On 31 December a reporter for the *Egyptian Gazette* interviewed McClean at the Arsenal at Alexandria, where he was superintending the assembly of S.80, describing him as 'most courteous and patient throughout'. Initially McClean stated: 'I don't want to say much be-

forehand, except this, that mine is purely a pleasure trip; I feel under no obligation to the public and so should prefer that no itinerary of my doings is published in advance.' He underlined the casual nature of the flight at the end of the interview, saying '. . . mine is a pleasure trip, so there's no need to train. I am "going-slow," traversing a sufficient distance each day as not to make the journey tedious'. As it transpired, however, things would go slower than even he intended.

The adventure begins

As related above, after erection at the Naval Dockyard by McClean, Alec Ogilvie, Horace Short and mechanics Gus Smith and Graves the S.80 underwent trial flights on 2 January 1914, the day the *Egyptian Gazette* published

The beginning of the great adventure. The S.80 seaplane during assembly at Alexandria, on 30 December 1913. (ROYAL AERO CLUB)

its interview. The next day McClean, Ogilvie, Horace Short and Smith took off from Alexandria at 9.20am, flew over the sea to Rosetta and then along the Nile to Cairo, a 160-mile trip, arriving at 1.18pm, having stopped at Kafr el Zayat for petrol. The *Egyptian Gazette* reported in its 5 January issue that the aeroplane's arrival at Kafr el Zayat had been awaited by 'a huge crowd of boats and a vast concourse of natives', and that 'the majority of the latter gazed awe-struck at the machine as it approached, while others threw themselves to the ground in abject terror or took speedily to their heels'.

On the 6th McClean departed from Cairo at 11.15am accompanied by his sister, Ogilvie and Spottiswoode and flew to Minieh, taking on fuel at Beni Suef *en route* and delayed only by a faulty sparking plug, while Horace Short went on to Assiut, ready to take Anna's place. At 9am the following day they took off for Assiut, and Deirout was reached at 9.40. After leaving Deirout a broken ball race 'distributed itself in the crankcase', and they proceed by short flights as far as the Assiut Barrage, which was reached at 1.30pm. The aircraft then had to be 'ignominiously towed through the locks at Assiut with its planes folded back'. Several days were spent there, replacing one cylinder and piston, Horace Short returning to Cairo on the 10th to obtain a component. At Assiut Anna left the party and returned to Cairo.

Following a test flight on the 13th, McClean, accompanied by Ogilvie and Gus Smith, con-

The assembled S.80 on the Nile at Cairo, 3-4 January 1914. Horace Short is standing on the nearest float. (AUTHOR)

tinued to Luxor on the 14th, with a stop for fuel at Girgeh, the leg from Assiut to Girgeh being described as 'very rough'. The only trouble was a broken oil pipe, which Gus Smith had to hold in place for half an hour. At 9am on 16 January McClean left Luxor and, after stopping at Edfou 'for petrol and a smoke', reached Aswan at 11am, alighting near the Savoy Hotel off Elephantine Island after an 'uneventful and pleasant' flight with only 'a falling off in power' and being met with an 'enthusiastic reception from the natives'. It was reported that the broken desert ground for the last 20 miles had 'made the machine fret a good

The S.80 at Assiut during 8-13 January 1914 with its wings folded. This capability proved useful when the seaplane had to be manoeuvred through narrow waterways. (ROYAL AERO CLUB)

Removing the big two-row Gnome engine at Assiut, 8-13 January.
(ROYAL AERO CLUB)

deal'. The S.80 was later taxied under its own power to a site by the railway station, where they ground in the valves. McClean left the aircraft and visited the Mudir, who invited him to dinner at the Cataract Hotel, where McClean was staying. Two days later McClean made some flights to entertain the 'great crowd' who had come to see the aeroplane. In its 15 January issue *The Aeroplane* reported that the aeroplane 'has been having engine trouble owing to the immoderate consumption of petrol'.

After they had taken off at 9.50am and flown 30 miles south towards Khartoum on Monday the 19th they crossed to Cataract and put down above the dam to refuel. Then they 'went on A1 for 60 miles', as McClean recounted in a letter to Jim Lockyer dated 27 January, but 'came down unexpectedly having got careless and found that one cylinder had nearly seized'. They filled it with oil and cut out its ignition. The return to Aswan was mostly made by taxiing on the Nile, and they 'got back to the dam with an inch of petrol in the bottom of the tank'. Ever the optimist, McClean said: 'I must say that our bad luck is somewhat helped out with good luck.' The engine was then dismantled with the help of a Gnome mechanic from Cairo. On the 26th the repair was completed, but five minutes into the test flight they had to descend with another cylinder badly heated. Of this brief flight McClean told Lockyer: 'Half a gale was blowing right at the dam & making a fine commotion at the top. We got into it & had a real worry worry. Getting out of that we had to get through a nasty gorge. Then we descended.' The next day the engine was again dismantled and a telegram was sent to the Gnome engine factory in Paris requesting four new cylinders, 'and many other parts'. In a letter to a friend in England, dated 20 January, McClean wrote: 'It is most annoying. The flying out here is perfect except for occasional bumps. The dam gave us a beauty on Monday and we shall avoid that spot in future.'

Ogilvie later recalled:

During the first part of the trip from Alexandria to Aswan, my flight maps are missing, but when getting away from the big expanse of water above the Dam, the power was so much down that I had to get on to the back of the plane, or rather the floats, before Frank could get her off. This was a bad sign and the engine was only making 1,160 revs instead of 1,200. During the next 40 miles, it slowed up still more and we had to anchor.

It was obvious that the back row of cylinders had been getting seriously overheated and after another short trial, Frank decided to go back to the workshops at the Dam and take the engine right down.

As a result of the examination, he found it necessary to order a lot more cylinders and other spares, which would have to come from Paris and would take about a month to reach us. We felt that a month's hang up, and a prolonged spell of "Bar to Barrage and back," as Frank put it, would seriously impair our morale, so a trip was planned to enable us to have a look at the Cataract between Merowe and Abu Hamed.

All reports on the state of the river showed that the Nile was lower than it had been for 50 years with the result that many unusual areas of rocks were appearing above the surface and this particular patch should be investigated.

Frank's sister came with us, we inspected some of the worst places and had a very enjoyable trip.

A reconnaissance trip

Frank and Anna McClean and Ogilvie went on a river steamer to Wadi Halfa, just across the border in Sudan, *en route* to Abu Hamed to look at the rapids, or, as Frank put it to Lockyer, 'to look at our future troubles'. Meanwhile, Spottiswoode went off to Luxor and Cairo for other spares. The trio left Halfa for Kareima on 29 January. Anna had been staying with the railway people and had secured a saloon carriage, borrowed a cook and got in a supply of food and drink. She joined the party, sleeping in the saloon while her brother and Ogilvie were turned out when the train reached Abu Hamed on 2 February and were put up by another railway man. The next day they set out for Kareima across the desert, only sighting the Nile near El Keb, where a supply of petrol was awaiting them.

At Kareima they were lent a river steamer in which to live, 'with a bath & all'. On the Sunday they called on Colonel Jackson, the governor of Dongola Province, at Merowe, and in the afternoon they 'visited some temples & climbed a hill to get our geography correct'. The next day they investigated the bottom 5 miles of the cataract; 'about 4 hours on camels. Beastly things,' McClean commented to Lockyer. 'Next day,' he continued, 'we were in our glory. We had a special train – starting at

6.30am, stopping 6 hours at a place called Amralo & continuing on to Abu Hamed.'

Those 6 hours were fair hell. Across the desert for 5 miles then up & down gorges, crossing dry water courses getting as much idea as possible of the middle of the cataract, & back to the train 8am to 2pm and the camels smelt like it. A Mc [Anna] really lasted out best but even she had a A1 thirst. We, Ogilvie & I wallowed in it, beer, gin & ginger, whiskey soda, tea, all found a place in our systems.

Back at Abu Hamed, McClean and Ogilvie again stayed with the railway employee, and on the next day, Tuesday 3 February, they returned to Halfa.

On the Wednesday, after laying in a fresh supply of food and drink, McClean and Ogilvie started off up the second cataract, covering ten miles that afternoon and then sleeping in a native house. On Thursday they went '15 miles out to near Sarras & back to Gamai[?] with an hour's hard walking as a rest from the everlasting tango of the camel 7.15am to 5.30pm but luckily quite cool.'

On Friday they returned to Halfa and caught

French aviator Marc Pourpe's Morane monoplane at the Aswan Dam on 24 January 1914. (ROYAL AERO CLUB)

the boat for Aswan to await the arrival of the replacement parts. The exhaust valves were already there. Horace Short left to return to Eastchurch at this point. Because of all the problems they had already encountered, McClean informed Jim Lockyer in a letter dated 7 February: 'We shall not try to fly back down the river. The wind would be against us & there is little water left. If all goes well we shall continue to Khartoum & possibly beyond – but shall dismantle at Khartoum.'

During this hiatus McClean was present when the French airman Marc Pourpe landed in his single-seat Morane-Saulnier monoplane, and 'received his colleague in a very friendly way'. Pourpe also stayed at the Cataract Hotel, and McClean gave a big dinner to the French aviator and his friends in 'this celebrated hostelry'.

Back in the air

The engine parts arrived on 12 February and McClean made a 'very successful' trial flight at

noon on the 14th, the propeller being changed and then changed back. The engine was giving 1,200 revs. Although they were ready to depart at 9.15am on the 16th, rare persistent rain delayed departure until the following day, when the 192-mile flight to Wadi Halfa was resumed at 9.30am, with Ogilvie and Gus Smith as the passengers. McClean later explained: 'From Aswan to Halfa and on to Argo in the Dongola bend all went well. The machine, being a seaplane, had to follow the river, which entailed a distance from Halfa to Abu Hamed of 600 miles instead of the 250 miles direct across the desert, the route taken a month before by Pourpe in his Morane-Saulnier. He was the first person to fly to Khartoum.' At 9.25am on Tuesday the 17th McClean, Ogilvie and Smith, 'followed by the good wishes of everybody at Aswan, where [McClean] has made himself extremely popular' set off again. A stop at Korosco for petrol and oil at 11.05am, 116 miles

The S.80 with its starboard float removed at the Aswan Dam on 10 February 1914. (ROYAL AERO CLUB)

The S.80 beached at Wadi Halfa on 18 February for general repairs and adjustments after a turbulent flight from Korosko. (ROYAL AERO CLUB)

into the leg, was protracted because, as Mc-Clean described to Jim in a letter from Halfa on the 19th, the locals:

. . . took about ½ an hour finding a boat, then started out to us without the fuel, then went back & brought some of it, then had to bring out the head man of the village to shake hands. In the end it was almost 1 o'clock when we got going again. And it was going. Bumps of every sort & description. On the water below us were long streaky gusts, short triangular gusts & worst of all circular ones, raising spray and twirling while they raced across the river. Sometimes it felt as though we had hit a brick.

We reached the Sudan boundary & were received by a beauty that shifted Ogilvie in his seat & made him say things. We reached Halfa in a procession of right hand wing lifts that made me perspire.

Wadi Halfa was reached just after 2.40pm on the 17th, where the S.80 was pulled ashore.

Examination revealed that an engine frame wire was broken, the throttle stop had shaken out, there were two dents in the propeller and the bracing was generally slack.

The 18th and 19th were spent putting things to rights and studying maps. In his letter of the 19th McClean remarked:

Can't say I'm happy. The map 1/50,000 shews the Nile at full water & that is bad enough. Now the water level is lower than any recorded summer level. No stretch of actual rapid appears to reach more than 7 miles – but neither do the good parts. We have petrol at Sarras only 30 miles on but DV [*Deo Volente* – God willing] shall not call there. At Kosheh [*sic*: Kosha] 106 miles from here there is petrol & oil, again at Delgo 180 miles and at Dongola 280 miles from here. We've got to get there tomorrow for any kind of accommodation. The other places are mud huts.

From there we shall go to Debba & Merowi [*sic*: Merowe] for the night. Then Abu Hamed. Worst cataract of all. This Dongola reach of nearly 600 miles is the worst going of any on the river. Pourpe only had to do some 250 miles across the desert – good landing all the way.

Spottiswoode & our mechanic have gone on by train today to Merowi. Our van load of spares goes to Abu Hamed on Saturday. My sister is uncertain when she goes or where. She is enjoying life.

The leg from Halfa to Argo was flown on Friday 20 February, departing at 6.30am. There were cataracts only six miles ahead, so, after taking off, McClean rose to a height of 100ft and went five miles north of Halfa and back, 'rising gradually', so that on re-passing Halfa the aircraft was at 1,100ft and 'climbing very busily'. In a letter to Jim Lockyer, written at Argo on 23 February, he wrote:

The engine did its best, the air was smooth and we crossed Absuiv rock at 1,600ft. At that point if the engine had stopped we would have had difficulty in landing, but only for about a minute and then we could have glid down [*sic*] to the south end of the second cataract. However all went well and climbing, first to 2,000, and then to 2,800, we did some proper corner cutting sometimes being a couple of miles from the river. All the time the air was perfect, but the view below was horrible. Rocks projecting out of water cataracts, small and large; at one place the river narrows to 45 yards between high rocks. But all this time there were pieces within reach that looked good for landing and you bet that FK's eyes were on them all the time.

On either side was endless desert, seen as it had never been seen before in this neighbourhood. The local name meaning Belly of Stone suits it. On the east bank were endless black hills, with endless black valleys, twisting and turning and looking like black furnace slag. On the west bank was a certain amount of rock but mostly golden red sand. And the river twisting in the middle. It was wonderful and so interesting that it was impossible to feel nervous. And the engine ran well.

The first refuelling stop was made 80 minutes later at Kosha, 108 miles on. McClean remarked:

If you deduct 10 minutes for starting upwind and turning upwind at the end, it means some speed [about 92.5mph]. At Kosheh [*sic*] there was a nice little piece of water probably 1½ miles long, but so smooth that one could not see the surface and the landing had to be judged by the sand banks on either side.

After taking in petrol and oil we taxied to the upper end of the smooth water, turned and started off. We had got to about 150ft when broken water was reached, and did not turn till about 300ft up. Then we began climbing and did not level out till about 2,000ft. The country now was not quite so rough but the river was not pretty from our point of view. Then after half an hour, bumps began and we rose to 2,500 where they were not bad. Our next petrol place was Delgo [Delga] and when within ten miles of it and a nasty gorge below, the engine half struck work. Down went her nose for a smooth piece of water (there were actually two possible pieces) but when down at 1,500ft the engine took on its job again and we continued. By this time and at this height it was getting very bumpy and at Delgo we had a beautiful vertical drop which shifted Ogilvie in his seat. The turn just after this – to turn into the wind – was bad partly from the weather and partly from nerves which had been jolted, but we landed and finding a nice sandy shore we ran aground. Here we found the magneto were [*sic*] loose and had a general overhaul – in addition to taking in petrol.

Tricky flying and a bad landing

Between landing at Delga at 10 o'clock and departing at midday the heat increased, and as McClean puts it, 'hell was not in it when we again got going'. He continues:

A full diary of the hour and a bit between there and here [Argo] is impossible and even Ogilvie's maps are disjointed and his note book almost empty. He was too damned busy holding on to his seat and I was jambing myself tight between the rudder bar and the back of my seat and using the steering wheel as a safety stop when I rose to the bump. I did actually hit the wheel with my knees once. It started before our turn down wind, it got worse at 600ft, it developed into a corkscrew at 1,000 and I gave it up later. The wind was slightly from the east side of the river – though mostly behind. I tried the west bank and we were thrown up by hundreds of feet. I tried the left and down we went in spite of the machine climbing to the limits of its power. Over the river was a macedoine of movement when there was a clear channel but when there were 2 or 3 channels with various shaped islands – then there was real trouble. The poor air hadn't a notion where it should go to and we had to take pot luck. Gus saw one dust devil. I'm glad I did not. One time we rose 500ft in about a minute with the nose down. Again

in 2 seconds we rose 100ft. That means lifting 1½ tons at a speed of 50ft a second. Thank goodness Short builds strong.

The so-called third cataract was the worse we have passed. As a matter of fact we have crossed twenty or thirty. It was just a bristle of rocks with a few inches of water between. Here again if the engine had petered out we should have found trouble. But the engine ran well. After crossing it I shouted to Ogilvie if we should come down but he called back that Argo was near where there was a telegraph station. He was no keener than I was but there would have been much alarm if we had landed nowhere in particular. So we stuck to it and then from 2,500ft we descended. It was impossible to cut the engine off as it was continually required when the bumps threw the nose up. It had to be shut off suddenly when the nose took charge. It had to be left alone when both hands had to control the warp [ailerons]. It was the devil. Finally close to Argo we landed on a good bit of water. I thought it was a good land[ing] at first, until the left wing caught in the water and turned the machine round and tore the tip off. Ogilvie says that one float was several feet above the other. I thought it was level – but it could not have been. Certainly we were all glad to be down and I'm damned if I could tell one position from another. As the machine righted I saw water come off the top plane.

We dropped anchor but it would not hold. Then Gus tried to restart the engine and nearly broke his wrist. In the end the engine started and we ran ashore. Crowds cheered – half-naked persons of both sexes crowded around until removed by police. Then the Mamour (head local magistrate – a native) came on to the float and we all shook hands. Then another native was carried on to the machine. We ordered him off and he was carried to a boat. We cleared the boat off and found later that the man was a direct descendant of Mahomet and worshipped as such. Finally 10 men pulled us by rope to a sand bank opposite the Government Offices and there the machine is still.

Ogilvie's recollections of this turbulent flight add some detail:

After a day or two we made a very early and easy start down stream. In an hour and a quarter we reached Kosha (105 miles from Halfa) where we had a petrol depot. We restarted within an hour and climbed to 2,000ft. After 20 minutes I could see that the river, which had been glassy smooth, began to show ripples from a surface breeze which we began to feel at our height a quarter of an hour later. This phenomenon we noticed on several occasions. Early a glassy calm; after an hour or so, a surface breeze starting, and 15 minutes later reaching the machine at 2,000ft. At Delgo [sic], 180 miles from Aswan, we stopped for more petrol and it is a pity we did not wait till next morning.

For the next hour the map records very tough going, such as "Tremendous bumps. ASI [air speed indicator] jumping from 55 to 69; aneroid from 1,500 to 1,750ft in half a minute, down draughts of 300ft per minute." At Argo Frank decided that it was too bad to continue and after a very rough descent we got caught in a minor whirlwind and landed heavily, doing some damage to the left wing tip which struck the water and broke off.

The relatively enormous span of the wings, the aileron flaps only to be controlled downwards [i.e. single-acting] and the heavy floats below, constituted a calm weather aeroplane

but not one to be comfortable in a dust devil.

This run of 245 miles was the most we ever did in one day.

McClean unhesitatingly shouldered the blame for the incident that caused the mishap, writing in 1938:

The troubles . . . were caused, of course, by an error of judgement on the part of the pilot. The machine was being flown near its ceiling of 2,000 feet when it met a dust devil reaching far above it. Not even a modern aeroplane will take on the air currents in one of these, and our engine being what it was, a quick landing was indicated and made. But there was no need to make such a crooked one.

In a second account written another twelve years later McClean expanded on this, but cited a different altitude:

The second, third and fourth Cataracts are situated in this bend of the river and a stretch of country known by the native word for 'Belly of Stone'. As the machine's ceiling was only some 3,000 feet, every atmospheric disturbance from every rocky hill found its mark. Finally, approaching Argo, a dust-devil towering high above the machine took up the pursuit and in the hurry of the moment a poor alighting was made. One float and one wing-tip reached the water first. The wing-tip was torn off and the lower main spar broken. But nothing else suffered.

They had arrived at Argo at 1.20pm, and the *Egyptian Gazette* had optimistically stated '. . . there seems to be no reason to doubt that he will be at Khartoum in a very few days', but it was not to be. McClean explained the problems in a letter to Lockyer:

Alec Ogilvie poses by the damaged wingtip at Argo on 20-22 February 1914. (Royal Aero Club)

Having got the machine ashore, we examined the trouble and Ogilvie said he could repair it. I was doubtful as Argo had no facilities. The local carpenter arrived with an adze and some pieces of packing case and wanted to start off on his own. We stopped him as we wished to have a say in the matter. In the end he found a saw and a plane and some fairly decent planks. Then a river steamer arrived from Dongola with an English engineer on board. Having asked if there were any beer or whiskey on board and been told no, we got him to cut some pieces of iron out of his galley floor. These were made into boxes to go round the break in the main spar. Hoop iron and biscuit box lid made strappings. Thus the repair was made and the tip covered with calico – all being finished on Sunday night at 7pm. During this time we had consumed gallons of water. The Mamour . . . had some whiskey which we investigated at dinner but during the day it was OH2

until an English Inspector Willis arrived on Monday morning.

The Aeroplane reported in its 5 March issue that 'The engine has been consuming too much petrol and overheating badly'. The 20th to 24th were spent repairing the aircraft at Argo. With his customary disarming modesty, McClean later wrote that the success of the trip 'was due in great part,' to Alec Ogilvie's improvisation, saying, 'Whatever the pilot did to the machine, he [Ogilvie] put it together again'. Ogilvie recalled: 'There were no white people at Argo, but the Sudanese Mamur or Inspector gave us all the help he could and entertained us in his house most hospitably. After two or three days of rather comic repair work to the wing, we got going again . . .' McClean was rather more complimentary regarding Ogilvie's handiwork. In 1950 he wrote:

Luckily Argo is the terminus for river steamers from Merowe and one arrived the next day. Pieces of iron chiselled from the galley floor were made into boxes for the broken main spar. Hoop iron from biscuit boxes made strappings. Sugar boxes were converted into three-ply inter-spar ribs, and two layers of calico, usually employed for native clothing, with a liberal coating of Assyrian glue, made the covering. This latter was replaced at Merowe as it billowed up in the bumps and gave birth to a lack of confidence. The other repairs were without reproach, thanks to the ingenuity of Alec Ogilvie.

In 1938 McClean wrote that, apart from the fabric repair, Ogilvie's work '. . . would have supported the Pyramid of Cheops . . .'.

They were ready to resume their journey on the Monday morning, but a dust storm arose and they hurriedly pegged down the aircraft. The storm was so bad that the trio expected it to break free and sat alongside to get a photograph when it happened, but it stayed put. They then lunched with Willis 'and were re-introduced to beer which we had not seen for days'. They had intended to fly the 25 miles to Dongola by that night if the wind dropped, so that they would have a clear start for Debba in the morning, but the wind persisted.

Despite 'a bit of a wind' they set off for Debba a little before 7am on Tuesday 24 February, stopping at Dongola for fuel and oil after covering the 25 miles in 18 minutes. The leg to Debba was flown in a wind that had 'got a bit rough' and they could see only three or four miles because of sand. That evening McClean wrote to Lockyer:

It was quite uninteresting after the cataract stretch but felt a trifle more safe.

Mostly it was flat yellow desert with just a line of trees on either bank and a few cultivated islands. We kept at about 800-1,000ft and had very few bumps. Landing was uncomfortable as we misjudged the direction of the wind and bounced quite a lot. We ran ashore and decided not to go on.

Before leaving Argo we borrowed a bottle of whiskey off Willis so we are not entirely dependant on the Nile supply. The Mamour gave us tea and biscuits and jam on arrival. He is also giving us lunch and dinner. What they will be like I don't know but let's hope. Tomorrow for Merowi [*sic*] where we recover the wing tip with proper material and examine valves before the bad rapids.

The wingtip after Alec Ogilvie's resourceful and ingenious repair work. (ROYAL AERO CLUB)

The Nile seaplane beached at Debba on 24 February.
(ROYAL AERO CLUB)

In accordance with their plans they took off at about 7.45am on the 25th and Merowe was reached at 8.40, McClean observing that they were in the air for 1 hour 59 minutes, 'including a turn at the start and a circle at the finish'. 'It is only 76 miles,' he added, 'but the Nile runs from north-east to south-west and the wind is always north. It gives us a puzzle from here, where the rapids start, as we can only last out 2¼ hours. It was quite smooth and we varied from 1,500ft to 50ft.'

Merowe was on the railway, and Spottiswoode was there with the spares and superintended their arrival along with Colonel Jackson. McClean circled round 'as a show off'

McClean, mechanic and Ogilvie with the S.80 at Merowe on 25 February.
(AUTHOR)

and they alighted amid cheering spectators and bands playing. 'The head man of the village presented me with a large silver plaque,' wrote McClean, 'a little girl brought roses and altogether it was a disgraceful show.'

On Thursday 26 February and the Friday morning the makeshift wingtip covering was replaced, and rents in the tailplane and rear elevators were repaired. They also adjusted the elevator and aileron control wires and replenished the petrol and oil tanks. In addition McClean wanted the engine to be seen to, as the rapids now before them beat anything they had hitherto encountered. As a precaution against headwinds on the next leg, petrol and four gallons of oil were sent to a place called Kulgeili, 25 miles distant, so that they could land there and reduce the next leg to 70 miles or less. Beer was also sent. Meanwhile, the crew had a rather enjoyable respite from their traumas. They shaved and brushed their teeth for the first time since Halfa, and McClean simply wrote that 'Two nights were spent in luxury at Merowe', but Ogilvie stated:

Frank's reference to our stay 'in luxury' there is an understatement.

The Governor of [Dongola] Province, Col. Jackson, was a fabulous figure and had a fabulous mansion if not a palace. My recollection is of a dinner for four, a magnificently uniformed servant behind each chair and on the table in front of each, a bottle of champagne, instantly replaced when the first one had been lowered. This was just what we needed to cheer us up. Jackson was apparently oblivious of our necessarily grimy and dishevelled appearance and entertained us with lively stories of Lord Kitchener.

We two and Spottiswoode were housed very comfortably in the Governor's river steamer. On our arrival at Merowe, we were introduced to a very holy man, the direct descendant of the Mahdi, but I don't think he was much interested. The natives throughout the trip were not much interested in the aeroplane as such, but were so in us. There was never any excited rush as there would have been if the situation had been reversed and a Sudanese had made a landing for the first time on the beach at Brighton. They walked straight out into any depth of water to give us a hand or a tow and on one occasion carried us and the machine bodily on shore.

On 27 February the aircraft set off for the fourth cataract. Writing to Lockyer from Abu Hamed on 1 March, McClean wrote:

Friday morning (Feb 27th) we made up our minds to start in the afternoon for Kulgeili; but allowing enough time to get to El Keb if the wind was not bad against us. Early in the afternoon Col Jackson . . . let off a gun to give everyone a chance of seeing the *Tyara* (kite) start. That did it – we had to go whether we liked it or not. I did not go near the machine till 4 o'clock & then I forgot the bottle of whiskey which was our passenger.

At about 4.20 we started – hot was not the word for it, but there was little head wind and strange to say no bad dunts only side gusts that did not throw us about. Ogilvie was damned busy. He had to settle by the maps whether or no we could go on or whether stop at Kulgeili for the night. The air over the river was one big down current. First we stuck at 600ft although the nose of the machine well up – then we got to 1,100 after 10 miles and then the cataracts started & we should have been at 2,000ft. When we reached Kulgeili we were 1,600ft up and only averaging 44 miles an hour. That meant in 2¼ hours which was our petrol limit & also daylight that we should do 99 miles. El Keb was 95 miles.

But we settled to go on.

We never got above 2,600ft. Every few hundred feet climb ended in a down drop – not violent but irresistible. Below were endless rocks & islands but made more palatable owing to the fact that every five miles or so the river joined up into a single stream & a possible landing place existed. There was no danger but if we had had to come down it would have taken days for anyone to get near us & the machine would have had to be dismantled.

This (known as the 4th cataract) extended from mile 10 to mile 78. In the middle the engine started missing but not badly. It was some relief to get beyond it although the river above was nothing much to swear by. When we landed the sun had set some time & before we ran ashore on the mud it was practically dark. We landed [at El Keb] at 6.5.

The ignominious Gnome

While Ogilvie & Gus fixed up the machine, I trekked across loose sand to the railway sta-tion a mile away. It was a desert station – no houses – nothing but a station & large water tank. Nobody spoke English. I got out the petrol & oil – & then luckily a train came in which should have gone hours before & on it was an Irrigation Officer who spoke Arabic. He explained everything to the station master. After the train had gone they carried our stuff down – we filled up & returned to the station. A tin of meat was cooked & we made tea in one of the petrol cans – enough for the night & for the morning cold. Then we all three slept in the booking office.

Up before dawn next morning we made a start at 6.50. There was good open water & we got off easily – but the engine was missing badly.

So we came down at the next open stretch of water, ran on to a mud bank & tried the engine stationary. We got it a bit better & went on. After 35 miles & when only 15 miles from here, an inlet valve began to fire back. Ahead was very bad broken water – in

The S.80 near Mehaiza on 28 February 1914. (AUTHOR)

fact more rocks than water. We daren't go on – so we turned back & after 5 miles found a stretch of a mile long where we could expect to get off again. We were about 1,300ft up. The landing was not good as the water was too smooth & we fell the last 5 or 10ft. From 8.25 to 4pm we were fooling around with the engine – running it at intervals.

The place was a mass of small flies which drew blood at every bite. It was here that we discovered that the whiskey bottle had been left behind. We made tea in the castor oil jug by means of a petrol blow lamp.

At 4 o'clock we again started. Before we were 150ft up we were over rocks – but the machine climbed well and we reached Abu Hamed at 1,700ft. Practically the whole 20 miles was unlandable. Certainly the last 14 as everywhere were rocks & the water between looked a few inches deep.

Matters were rectified at Abu Hamed, where the two mechanics, Gus and Ogilvie's mechanic, Graves, worked on the engine. They also had to mend a broken wire, repair a cracked float cross-strut and 'doctor up the starting magneto'. McClean planned to start for Atbara early in the morning on 2 March, then 'DV [*Deo Volente* – God willing] next day for Khartoum'. Anna McClean was awaiting them at Atbara, and it was thought that she would occupy the fourth seat in the S.80 from there to Khartoum.

The journey was resumed on 2 March, but not for long. As McClean recounted to Lockyer in a letter of the same date from Shereik Station:

More trouble. Yesterday the heat was of the next world; today is the devil's delight – best Powell Duffryn brand [an allusion to the colliery company of which McClean was a board member]. Yesterday we ransacked the Greek shop at Abu Hamed & laid in sardines, tea & sugar – then we boarded the express & secured biscuits & incidentally made the acquaintance of some beer. Gus & Graves got the engine running well & all was serene except that the sun shone. This morning we were out of bed at 5.30 & the stores were on board by 6.0. Allah be praised we did not forget the whiskey bottle this time. At 6.15 we were pushed off & ran out onto the river at 15 miles an hour not a bit more – we gave it up & returned. More play with the d-d engine & pumping out some water from the float. Next time all was well & we got away in great style. But a south wind had got up. Now – a south wind does not blow at this time of year it is unknown – but there it was.

The first 10 miles were good water – then it got a little worse & later became rocks with water between. At 1,000ft our speed decreased to 37mph so we had to go lower whether we liked it or not & we didn't like it. At 45 miles after an hour and 10 minutes I got a thump on the back from Gus who shouted that the oil pump had broken. It had to be done & we landed – a real bad pancake from 10ft but no harm. The machine was run ashore. We were 8 or 9 miles from here where we have petrol & which is a fairly important station without a town. We found that there were a few miles of fair water ahead. So oil was poured into the engine & after some persuasion we got a Rice (local boatman) to come on board. He went to his village to get some clothes on & came back with 2 rags & a spear & sat on the float.

Off we went again taxying on the water. Rocks to the right & rocks to the left & between them we zigzagged for 3 miles. It was hair raising but we daren't risk flying & we didn't appreciate 9 miles walk to the telegraph. The old chap signalled the direction & grinned from ear to ear. He shouted at anyone on the bank – probably to swank – and now he is probably the hero of the cataract. When we finally ran ashore because we couldn't go any further we were still 6 miles from here.

When the machine was well on the mud – we quaffed some whiskey & Nile water & Ogilvie & I took off what we could, filled our pockets with boxes of sardines & not forgetting the whiskey flask – set off on our flat feet. My gawd – it was awful. Over soft mud, through sand drifts & finally over a red-hot plain we marched along. But now we blessed the south wind which kept us from frizzling. At intervals I poured pints of Nile water over my head & let it run down inside my clothes. Ogilvie only did so once & survived better than I did. I found a very old man on a donkey & tried to turn him off – but found he was too infirm to walk – so had to let him be.

In the end we arrived [at Shereik Station]. Then we let ourselves go on water till the station master brought us tea & over the third or fourth cup we felt that we could eat. A tin of sardines & a dozen biscuits between the two of us made us better & after a few more cups of boiling tea we went back to water. You may not believe it but tea is far better than whiskey. Tell them in town that at 11 o'clock I shall demand it & again at 12.45 and during the afternoon. Will write more some later day as I must return to the Kite as they call it here. By trolley – not by foot.

In a 1938 account of this incident McClean waxes more lyrical about their native guide:

The fifth of these cataracts lies above Abu Hamed. Here the engine again faded, and we landed among the scattered rocks. By signs we induced comprehension into a gigantic native who, after donning his most elaborate ceremonial dress and with an 8-foot spear in his hand, (we thought our last day on earth had come when we saw him armed to the teeth), stood on one of the floats and for three miles guided us between the rocks by pointing with his spear. This was not too easy since at frequent intervals he saluted his friends on the bank and forgot us.

Ogilvie recalled:

The night was spent on 'angarebs' in straw mat shelters, which the local natives put up in a very short time, to shield us from the cold wind from the North.

The angareb is a bed constructed of very crooked bits of timber with a web of string or thongs; airy and very comfortable.

In the shore party was Frank's dragoman, a high class Arab, named Abdul, who used to turn up in the strangest places and take over our welfare.

Before Abdul arrived at Shereik, we kept going on the few supplies we had on the aeroplane. As a measure of our situation, I might recount that a sardine dripping with oil was dropped on the sand, picked up, brushed off and consumed.

Continuing his 2 March letter on 6 March, now on headed paper from the Grand-Hotel at Khartoum, McClean described what happened next.

We got our repair done by the following morning. Graves . . . was brought by motor trolley also Abdul and the spare pump. They arrived just at dark and as our only light was a candle belonging to a native inspector who also turned up there could not be much work. We got some beds & slept out by the machine after a little tinned dinner. During the night a strong north wind got up and by morning was blowing a gale. This went on all that day & half the next. We were covered with sand & filthily dirty. The nights were cold I put on my spare shirt & used a handkerchief as a nightcap.

On Wednesday 4th we got a shelter put up and immediately the wind dropped. At 4pm we started off – down stream & against a strong wind. As we got off there was a rock under each wing & a mill race current between. We climbed to 300ft & turned. For a bit all was smooth. Then came a vicious bump followed by more. We only had a few bad ones but much worrying. There were two fine cataracts of 3 or 4 miles each. Low down the wind was strong behind us – but we couldn't stay low. High up it was across us & slowed us down. After about 40 miles we came to a fine rocky stretch & rose from

1,100 to 1,900 without elevating. All looked well when suddenly the oil stopped & we had to come down. Then the engine stopped but over good water.

I judged my landing 30ft too high and we pancaked, smashing one float & breaking 2 struts below the planes. Out came dozens of natives swimming & pulled us ashore – but first insisted on shaking hands. After we had got ashore 2 of the struts to the other float collapsed with a bang. We examined the engine and found that a large section of the timing wheel had broken clean away & that both oil pump spindles had sheared. We left it and crossed from the island we were on [Fitwar Island] to the mainland. A 3-mile walk brought us to a railway station [Gananita] but no English speaking man. After a time we got through on a telephone to an inspector who came by trolley & next day one of the head railway men came out by motor trolley from Atbara 50 miles away [where the main stores were kept]. I went in to Atbara with him & sent our trucks back to Gananita

The beached S.80 on Fitwar Island, 4-14 March, with collapsed float struts. (AUTHOR)

along with much wood & food & a cook, a carpenter and a mechanic. Ogilvie & the 2 mechanics are there now. I came on here [to Khartoum] by train & have done much shopping. Tomorrow night I go back to Atbara – & later to the machine. There are a week's repairs at least. Luck is out again.

In 1955 Ogilvie provided his own impression of the dramatic departure from Shereik on the 4th:

The start from this riverside camp was sensational. According to my map notes: 'Charging between two rocks 20 yards apart (our wing span) against a 10mph wind and with a 5 mile current, we were in the air in about 10 yards.' In a letter to me last year, Frank referred to this incident as follows:–

"You only once I think showed a well deserved distrust of me, when we were getting away from Shereik, with rocks to the right of us and rocks to the left of us. I had put my foot whole-heartedly on the gas, you shouted in my ear, 'Don't change your mind.'"

I don't remember this at all and the map note as quoted above and written at the time indicates a critical situation handled with much determination and skill. I don't remember any distrust. I always felt Frank would always get away with it if it could be done.

What McClean failed to mention in his letter was that, in the process of departing from the aeroplane, a large section of the timing gear had damaged two of the four tailbooms supporting the rudders and rear elevator. 'This,' said McClean, 'may or may not have been an adequate excuse for the bad landing.' He omitted to say that it could easily have resulted in a disastrous in-flight structural failure. In addition, both oil-pump spindles had sheared.

In his 1938 account McClean mistakenly and confusingly combines this incident with the later one at Kabushia on 15/16 March, writing:

. . . The timing gear and its ball race, probably irritated by a surfeit of sand, resolved itself into its component parts, and in doing so crippled two of the tail booms, thereby giving to the elevators and rudders an element of freedom which was inconvenient but luckily nothing more.

Having no tackle for lifting out the engine, we pushed it off its bearings on to a mound of sand, and placed it on a native bed. It was then carried to the railway and so to Atbara, where repairs were made in the workshops by the courtesy of the Engineering Staff.

However, from his letters written at the time, his 1950 account and Ogilvie's version of 1955 it is evident that the timing-gear failure and the engine removal after a connecting-rod failure were two separate events. In his 1950 account McClean states that the S.80 had a 140hp Gnome, whereas all descriptions and reports contemporary with the event clearly say it had a 160hp Gnome. Both versions of the engine had fourteen cylinders and were created by joining two seven-cylinder engines together.

Of this episode, Ogilvie recalled:

This was near Gananita and we were carried ashore to an island in mid-stream by natives who appeared in large numbers from nowhere. All insisted on shaking our hands before taking any practical steps towards salvage.

The situation seemed to require a look into the structure to check up for possible further damage and with the consent of the old Omda or chief, who was the owner of the island, we decided to set up a regular camp, getting tents and supplies from Atbara, not very far away, and make ourselves really comfortable. This was soon arranged and we were there for 10 days having been joined by Spottiswoode and my mechanic Graves.

I enjoyed this camp more than Frank, who was getting very fed up with our snail-like progress. But there was never a word of anger against anyone, merely a grim determination to get to Khartoum somehow or other.

The engine was lifted out with a pair of shear legs and stored in a small shelter on the extreme north tip of our island to avoid as much flying sand as possible. Wings were taken off and examined but I am ashamed to say that a complete fracture of the main top back spar in the centre section was not discovered till the machine was back in Short Works at Eastchurch undergoing a thorough overhaul before being converted (doubtless at Frank's expense) into a torpedo carrier for the Royal Naval Air Service.

It was as well we did not know this as it would have been very alarming to think of during the rest of our journey.

'In 10 days,' wrote McClean, 'with very great help from the Sudan Railway, the machine was in the air again.' During the interlude he wrote to 'Bill' from Atbara on 9 March, saying: 'We left Abu Hamed a week ago & the machine is now only 100 miles on'. Describing the aircraft as 'a comparative wreck', he commented: 'I am supposed to be on holiday but should have gone back today only there is no way except camel & it is 50 miles distant.' 'We still hope to get to Khartoum,' he added, 'but when God only knows.' Anna was staying in Atbara, hoping to see the S.80 soon, but McClean said: 'Her chance of another flight is small as it would not do for her to be lying about on sand banks as we are. There are a few crocodiles about in these parts – saw one at Gananita.'

McClean got back to Gananita late at night on Tuesday 10 March, where his train was met by Ogilvie, Spottiswoode and Abdul. Inexpli-

Two views (below and overleaf) of the dismantled and engineless seaplane at Gananita, during the hiatus there. (AUTHOR)

cably, his telephone message to say that he wanted a felucca (boat) had been altered into a statement that he wanted to see them on his way to Cairo. 'They were wondering what the hell was the matter,' McClean wrote in a letter to Lockyer from Kabushia Station dated 16 March, '& were quite annoyed when they found that they had been kept up for nothing.'

More breakdowns

In the same letter McClean described what next ensued.

Graves had come to Atbara to see the final touches to the oil pump wheels & spindles [in the Sudan Railway workshops] & returned with me. We stopped the train 4 miles north of Gananita & walked & boated across to Fitwar Island. A fine camp had been put up & all the structural repairs were finished. Ogilvie, Gus & Graves with the help of 2 Greeks – one a mechanic & the other a car-

penter – had made a fine job of it. Ogilvie is wonderful when repairs of any sort are doing.

Next day we had another shock. Late in the afternoon when the two magnetos were being taken to pieces for cleaning it was found that the spindles of both were broken. It looked like another Atbara repair – but next day Graves propounded a scheme & he and Gus repaired one with parts out of the two.

By Friday the 13th the machine was assembled and the following day [was] spent in truing up & fixing controls. At 12.30 the engine was run & by 1.30 all was ready for a start. During the afternoon we packed up etc & at 5pm the machine was lifted back into the water. At about 5.20 we started. Ogilvie wanted me to do a straight & land, being a bit nervous after my three previous bad landings – consecutive. However I assured him and we cut it out. Before we got high enough for a turn we were over rapids but we are getting used to that. We climbed gradually to

1,500. A few small rapids occurred south of Gananita & then some fairly bad ones between Berber & Atbara – especially just up to Atbara. The sun set clearly in this part of the flight & looked quite below one. It was over endless flat desert. We reached Atbara [after a 40-minute flight] at 1,500ft & circled over the railway shops, down over the railway bridge & touched opposite the houses where all the population was assembled. My sister had been waiting a fortnight. The last time she waited was at Halfa when a month elapsed. The same night after dinner we filled with petrol & got up before 5 next morning to put the oil in. We got to bed about midnight.

Our intention was to start at 5.45 when it would be quite light but it was after 6 when we pushed off. A run up stream, turn on the water & sprint back & we got into the air opposite the start. Again we had to turn over rocks but the engine was pulling like the devil. All went well for 13 minutes then an inlet valve broke. Bang after bang & we came down & anchored in midstream. It took the better part of an hour to locate & change the valve & again we went away like the devil.

The air was roughish but not bad and our speed a bit over 70mph. Then opposite here [Kabushia Station] the machine started vibrating & corkscrewing. I had had the symptoms twice before in England & it was necessary to cut the engine out at once. It was a broken connecting rod. We anchored & tried to work out a method to drift to the east bank – on which side was the railway. But it was no use – the wind took us eventually to the west shore. We were at once surrounded by a semi-naked crowd & got them to pull us along till opposite a good spot on the east bank. Then we made them swim & pull. Six on the end of a rope & 6 others holding to the floats & striking out with both

legs. But the wind beat them. After many hours a boat was brought & the machine pulled across. I came to the station & telephoned. Graves who had started for Khartoum – had got off at Shendi when he found that we had not arrived there & came back – bringing a dozen beer, a dozen soda & a bottle of whiskey & some tins of food. We drank his health unanimously.

We then got a shelter of sticks & mats – borrowed some beds & after a good meal turned in. One thing about this country is that you can always get beds & a blanket. It was not comfortable. The bed was hard, the blanket rough & our legs badly burnt by the sun when paddling along with the machine.

This morning [16 March] the engine was lifted out by hand. A high mound of earth was built below the propeller on which 6 men stood. Two more stood below the forward end of the shaft & by the help of two on the nacelle with a rope it was got out. Then it was laid on one of the beds and two batches of eight men carried it 3 miles to the station. It was a comic sight. We had not previously thought of moving the engine without block & tackle. Necessity is the mother of invention. The four of us came on donkeys & our supplies on a camel. The supplies included 4 bottles of cold tea. Not half bad either when you must. We allowed two hours to carry the engine but they did it in 45 minutes.

Thank heaven there is a daily tram each way here. At Gananita it was twice weekly & if we wanted to travel otherwise than by 4th class we had to stop the mail train.

We all go to Atbara now & probably Ogilvie & I shall go to Khartoum tomorrow for a couple of days.

Ogilvie recalled the difficulties that had to be overcome to remove the engine:

Landing presented no difficulty to Frank but we had to run ashore at a place where, owing to the unusual lowness of the river, the bank was 20ft high and very steep.

The first problem was to remove the engine with no lifting tackle and not even a stick more than 6ft long and crooked at that. This problem was solved by getting the large gang of natives who appeared almost immediately to build a solid ramp of earth high enough and wide enough for a strong-arm gang to draw the engine bodily out of its cradle and put it on an 'angareb' with its crank-shaft sticking down through the webbing to keep it in place.

The next job was to get this up on top of the bank and was done by turning our gang on to making a cutting at a slope up which the angareb could be carried. On top, donkeys appeared; carrying teams were selected and we set off in style for the railway station a few miles away. I remember that Frank had difficulty in keeping his long legs off the ground.

Once the engine had been carried to the railway it was transported back to Atbara, where the railway workshop took it in hand. Of their stay there, Ogilvie recalled:

Poor Miss McClean, I remember on one occasion Frank and I were summoned by her from our work bench in the railway works at Atbara, where we were working on the engine, to come to the station to meet the Governor-General, Sir Reginald Wingate. When we reached the platform, in the far distance we could see a glittering body of white uniformed and bemedalled officials with Miss McClean hovering around. We were bedecked with patches of pure castor oil, considered necessary for those air-cooled Gnome

engines, and the patches had collected dust and sand. I do not know if we had shaved but our appearance did no credit to Frank's sister. I remember that the platform seemed to be a very long one.

The repaired engine was then taken back to the aeroplane. McClean wrote:

The reinstallation with a borrowed derrick was simple, but had to be carried out in the lee of smoking fires lit to create an atmosphere in which sand flies could not breathe, while a native boy carried the spanners and other tools to and from the river to keep them cool.

The river was not cold, but no refrigerator was ever such a welcome neighbour, and when we discovered a Greek shop only thirty miles away and a camel load of beer found its way to our temporary home, the temperature of the consignment was reduced from blood heat to mere tepidity before being returned to the temperature of the body.

Khartoum at last

On 22 March, seven days after the forced descent, the aircraft was ready to embark on the final leg of its arduous journey. Ogilvie wrote:

After a few days in the Atbara workshops we were back and made another early start on 22nd March with 138 miles to go to Khartoum. Our average speed was 80 and at times the tailwind was 30mph, but the going was fairly good.

The Shabluka Gorge, about which we had heard some alarming stories, was about half way and presented a very fine sight. Thousands of duck could be seen getting up from the sandbanks 1,600ft below.

The vast area of Omdurman soon came in sight on our right, then the junction of the two Niles and Khartoum at last. Frank landed in style opposite the Governor General's white palace and taxied across to the Dockyard, where we hauled out.

Many kind people invited us to dinner during the next few days but as guests we were poor value as we both invariably fell asleep after dinner. [McClean recalled that, as they stepped ashore, a lady had invited Ogilvie and himself to go for a picnic on the river on the afternoon of their arrival!]

We dismantled the aeroplane in the Dockyard and despatched it to Shorts.

It will be admitted that this was a very trying and arduous trip for all but particularly for Frank McClean. He got very exhausted and haggard but I do not recall a cross word to me or to anyone else. He remained his genial and stout-hearted self to the end.

Thus Khartoum was finally reached at 8.55am on 22 March. Ogilvie said, 'Everyone throughout Egypt and the Sudan was extremely kind and seemed to be determined to push us through to our destination. Unfortunately I had my pocket picked at Khartoum after arrival and so lost my notebook and diary as well as a considerable sum of money.' Consequently the account of the expedition that he penned in 1955 was compiled from pencil notes made on the margins of the roll-up maps, many photographs, and from some dates and details given by McClean in an article published the *Royal Aero Club Gazette* in May 1950.

Clearly frustrated by the persistent engine problems, McClean, who had already abandoned any idea of making a return flight, wired *The Aeroplane* to say that the S.80 was coming back to England by boat. 'The delay in his journey,' the magazine reported in its 9 April issue, 'was caused entirely by trouble with the 160hp Gnome. Apparently this sized Gnome is particularly prone to go wrong.' On his epic flight down the Nile McClean suffered no fewer than thirteen engine breakdowns, and 'three bad landings were made'. In 1938 McClean somewhat understated the case when he wrote:

The whole trip would have been rather colourless had it not been for that engine. At Assiut it faded out, and we had to be towed through the lock before we could make repairs. Thirty miles beyond the Aswan Dam it lost most of its horses, but enough remained for us to taxi back to civilisation, where a lady visitor at the Cataract Hotel, hearing that we had done this, expressed surprise that we should have found a 'taxi' so far out in the desert. A month went by while new cylinders were coming from Paris, and the time was spent exploring the second and fourth cataracts. One realised after sitting on camels for seven or eight hours a day how much harder a world it would have been if engines had been endowed with camels instead of horses.

The second cataract was passed without incident. The third was left behind before the encounter with the dust devil. The fourth was enlivened by a broken inlet valve, and one of our usual hurried landings, followed by the discovery that our commissariat had been left behind; all we had that night was tea boiled in a castor oil tin. Healthy is as healthy does!

He concluded:

All this must sound strange to those who today travel by Imperial Airways or in service machines, and who in one day cover our two months' pilgrimage. They have no happy recollections of sand banks, of cataracts, of mud villages, camels and sand flies. Beer they may know, but not nectar. . . . . The unsophisticated inhabitants had never dreamed of human beings appearing from the skies, and though I had once been mistaken for an angel by a small boy in Kent, I was quite unnerved when greeted by the natives as the Almighty (or his arch-enemy) – and worshipped.

Various people, including Major-General Sir Rudolf Slatin Pasha, Inspector-General of the Sudan, were given joyrides at Khartoum on the 23rd, and then S.80 was dismantled the next day for shipment back to England. McClean and company left Khartoum by train on the 26th, and sailed for England from Alexandria aboard the Austrian Lloyd steamer *Helonan* on 2 April.

During McClean's absence abroad, his praises had been sung in the 17 January 1914 issue of *Flight* by 'Will o' the Wisp', the contributor of a regular chat column entitled 'Eddies':

It's a pity aviation cannot boast a few more sportsmen like Frank McClean in its ranks. Possessed of a fair share of the stuff that makes the world go round, and with a huge interest in all that pertains to aviation, either in his own interests or in the interests of others, he has probably done more for the advancement of flying than any other single individual. In the very early days he obtained possession of a large tract of land in Sheppey, round about Eastchurch, which he made over to the Royal Aero Club at a mere peppercorn rent as a practice ground. It would not be wrong either, I think, to call him the father of the Navy flyers, for he it was who at his own expense bought and placed machines at the disposal of the Admiralty to enable the first quartet of naval pupils to be trained at Eastchurch, when the Navy had not a single machine for them to learn on.

A very reticent man, so far as his own good deeds are concerned, he has done more for aviation than most people are aware of, and there is not much doubt that his recent flight up the Nile is as much in the interests of other people as for his own pleasure; nor must we forget his sister, who is frequently his passenger and companion when flying. The enthusiastic private owner is the man for aviation – would to goodness we had more like him.

Shortly after the completion of the Nile flight, and while McClean was still abroad, *The Times* for 27 March carried a reference to a case brought before Mr Justice Darling in the King's Bench Division of the High Court of Justice. The plaintiff, Mr George William Hare, was suing McClean for damages for personal injuries in a motor-car accident, and McClean had applied for an adjournment because he was unexpectedly delayed in Khartoum, awaiting spares for his aeroplane. Mr Patrick Hastings, speaking on behalf of the plaintiff, opposed the application, asking 'why it should take a gentleman, with or without an aeroplane', such a time to come home, whereupon Mr Justice Darling commented: 'If he is coming in the aeroplane he will probably never get here at all'. The case was allowed to stand over until 27 April.

The growth of Shorts and naval aviation

By the beginning of March the new Shorts' factory at Rochester was virtually complete. It comprised general offices and two workshops, each 60ft wide and 240ft long. The one nearest the River Medway was to serve as an erecting and assembling shop, with the separate drawing office in one corner, while the other was to be divided into four to house the sawmills, machine shop, fitters' shop and covering department. A slipway into the river was to be built at the end of the erecting shop. Sufficient additional land had been acquired to allow for future extensions, there being room for four more shops similar to those already built. The new factory was expected to be ready for occupation in April.

Introducing the Navy Estimates in the House of Commons on 17 March, Winston Churchill stated that £375,000 was to be spent on 'aircraft, building and repairing by contract' in the 1914/15 budget, compared with £113,300 the previous year. The total to be spent on naval aeronautics was £900,000. He stated that the Naval Wing now had 103 aeroplanes, of which 62 were seaplanes, 120 regular pilots and 20 officers who had taken their Aero Club certificates in addition. Five seaplane stations had been established along the coast and two more were under construction. There were now 125 officers and 500 men in the service, and by the end of the year there would be 180 officers and 1,400 or 1,500 men. He said, 'This new service is thoroughly naval in spirit and character, but at the same time it contains, and must contain, a large element of civilians, both officers and mechanics.' At Eastchurch a large amount of training work had been carried out, particularly in the training of engine-room artificers, artisans and other ratings in flying and in the general care and maintenance of aeroplanes of all kinds and their engines.

Frank McClean arrived back in London on 6 April, attended an RAeC Committee meeting on the 7th, and on Sunday 19 April made his first flight from Eastchurch since his return from Egypt, taking up a lady passenger. He was flying again on Friday 24 April, and made two flights with passengers the following day.

On Saturday 23 May Gustav Hamel disappeared over the Channel while flying a Morane monoplane from France to England. Hamel's body was never recovered, and McClean attended his memorial service in London on 24 June as a representative of the RAeC. Doubtless he was reminded of the similar disappearance of Cecil Grace in one of McClean's own aircraft on 22 December 1910.

At a Committee of Imperial Defence Sub-Committee meeting on 25 June the chairman expressed 'deep anxiety' concerning the defence of the Medway against attack from the air, saying it was doubtful whether the most active form of defence could intervene in time. The chief vulnerable points were the dockyard powerhouse, Chattenden magazine, the oil tanks and Kingsnorth airship station, and at that time the navy was undertaking the defence against the aerial threat. He added that a war station was about to be established at Eastchurch in addition to the school, and that there was also the seaplane station on the Isle of Grain.

On Sunday 5 July McClean made two flights with a lady passenger at Eastchurch on his '70hp Short biplane'. On Saturday the 11th he took part in the Hedges Butler Challenge Cup balloon race as a passenger in John Dunville's balloon, *Polo*. Ascending from the Hurlingham Club at 4.15pm, they alighted near Oxford at 8.55 in the evening. The race was won by Dunville's wife in the balloon *Banshee II*, who was accompanied by Mr C F Pollock and Captain B Corbet. They descended at Nesscliffe, near Shrewsbury, in the early hours of Sunday and, this being Mrs Dunville's third consecutive victory in the race, the cup became her 'absolute property'.

The dismantled S.80 back at Harty Ferry in April 1914 after being shipped back from Egypt. (ROYAL AERO CLUB)

The damaged wingtip uncovered at Harty Ferry, showing Ogilvie's improvised but still sound repair. (ROYAL AERO CLUB)

The S.80 Nile Seaplane spent some time under refurbishment in the Shorts factory, but on Monday 13 July McClean took a passenger aloft in it on a 'fine flight' from Harty on its first outing since its return from Egypt, and he carried two passengers and a mechanic later in the month. In its 31 July issue *Flight* reported that the aircraft had been doped with Cellon for its Nile flight, and that when some of the fabric was removed upon its return it was 'extraordinary to notice the effective way in which it has stood up to the hard usage. In spite of the fact that the machine was left exposed to the atmosphere for the whole of the time it was on the Nile, the condition of the fabric is extremely good.'

With war looming, on Wednesday 29 July McClean made a flight from Harty to Ramsgate with two passengers, and returned to Harty on Saturday 1 August. The next morning he flew to the Isle of Grain with Perrin and Gus, his mechanic, and placed the aeroplane at the Admiralty's disposal.

Major Christopher Draper was stationed at Eastchurch with the RNAS at this time. He recalled that it was a 'madhouse', and that '. . .

Frank McClean takes off from Ramsgate, Kent, in his repaired S.80 Nile seaplane, probably on 1 August 1914, the day before he flew the aeroplane to the RNAS station on the Isle of Grain and placed it at the Admiralty's disposal. It became '905' in RNAS service. (AUTHOR)

there were continuous alarms and excursions all over the island. Germans were reported landing everywhere and "Sammy" [Samson], with two or three others, armed to the teeth, would rush off in a lorry to repel the "invaders".'

Early wartime activities

War was declared on 4 August 1914, and in its issue of 14 August *Flight* reported that Mc-Clean had 'joined the Navy at the Isle of Grain, receiving the rank of Flight Lieutenant' in the RNAS. He was commissioned on the 6th. The first volume of the official history *The War in the Air* (Clarendon Press, Oxford, 1922) records that he 'offered to the Service his three motor-cars, his motor-boat at Teddington, his yacht *Zenaida*, with two machines, and his pri-

vate house at Eastchurch [Aerodrome], which was converted into a hospital. A nation which commands the allegiance of such citizens,' the author continues, 'need never fear defeat.' The naval pilots were reported to be flying 'Lieut McClean's biplane' in the third week of August, and in its 11 September issue *Flight* reported that Flight Lieutenant McClean's Short was one of four Short machines being used for instructional purposes for young officers at Eastchurch during the first week of the month.

On 8 August the Admiralty ordered the establishment of a coastal patrol for the whole of Britain's East Coast, from Kinnaird's Head in Aberdeenshire to Dungeness, between Dover and Hastings. Incomplete squadrons of the RFC not yet ordered abroad undertook the northern and southern extremities of this patrol, but the most vulnerable part of the East Coast, from the Forth to the Thames, or from North Berwick to Clacton, was to be patrolled by the RNAS. However, these arrangements were soon changed, because shortly after the outbreak of war the Germans became established in Belgium. In the belief that the enemy

McClean also donated his S.58 biplane to the RNAS; it was allocated serial number 904. (AUTHOR)

would use Belgium as a base from which to launch formidable aircraft raids on the Thames estuary and London, the RNAS forces were now concentrated between the Humber and the Thames, from Immingham to Clacton. Moreover, the most likely landfall for German airships raiding London was thought to be The Wash. Consequently regular patrols of the coast were carried out in the early days of the war, with the aim of observing and reporting the movements of all enemy ships and submarines. It transpired that there was little to report, and, in the words of the official history, 'it was weary work waiting for the enemy to begin'.

When the British Expeditionary Force (BEF) was ready to go abroad, the RNAS was charged to monitor its passage across the Channel. Seaplanes, following one another at two-hourly intervals, maintained a regular patrol between Westgate, close to the north Foreland, and Ostend. A temporary seaplane base was established at Ostend on 13 August but was withdrawn, and its men and supplies returned to England, on the 22nd, when the BEF was safely landed and Ostend's occupa-

tion by the Germans seemed imminent. The routine patrols were then discontinued, but seaplanes and airships continued to make special scouting flights over the North Sea and the Channel. Dawn and sunset patrols scouting the coast were carried out on every possible day, defence of the Thames estuary being entrusted to the group centred on the Isle of Grain. They were charged with reporting any approach of hostile ships and aircraft, helping submarines deliver attacks and warning friendly craft.

Frank McClean continued to attend RAeC Committee meetings whenever possible. From 6 to 11 August he was serving as a flight lieutenant at Grain on the Channel patrol. On 11 August he made a 35-minute flight to Westgate and then flew with 'Williamson' to 'Sangatti' (Sangatte) and back to Westgate. The next day he flew back to Grain. On the 13th McClean went to Eastchurch, and he records that on the 15th he was '1st Lt of Eastchurch'. This really marked the end of his active flying career, though he headed the instructing staff at Eastchurch, flying when the opportunity presented itself.

On 21 December 1914 a special meeting of the RAeC Committee was convened to resolve a conflict of opinion as to whether £1,000 should be contributed to a Fund for the Air Services. While a majority of the Committee was in favour, a majority of the Finance Committee was opposed, arguing that the Club's financial position did not justify giving any payment at all. At the meeting Griffith Brewer moved that the Club contribute £1,000 to the Flying Services Fund, and this was seconded by Flight Lieutenant McClean. The motion was carried by twenty in favour and eleven against, an appeal for subscriptions being issued immediately. As a result, two members of the Finance Committee, including the honorary treasurer, resigned.

On 22 December the Admiralty requisitioned Eastchurch under the Defence of the Realm Act, instructions being given to take over all of the privately-owned sheds. Although the Admiralty agreed to house old aircraft of historical value safely elsewhere, this promise was not kept, but Ogilvie was allowed to retain his shed, where he was manufacturing speed indicators. At this time there were eighteen sheds in all, three of which belonged to the RAeC. Seven were in active use, including four belonging to McClean. This remained the position until 12 June 1917, when the Superintendent of the Dockyard, Sheerness, formally took possession of all buildings and the RN Air Station, Eastchurch, passed from private ownership. However, the matter was not concluded until 23 September 1919, when the Admiralty exercised its option to purchase the flying ground and Mr G Hayley Mason of the Government Valuation Office wrote to the RAeC,

offering £13,500 for the Club's interests at Eastchurch. The Club had already rejected an offer of £9,000, and only after careful consideration was the new offer accepted. The final figure, paid in May 1920 and including accumulated interest, was £13,621 8s 11d.

Harold Perrin, Secretary of the RAeC, pointed out that McClean had insisted that all he should receive was the actual amount paid by him for the property, and did not wish the RAeC to profit by the transaction, but after many arguments with Perrin he was persuaded to agree to the Club being reimbursed at least the amount it had expended on sheds, roads, etc, during 1908–18. This splendid gesture by McClean resulted in a substantial addition to the Club's exchequer, out of which the Club voted £2,000 for air racing and £1,000 for the Flying Services Fund.

As Hurren commented in 1951, the foregoing

. . . does not give full justice to the debt that not only the Club but the nation as a whole owes to Sir Francis McClean. Perrin tends to emphasise the gift of money; but a financial transaction tells of nothing but the skeleton of the story: for what Sir Francis really did was personally to give naval aviation a splendid start. It is often thought that the Royal Aero Club itself gave this facility. In fact, any true assessment of the story will show that it was one of the members, Sir Francis McClean, rather than the Club itself, which set in train the long and glorious tale of naval flying.

From February to March 1915 McClean commanded the naval flying school at Eastchurch. It must have been satisfying for him to see that his unstinting efforts to set British naval aviation on a sound footing had borne fruit and contributed to the nation's preparedness for the great conflict in which it was now involved.

CHAPTER 8

McClean's Post-flying Activities

The following is a summary of Frank Mc-Clean's principal aviation-related activities from the time he had largely ceased active flying up to his death in 1955.

1914

On 6 August 1914 McClean was appointed Flight Lieutenant, HMS *Pembroke* (HMS *Pembroke II*, alias RNAS Eastchurch, 1913–18), and from that date to 11 August he went to 'Grain Air Station as a Flight Lieutenant'. He flew on Channel Patrol/North Sea patrols during the BEF's crossing to continental Europe. On 16th and 22nd September he recorded that the 'Flights leave Eastchurch for continent'.

Christmas Day 1914 was memorable owing to a German air raid. At mid-day on 25 December *Oberleutnant-zur-See* Stephan Prondzynski, flying Friedrichshafen FF 29 seaplane No 203 with *Fähnrich-zur-See* von Frankenburg as his observer, crossed the English coast on a hit-and-run raid against London. Anticipating the possibility of attacks on Christmas Day, RNAS Dover had sent up standing patrols from 08.00hr, but the raider made landfall 30 miles north-west of the patrol line. In addition, one sortie was flown from Eastchurch, RNAS-operated Albatros B.I 890 (which had been impressed into British military service upon the outbreak of war) went up from Grain, and RFC sorties were made from Joyce Green, Farnborough and Brooklands. The Vickers Gunbus from Joyce Green exchanged fire with the raider, who turned away and dropped two bombs in a field near Cliffe railway station. Prondzynski later claimed to have attacked oil storage tanks at Sheerness.

1915

On 4 February 1915 McClean was appointed Acting Flight Commander, HMS *Pembroke* (HMS *Pembroke II*). From February to March he commanded the Naval Flying School at Eastchurch, being replaced by Squadron Commander Alec Ogilvie, who remained CO for a year and then left for Dunkirk.

After leaving Eastchurch on 6 May McClean spent some time 'prospecting for aerodromes' for the RNAS, and on 20 September he commissioned the RNAS night-flying ground at Rochford, Kent, one of Yarmouth's early sub-stations, and the first of several that came into being in September, October and November 1915. The ground was in use as early as 31 May, when a Blériot monoplane was sent up in a vain pursuit of German Army Zeppelin *LZ 38* when it made the first airship raid on London.

On 26 November McClean was appointed Acting Squadron Commander, HMS *President* (RNAS Chingford).

On 29 December the Admiralty announced the promotion of McClean from Flight Commander to the rank of Squadron Commander: 'Francis Kennedy McClean (for temporary service) (now Acting Squadron Commander)'. (*Flight*, 6 January 1916, p 4)

1916

On 1 January 1916 McClean was Appointed Temporary Squadron Commander, HMS *President*. He left Chingford on 12 March.

Around March–April 1916 McClean was involved in planning, with Commander C R

Samson and Lieutenant R B Davies (who had been Samson's First Lieutenant at Eastchurch when Samson was commanding the Naval Flying School), to send 3 Sqn RNAS to France to carry out bombing raids into Germany, however, the project was abandoned in April.

In his book *The Mad Major* (Air Review, Letchworth, 1962, p 53), Major Christopher Draper records that in April 1916 he was relieved of his command of the RNAS aerodrome on Scarborough Racecourse by 'Flight-Commander Frank McClean'. Draper was then put in charge of the War Flight at Eastchurch. McClean was not at Scarborough for long; he notes that he went there on 7 April and left on 25 June.

From 28 June to 18 September McClean was in France, and on 16 July he made an ascent in a kite balloon near Meudon, Paris.

On 10 November McClean moved to Chatham, where he was "stationed in DCA [Deputy Chief of Air Staff?] office."

1917

McClean left Chatham on 3 March 1917, and that month went over from Dover to Dunkirk, and visited the trenches on the 22nd. He went back to Dunkirk on 15 June, on the 30th was promoted from 'From Squadron Commander to Wing Commander'. For the remainder of the year he divided his time between England and France.

1918

On 16 February 1918 McClean married Aileen Wale, elder daughter of W H Wale of Lapworth (two daughters: Francis Aileen and Iona (married Peter, later Lord Carington) at St Pauls' Knightsbridge. On 4 April 'Acting Wg Cdr F.K. McClean' was listed as being in command of Dover Aerodrome, RNAS.

McClean records for 22 April 1918, 'Send off machines for Zeebrugge raid'. This refers to aircraft that were despatched from the 61st Wing at Dover to escort the naval forces across the North Sea that were to launch an attack in an effort to block the entrance to the Bruges

On the night of 9/10 May 1918 McClean sent off the Handley Page O/400 bombers of 214 and 215 Squadrons to bomb the German defence batteries at Ostend and drop flares. This O/400, C3491, is known to have been on the strength of 215 Squadron. (AUTHOR)

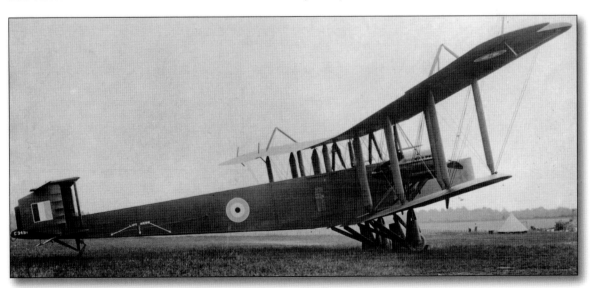

ship canal at Zeebrugge, and thus close the waterway connecting the port with the inland naval base at Bruges. The operations were originally to take place on the night of 11 April, but were postponed. On the night of the 22nd/23rd the weather prevented any air night bombardment by the Handley Page bombers of 214 and 215 Squadrons, based on the European mainland, during the attack, but the operation at Zeebrugge was deemed successful, though in fact it was not. An attempt to block the harbour at Ostend that same night was a failure.

On 9 May McClean records 'Send machines to Ostend raid'. A second attempt to block the harbour at Ostend was made this night, and another escort was provided. In the early hours of the 10th seven Handley Page night bombers bombed the German defence batteries and dropped flares. This time the operation was partially successful.

McClean left Dover on 6 September. An ascent in a kite balloon with his old friend Griffith Brewer was made at the ballooning school at RNAS Roehampton on 11 October to conduct a 'rip experiment'. Brewer was now Honorary Adviser to the Kite Balloon and Airship Services, acting as an aerostation instructor and lecturer and conducting experiments, and this was probably a test of Brewer's balloon diaphragm rip for ripping kite balloons to bring them quickly and safely to earth after they had broken away from the cable, which has been described as being 'far superior to anything in service'.

On 21 October McClean made a balloon ascent from Hurlingham with 'Clinton in charge', and Powter, Glasson and Guinness; the

McClean sampled airship flight on 25 October 1918 when he flew in Submarine Scout Twin non-rigid SST 11, which had been delivered to the RNAS earlier that month. This study of sister-ship SST 5 gives a good impression of the airships of this class, which had an envelope capacity of 100,000 cubic feet, were 165ft long and were powered by a pair of 100hp Sunbeam or 75hp Rolls-Royce engines. (AUTHOR)

balloon descended at Wanborough. Another ascent from Hurlingham was made on 24 October, the voyage ending at the Burford Bridge Hotel near Dorking in Surrey. Powered lighter-than-air flight was experienced by McClean on 25 October, when he flew in RNAS dirigible SST 11, piloted by 'McDonald', from Wormwood Scrubs and travelled over Trafalgar Square and back to Wormwood Scrubs.

McClean made his last balloon flight on 30 October, recording: 'Balloon *Violet* 11.30 to 4.15 Hurlingham to Langdale End 12m NW of Scarborough. Pilot Wilkinson. Drop one passenger *en route*.'

The signing of the Armistice on 11 November 1918 heralded the end of his RNAS service. He was commissioned as a Colonel in the RAF on 1 December. During war McClean had been awarded the Air Force Cross and mentioned in despatches.

1919

Demobilised on 3 February 1919, McClean wasted no time in getting involved with civil aviation again. On 17 May he travelled to Paris with Mervyn O'Gorman, Frederick Handley Page and Harold Perrin of the RAeC, and the 19th to the 22nd were occupied in a meeting with the Fédération Aéronautique Internationale (FAI), the supreme body ratifying aeronautical records, represented in the UK by the RAeC.

On 28 May McClean attended a special *Daily Mail* lunch at the Savoy Hotel in tribute to Harry Hawker. Hawker and his navigator, Lieutenant-Commander Kenneth McKenzie Grieve, had been assumed drowned during an attempted non-stop transatlantic flight on 18–19 May, but were rescued, and upon their safe return to England a dinner was held in their honour. Two days later McClean gave a speech at an Aero Club lunch for Hawker.

The following month, on 14/15 June, Captain John Alcock and Lieutenant Arthur Whitten Brown accomplished the first non-stop transatlantic flight, flying a Vickers Vimy from St John's, Newfoundland, to Clifden, County Galway, Ireland. McClean met the two fliers at Euston Station in London on 17 June, and drove them himself to the Aero Club's offices in Clifford Street in his Rolls-Royce. Three days later he was at the *Daily Mail* lunch for Alcock and Brown. The following day, the 21st, he attended the first post-war Aerial Derby at Hendon, and on the 23rd he was at the Aero Club dinner for Alcock and Brown.

A month later, on 23 July, there was yet another dinner, at Princes, to mark a transatlantic flight. This time it was in tribute to the crew of the airship *R.34* after it had accomplished the first out-and-return transatlantic flight from England to the USA and back, from 2 to 13 July. On 24 July McClean attended the investiture at which Alcock and Brown were knighted.

McClean was also involved in the planning of the first post-war Schneider Trophy contest for seaplanes, for which Great Britain was the host nation, and on 20 August he went to Southampton and Cowes with Perrin. At Southampton they visited the Supermarine works and met Scott Paine, Commander Bird and other company worthies. The next day he flew to Bournemouth to arrange the event, which was scheduled to take place there on 10 September. On 3 September he went to Southampton and Cowes for a meeting with Perrin, Jimmy Bird and Scott Paine, and on the 8th he was at those locations again to witness the preliminary trials of two of the British entrants, the Avro Type 539 seaplane and the Supermarine Sea Lion flying boat. Alas, after all their efforts the event on the 10th was a 'fiasco', to use McClean's description. Fog, dense

On 17 June 1919 McClean drove Alcock and Brown from London's Euston Station to the Royal Aero Club's offices in Clifford Street for a reception. Here the car is en route, with McClean at the steering wheel and the Atlantic's conquerors standing up in the rear. This print, from McClean's personal collection, has been autographed underneath by the two national heroes. (Fleet Air Arm Museum)

in places over the course, turned the contest into a chaotic shambles, with disorganisation, turning markers becoming obscured and aircraft becoming lost. Sergeant Guido Jannello, pilot of Italy's Savoia S.13 flying boat, completed 11 incorrect laps. Of the three participating British entries, the Sea Lion sank at the end of its first lap, having damaged its hull when it struck and unseen object while taking off after an interim alighting, and the Fairey IIIA and Sopwith aircraft had both retired on their first laps. Neither of the two French machines started. In the end the contest was declared void. The Italians, who felt that they were entitled to be declared the winners, objected vehemently, and the RAeC subsequently recommended that the trophy be awarded to Italy and the prize to Jannello. However, the FAI rejected the recommendation, but asked the Aero Club of Italy to organise the event in 1920.

Sir John Alcock, now serving as Vickers's chief pilot, was flying the Viking I amphibian

Succinctly summed-up by McClean as a 'fiasco', the 1919 Schneider Trophy contest, held off Bournemouth on 10 September 1919, was declared void owing to fog obscuring the course. McClean witnessed the preliminary trials of Supermarine's entry, its Sea Lion flying boat, seen here, but it sank at the end of its first lap after its hull had been pierced by an unseen object. (AUTHOR)

G-EAOV solo to the Paris Aero Show when he encountered thick fog and struck a tree in an orchard near Rouen while attempting a forced landing. He was killed in the crash. On 24 December McClean met Alcock's coffin at Waterloo, and on the 27th he attended his memorial service.

When B F S Baden-Powell, brother of the Chief Scout and long-standing member of the RAeS, asked McClean to endorse his application for Fellowship of the society, McClean wrote: 'The old order changeth and the new forget the foundation of aviation on which their success rests. Most of those who now rule the air and make speeches have probably never heard of you and me.'

1920

In its obituary of McClean, published in the issue for 19 August 1955, *Flight* recorded that 'In the post-[First World War] years he was to be seen at every aeronautical sporting event, usually visiting them either by air or in his big white Rolls-Royce'. This is evident from his listing of the events he attended. In 1920 McClean was appointed, with Brigadier-General Sir Capel Holden, to represent the RAeC on the Air League's executive committee.

1921

After holidaying in Egypt during January and February 1921, McClean was at the Aero Club on 30 March to meet the brothers Ross and Keith Smith, who had accomplished the first flight from England to Australia from 12 November to 10 December 1919, and were subsequently knighted.

Griffith Brewer had become closely involved in a long-running dispute between Orville Wright and the Smithsonian Institution in Washington, D.C., in the USA. In 1914 American pioneer Glenn Curtiss, seeking to win a patent infringement battle with the Wrights by proving that a machine capable of powered fight had been produced before the Wrights' 1903 Flyer, had obtained the remains of Samuel Pierpont Langley's tandem-wing 'Aerodrome' aircraft of 1903, which had twice failed to fly after being launched by catapult from a houseboat.

Curtiss was in cahoots with Charles D Walcott, Langley's successor as secretary of the Smithsonian, who had also been his friend. By rebuilding the machine at Hammondsport as a floatplane and incorporating modifications in two stages he had persuaded it off the water, and the Aerodrome was then returned to the Smithsonian and displayed with a label proclaiming that it was 'the first man-carrying aeroplane in the history of the world capable of sustained free flight'. Enraged, Orville embarked on a bitter campaign to obtain justice (Wilbur had died in 1912). Brewer had made a clandestine visit to Hammondsport in 1914 and, with other information obtained by Lorin Wright, in 1921 had delivered a lecture exposing the chicanery of Curtiss and others, which was also published in England in the December 1921 issue of *The Aeronautical Journal*. In response the magazine *Nature* published controversial article refuting Brewer's paper and siding with Walcott.

On 9 February 1922, in a letter to Brewer, Katharine Wright, sister of Orville and Wilbur, remarked: 'I do think it is pretty bad to have a paper in which Mr McClean has interest and certainly some influence playing the game for Walcott as it is'. Brewer quickly responded, saying that McClean and T P Searight, a director of the British Wright Company, proposed that the company should bear the expense that Brewer had incurred in the controversy, but Katharine replied that she wanted to bear all of the expense. While the dispute continued, Orville had the 1903 Flyer sent to the UK, and it was displayed in the Science Museum from

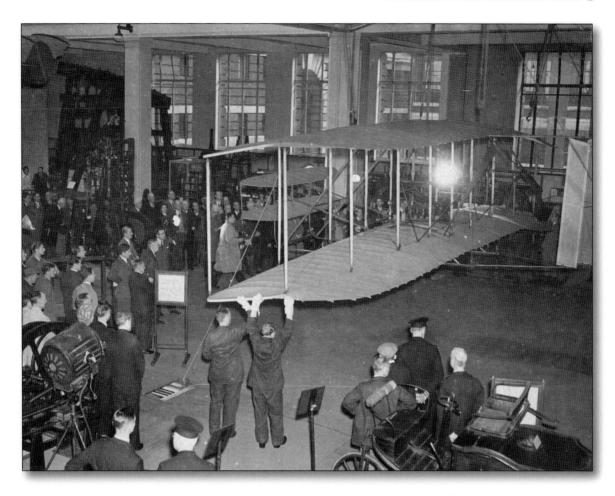

In 1922 McClean became involved in the controversy between the Wright family and the Smithsonian Institution in Washington, DC. Enraged by the Smithsonian's misleading labelling of the Langley *Aerodrome*, Orville Wright, through McClean's friend Griffith Brewer, had arranged for the historic 1903 Wright Flyer to be loaned to the Science Museum in London. When the magazine *Nature* published a piece refuting a paper on the subject written by Brewer, McClean and J P Seawright proposed that the British Wright Co should bear the expenses incurred by Brewer, but Katharine Wright declined the offer. The long-running dispute was finally settled when the Smithsonian recanted in 1942, but the Flyer could not be returned to the USA until the Second World War had ended. On 18 October 1948, as seen here, the aeroplane was lowered from its position in the Science Museum during a ceremony marking the first stage of its journey back to the USA. (AUTHOR)

1928, being removed for safety during the Second World War. The dispute was settled in 1942, when the Smithsonian recanted, and the Flyer was returned to the USA in 1948.

1922

McClean attended a flying meeting at Waddon Aerodrome on 17 April 1922.

On 13 April, while test-flying Vickers Viking IV amphibian G-EBBZ, in which he planned to attempt a round-the-world flight, Sir Ross Smith died in a crash at Brooklands. McClean attended the Memorial Service on the 20th.

McClean was at the Hendon Aerial Pageant on 24 June.

The King's Cup Circuit of Britain Air Race was to be held on 8–9 September and, probably remembering his disappointment in the *Daily Mail* Waterplane Circuit of Britain in 1913, McClean decided to take part, though not as a pilot. On 4 August he went to Horsley Towers, where he met Sir Thomas Sopwith, who was to provide an aeroplane, and Flight Lieutenant Walter H Longton DFC AFC, who would pilot it.

On 22 August McClean attended a reception held by Supermarine to celebrate the winning of that year's Schneider Trophy contest at Naples by Henri Biard, flying the company's Sea Lion II flying boat.

McClean's entry for the King's Cup Circuit of Britain Air Race was Sopwith Gnu G-EAGP, powered by a 110hp Le Rhone rotary engine, flying as Race No 3 and piloted by Longton. (The aircraft was not registered to McClean at this time, but was still Sopwith-owned.) The event started from Croydon, but trouble was encountered in starting the engine, and the Gnu got away from Croydon 25 minutes late. It was in ninth position at end of outward leg, and in eighth position at end of homeward leg. *Flight* for 14 September 1922 remarked: 'Even the old Sopwith Gnu entered by Col McClean, and flown by Longton, stuck it to the bitter end, once it did get going.'

For the last Coupe Deutsche de la Meurthe air race in Etampes, France, held on 29–30 September, Britain entered Jimmy James with the Gloster Bamel. The British sent a strong contingent of supporters, for whom Frank Mc-

In 1922 Frank McClean entered Sopwith Gnu G-EAGP in the King's Cup Circuit of Britain Air Race. It was piloted in the event by Flight Lieutenant Walter H. Longton, but was unplaced. Longton is on the left in this picture. McClean subsequently bought the aeroplane. (AUTHOR)

Clean laid on an excellent lunch, but unfortunately James lost his way after his maps blew out of the cockpit.

At the other end of the speed range, McClean went to watch the gliding at Itford Hill on 16–17 and 21 October.

1923

McClean was elected Vice-Chairman of the RAeC for 1923/24, and at the Annual General Meeting on 31 March he was presented with the Gold Medal of the Royal Aero Club 'for pioneer work in aviation'. He was in illustrious aeronautical company, for this award had previously been given to Wilbur and Orville Wright, Louis Blériot, Henry Farman, Hubert Latham, the Hon. Charles Rolls, Cecil Grace (posthumously), Claude Grahame-White, S F Cody (Cowdery), Sir John Alcock and Sir Arthur Whitten Brown, and Sir Ross Smith and Sir Keith Smith. On 18 April he was elected Chairman of the RAeC for 1923/24.

This was evidently McClean's year, for on 23 June he achieved his long-sought-after racing success. He had entered Sopwith Gnu G-EAGP, now registered in his name and again flown by W H Longton, in the Grosvenor Challenge Cup Point-to-Point Handicap Race, staring from Lympne. Longton won the cup and £100. (Gnu G-EAGP, constructor's number W/O 2976/3, originally registered K-163, was awarded its Certificate of Airworthiness on 3 October 1919 and owned by the Sopwith Aviation Co, Brooklands. It was registered to Lieutenant-Colonel F K McClean in June 1923, passed to Major S A Packham of Cramlington in November 1924, went to the Southern Counties Aviation Company at Shoreham in July 1925 and crashed at King's Lynn on 2 May 1926.)

On 13 and 14 July McClean attended the King's Cup Race, and on 6 August he was at the Aerial Derby, held this year at Croydon.

The 1923 Schneider Trophy Race was held at Cowes on 28 September, and it was won by Lieutenant David Rittenhouse of the USA, flying a Curtiss CR-3 seaplane. That same evening McClean attended a dinner in the Americans' honour at the Royal London Yacht Club.

As part of the Motor Glider Competitions at Lympe the Duke of Sutherland, Under-Secretary of State for Air, offered a prize of £500 re-

Another view of McClean's Sopwith Gnu, G-EAGP. Designed as a three-seat tourer or taxi aircraft, the Gnu could be built with a cabin for the passengers or with an open rear cockpit, McClean's example being of the latter type. (AUTHOR)

Colonel McClean, centre, holds the trophy after winning the Grosvenor Challenge Cup Point-to-Point Handicap Race on 23 June 1923. Longton, who piloted Gnu G-EAGP to first place, is second from right, looking on, and Lord Edward Grosvenor, who donated the trophy, is on the left. (AUTHOR)

A happy team. McClean, second from left, Walter Longton and Lil Longton pose in front of the Gnu after winning the Grosvenor Challenge Cup on 23 June 1923. (AUTHOR)

stricted to British competitors flying British machines. Competition flying began on Monday 8 October, though there was a great deal of activity on the aerodrome over the preceding weekend. McClean was there on 6–8 October, and Longton was flying the English Electric Wren. At the end of the week-long event Longton shared the Sutherland prize with J H James, flying an Air Navigation and Engineering Company (ANEC) monoplane, and they also shared the *Daily Mail*'s £1,000 prize.

1924

From early January to late March 1924 McClean was on holiday, spending 22 January to 29 March in Egypt and visiting old haunts. Among several aeronautical functions, including the RAF Display, the King's Cup and that year's Lympne Light Aeroplane Trials, on 15 June he was at the Gordon Bennett balloon race, and on the 27th he visited the Supermarine works at Southampton. At Croydon on 16 July the American round-the-world flyers arrived in their Douglas World Cruisers, and two days later the RAeC held a banquet in their honour, which McClean attended.

1925

On 1 September 1924 the Air Ministry had announced a scheme of assistance for light aeroplane clubs, whereby ten such clubs were to be assisted financially for an initial period of two years. The first grant to each club would be £2,000, to be secured by a mortgage on club property, and would only be made if the club used 'approved types' of aeroplanes. The RAeC was designated as the responsible body, and was to put up financial and other contributions for at least £2,000 and insure equipment provided.

By 8 April 1925 Major-General Brancker had communicated with the Under Secretary of State for Air and the Air Member for Supply, and they had agreed to the purchase of de Havilland D.H.60 Moth aeroplanes out of the Air Ministry grant of £10,000. The Air Ministry agreed to appoint the RAeC as its agents for the purchase of the Moths for the five selected light aeroplane clubs, and the RAeC set up a committee which formulated a scheme. Frank McClean was on this committee, all but two of whom became directors of the duly registered 'London Aero Club, Ltd'. It started operations on 19 August 1925, and by 14 October was able to report that 200 hours' flying had already been completed. Many members had flown solo and one had gained his aviator's certificate.

1926 to 1955

In 1926 McClean appeared in the list of the King's Birthday Honours (publication post-poned from 3 June to 3 July owing to dislocation caused by the General Strike): 'Knight. Lieut-Colonel Francis Kennedy McClean. In recognition of his services to aviation.' An RAeC banquet was held at the Savoy on 27 July to celebrate the honour conferred on McClean and present the prizes to the winners of that year's King's Cup Race. After presentation of the prizes the Duke of Sutherland proposed a toast to the health of 'Sir Francis K. McClean' and then read letters from the Secretary of State for Air and Mr Holt Thomas, expressing their appreciation of Sir Francis's pioneering work.

Lieutenant-Colonel J T C Moore-Brabazon, who was now the Parliamentary Secretary for the Ministry of Transport, said that everyone attended the dinner in a spirit of better late than never, and that he felt it was rather like giving an award for services at the Battle of Agincourt. He said the dinner might have been held fifteen years ago, and that many of the pioneers would have liked to be present if they had survived. He recalled that he had himself been classed as an amiable lunatic on account of his early interest in flying. 'In those days,' he recalled, 'Frank McClean's purse had been a cornucopia for aviation.' Air Commodore A M Longmore paid a tribute to Sir Frank on behalf of the first four naval aviators. The veteran aviation journalist C G Grey, who covered the evening's proceedings for *The Aeroplane*, observed that Longmore referred to the guest as Sir Frank, rather than Sir Francis. 'One imagines,' wrote Grey, 'that everybody who has been associated with aviation for any considerable time will prefer the more familiar Christian name, even with a handle to it.'

In response, Sir Frank, whom Grey on occasion had described as 'the worst speaker in the world, bar one, and that is oneself', 'made a speech which would have been a good effort for the most practised speaker. He evidently forgot all that nervousness which with which his naturally modest and retiring nature afflicts him on public occasions, and felt that he was just speaking to a room full of friends – which he was.' Sir Frank said that to have done something, however small, was its own reward, but that the recognition of his friends was very pleasant. As to the honour conferred upon him by His Majesty, he felt that this was an honour to the Aero Club, and that the work of the RAeC before the First World War was not fully understood. It had paved the way for the flying done during the war. Describing Eastchurch as the home of pioneering, he said that before there was any real naval flying it had an amphibian that really amphibbed.

Grey reported that 'there were not so many people there as Sir Frank McClean deserved, but perhaps he was all the happier for that'. At any rate, almost all the survivors of his old friends in aviation turned up to celebrate the occasion with him. Grey recalled:

One first met Sir Frank McClean at Leysdown, or rather at Shellness, in the extreme east of the Isle of Sheppey, quite early in 1909, when he and the never-to-be-forgotten Horace Short were conspiring in the construction of an aeroplane which Frank McClean hoped to fly some day.

The Short Brothers at that time held the British agency for the Wright Brothers, which had been wished on to them, one believes, by Griffith Brewer. [This was not strictly correct; the Shorts merely had a contract for the construction of six Flyers. Grey harboured a long and strong bias against the Wright aeroplanes which he expressed whenever the opportunity presented itself.] Frank McClean had a Wright biplane at Shellness and on it he was launched along a rail by that catapult device which was necessary to the early Wright machine.

One well remembers one's first sight of the apparatus in action. The actual flight lasted fully fifty yards. And as usual something broke when the machine sat down. A little later the flight extended still further and the machine sat down still harder, with the result that the upper plane descended and enclosed Frank McClean as in a tent. In no wise discouraged, he climbed out of his machine time after time with that same good humoured smile which we all know so well, and merely set to work again. [Grey might well be remembering the trials with the first Short machine here, rather than the Wright Flyer.]

Apart from his generosity, which has helped so many lame ducks over stiles that it has justified the wealth which he has expended on entirely unworthy human objects in an equally earnest desire to help them, Frank McClean's outstanding characteristic is his good temper. Presumably somebody must have seen him lose his temper at some time or another, but one has not yet met the individual who has done so. Therefore there is nothing surprising in the fact that he has more real friends than any man can reckon.

If Frank McClean had not inherited wealth one doubts whether he would ever have made it, for he is far too good-natured and generous, and he would never have pursued any of the various hard-headed hard-fisted policies by which alone money can be made. But he would certainly have done good work in the world.

In spite of having been born with a golden spoon in his mouth, Frank McClean has always used his very considerable mental ability to good purpose . . . the fact that he backed aviation when he did, and that he devoted himself so particularly to the naval side of aviation shows that he has foresight and an appreciation of political developments . . .

It is only now, when war production has ceased and something approximating to peace conditions have arisen, that we can look back calmly on the history of aviation since it began in this country seventeen years ago and assess without prejudice the value of the work done by the real pioneers of aviation. And there is not one among those pioneers who will not agree with a whole heart that of all their number none is more worthy to be honoured by His Majesty than is Frank McClean.

On 28 April 1931 McClean said a few words at a dinner held to some of the pioneers of aviation at the Aviation Section of the Forum Club, under the chairmanship of the Hon. Mrs Forbes Sempill. Among other things, he described how,

. . . at Eastchurch, they used to look for the bumps on the aerodrome and then taxy hard at these bumps in the hope of being thrown up into the air and thus fly for a few yards. He recalled how, later on, they were always told that they could not turn to the right with a Gnome engine, but one day he nearly ran into a tree and had to turn to the right, and after that everyone else followed suit, finding it was not so dangerous as they had been told. He was very lucky to be able to have a photograph of himself in the air in those days, and this was done by getting a photographer to lay on the ground just in front of him and, by the Grace of God, he just missed the photographer, who thus got a beautiful photograph. The Short Bros., he said, were also at Eastchurch in those days, and on one occasion Horace Short wished him to fly into a large net in order to test out a method by which landings might be made on board ships, but he declined gracefully.

Sir Frank was High Sheriff of Oxfordshire in 1932–3, and was again elected chairman of the RAeC for 1941–3. From 1944 to 1951 he was again vice-president.

Hurren, in *Fellowship of the Air*, records that McClean had a series of gold tie-pins, 'unique in the world', fashioned after the balloons and aeroplanes he had flown. 'It arouses a profound sense of *nostalgia aeronautica*', he writes, 'to see this tall, twinkling eyed, virile airman wearing a tie offset by a gold aeroplane of a design 40 years old or more.' Hurren also recalls how the pioneer members travelled from London to Eastchurch in the early days.

The normal routine was to decide that the weather was satisfactory for flight, and then if no car were available take the boat train from Victoria to Sheerness – there was a service in those days of the South-Eastern and Chatham Railway from Sheerness to Flushing. At Queenborough, a light railway was taken to Eastchurch, and the flying ground was a mile distant. In the evening, or perhaps as much as ten days later, the boat train back to London.

Being a pioneer demanded determination as well as courage. No wonder McClean opted for private on-site accommodation in his bungalow.

In 1950 McClean was elected an Honorary Fellow of the RAeS.

At Eastchurch on 25 July 1955 Marshal of the RAF Lord Tedder unveiled a memorial to the pioneer airmen who began flying in the vicinity in 1909. Among those present were Lord Brabazon, Air Chief Marshal Sir Arthur Longmore and Air Commodore E L Gerrard. Sadly, Sir Francis McClean was unable to attend owing to ill health, and the last surviving Short brother, Oswald, was also absent, but sent a message of greeting, as did Alec Ogilvie. In his speech Lord Brabazon paid tribute to McClean and the Short brothers. Located on a corner site opposite Eastchurch Church, the memorial commemorates the original aero-dromes at Leysdown and Eastchurch, where the Shorts established the first dedicated air-craft factory in Great Britain, and the forma-tion of the RNAS station in 1911. Reporting on the event in its 29 July issue, *Flight* said '. . . Frank McClean, as he then was, could justifi-ably be called the father of the RNAS'. The idea of the memorial had been put forward in a letter published in *The Times* of 11 February 1950, signed by the then Mr Winston Churchill, Lord Brabazon and Oswald Short,

This sketch by Edward Newling, dated 5 February 1950, was made in preparation for a portrait of Sir Frank McClean that was subsequently hung in the lounge of the Royal Aero Club's premises in Londonderry House, Park Lane, London. McClean died five years after the sketch was made. (AUTHOR)

and it was designed by Sidney Loweth, BRIBA, and sculpted by Hilary Stratton, FRBS. The patrons of the fund opened to cover the cost of the memorial were the Prime Minister, the Rt. Hon. Sir Winston Churchill, Lord Brabazon, Sir Francis McClean and Os-wald Short.

The main part of the memorial is a wall of Portland stone, curved in plan on one side, like the camber of an aeroplane wing, and straight on the other. The wall incorporates panels in mezzo-relief depicting aircraft of the 1909–11 era, while a central figure representing Zeus, the mythological God of the Heavens, looks down from the clouds. Beneath the central fig-ure are four tablets recording the purpose of the memorial, the names of twelve pioneers, headed by Moore-Brabazon, Rolls and Mc-Clean, the three Short brothers and the names of the first four naval officers who learnt to fly. Two frieze tablets record Moore-Brabazon's first flight by a British subject and first circular mile in Great Britain in a British aircraft, and the facts that Mr F K McClean leased part of the site to the Aero Club for the use of mem-bers and also provided aeroplanes free of charge for the instruction of naval officers.

The pioneer passes

On 11 August 1955 Sir Francis McClean died, aged 79, in the London Clinic 'after a long ill-ness'. A private cremation on 15 August was followed by a memorial service at Christ Church, Down Street, London, on 25 August. The address was given by Lord Brabazon of Tara, who had written in *The Times* for 16 Au-gust 1955:

By the death of Frank McClean there passes the great patron of aviation. He was not known so much to the present generation, but his influence, his benevolence, and his enthusiasm in the early days were so remarkable as to leave him on a plane never equalled by another.

He could not have had an enemy in the world. His great size, his shaggy appearance, his gentle ways endeared him to all who were lucky enough to know him.

Those he leaves behind will for ever be conscious of the debt they owe him, and of the love they bear him.

In its issue of 19 August *The Aeroplane* published an obituary of McClean under the heading 'Godfather to Naval Aviation'. He had served on the RAeC's Committee from 1909 until his death, either by election or as a vice-president or chairman.

In a tribute in the November 1955 issue of *The Journal of the Royal Aeronautical Society* Alec Ogilvie recalled: 'My last glimpse of him was at the Society of Arts in 1953 when Captain Pritchard [of the RAeS] was giving a lecture about the Wrights. To me, he looked pretty well, but when I asked if he was coming to dinner next day to celebrate 50 years of flying, he said that the insides the doctors had left him were capable of absorbing a little food but no drink, which was no way to celebrate the first flight of the Wright brothers whom he knew and admired very much.' Ogilvie said the last letter he received from Frank McClean, dated 16 October 1954, began: 'My dear Alec, Thanks for your kind wishes for my health, but in view of the fact that for nearly 80 years I have survived the strain of finding enjoyment in this world and have very few stones unturned in the process, I can't complain.' Ogilvie commented:

This seems to me to express very well Frank McClean's point of view. He enjoyed life and took what was coming to him without complaint. As I really only saw a lot of him in a relatively short space of his life between the ages of 32 and 38, I daresay that he turned many stones, about which I know nothing, but I have seen him as the genial host of a children's party at his family home, Rusthall in Tunbridge Wells, as a balloonist, as a pilot of many experimental aeroplanes, as a wise Club committee man in the early days when nearly every problem was a new one, but chiefly as a stout-hearted leader of a long trip up the Nile in which I shared and during which the stones were sometimes heavy and sharp.

He was a wealthy man for those days and he was prepared to spend his money freely in getting to the bottom of things which interested him and in which he could see benefit to the country. His magnificent offer of providing aeroplanes for the Royal Navy, on which to learn to fly, as well as the aerodrome to fly from, was typical. The long series of his aeroplanes and seaplanes, a dozen or so, built for him by Horace Short, enabled Short Brothers to get going, and keep going, at a critical period when aviation in this country was staggering about apparently miles behind other countries in Europe. It is impossible to deny that McClean and Short did a very great deal to overcome the inertia in official circles and among the general public.

In a fitting final gesture McClean's ashes were scattered at Eastchurch, where he had spent so many happy hours aloft during aviation's pioneer years nearly half a century earlier.

Appendix: Frank McClean's Aeroplanes, 1909–1914

This new listing is mainly based on the Shorts brothers' order book. McClean's own listing of his aircraft did not include machines ordered but subsequently cancelled and unbuilt, and also omitted some aircraft, so his personal numbering system has been appended in brackets after the appropriate entries. Therefore, instead of the aircraft being listed in the order they were acquired by McClean, which would be confusing, they are listed principally in order of constructor's numbers, with the exceptions of the early Short aeroplanes, the unnumbered and unbuilt monoplane of 1910, and the Birdling monoplane. Entries for unbuilt and unfinished machines are enclosed in square brackets.

(1). Short No 1 Ordered January 1909. Built at Battersea and Shellbeach, delivered July 1909, exhibited uncovered at 1909 Aero Show. (McClean No 1)

(2). Short-Wright No 3 Built at Shellbeach, delivered 16 October 1909. Substantially modified in 1910. (McClean No 2)

(3). Short No 3 Ordered by McClean 3 August 1909 and delivered in mid-1910. Span 30ft 0in, but actual configuration and powerplant arrangement unknown. An undated entry in the Short order book between 30 July and September 1910 records 'repairs etc' to this aircraft, so it seems that McClean (or someone else) might have attempted to fly it, but there is no record of its fate, though it was probably obsolete before completion and therefore short-lived. McClean did not even include it in his personal numbering scheme.

(4). Short S.26 Colmore's Green-powered Short-Sommer No.3. Acquired by McClean late 1910/early 1911 and flown for naval training March–June 1911; 'Samson's Serials Navy Biplane No 1', 'The Dud' and 'Th' owd Bitch'. (McClean No 3, but correctly No 5)

(5). Short S.27 (Short-Sommer No.1; ex-Cecil Grace No.2) Acquired by McClean in 1911 (probably the machine advertised in the classified advertisements in *Flight* for 30 July 1910 and in eight subsequent issues up to 15 October 1910 at £300 without engine or £700 with 60hp ENV). Converted to Tandem Twin (see below). (McClean No 7)

(6). Short S.27 Tandem-Twin (rebuild of above aircraft) (became 'No.4 Biplane' under an early Admiralty numbering system, recorded by Samson on 2 December 1911). (McClean No 11)

(7). Short S.28 (Short-Sommer No.2; ex-Moore-Brabazon No.6, built at Eastchurch.) Entered for the 1910 Bournemouth meeting by Brabazon, not flown. Sold to McClean shortly thereafter; used for naval training, 1911. 'Samson's Serials Navy Biplane No 2'. Replaced by S.38 after crash on 1 May 1911. (McClean No 5, but correctly No 3)

(8). Short S.32 (Short-Sommer No.5; ex-Cecil Grace No.3.) Built at Eastchurch. Was to be converted to multi-engine aircraft *à la* S.27, but the plan was cancelled upon Grace's death. In McClean's possession 1911, still single-engined, and used by Territorials). (McClean No 8)

(9). [Monoplane for McClean, ordered September 1910. Not built.]

(10). Short S.33 (Short-Sommer No.6.) Ordered September 1910. Delivered to McClean 12 November 1910.) Lent (?) to Cecil Grace. Being flown by Grace during Baron de Forest prize attempt; lost at sea. (McClean No 4)

(11). [In January 1911, before departing for the Pacific, McClean instructed Shorts to build a 'possible (and entirely at Mr Short's discretion) new Multiple Plant Machine. This latter either for the Navy or other Pilots'. Gnome powered, it was to be ready for use upon his return in July 1911. Although this was not built, the idea clearly led to the S.39 and the conversion of S.27 as the Tandem Twin.]

(12). Short S.34 (Short-Sommer No.7); copy of

S.33 for McClean, delivered 8 March 1911 (first built for naval training; 'Samson's Serials Naval Biplane No 3'; became RNAS 1/B1/T1; Samson gained his aviator's certificate on this machine on 24 April 1911; it was sold to Admiralty for £550 between September and December 1911). (**McClean No 6**)

(13). Short S.36 Tractor Biplane, 70hp Gnome, for McClean. Shorts' first tractor biplane built '*ab initio*', at Eastchurch. First flight 10 January 1912. (**McClean No 12**)

(14). Short S.38 (Short-Sommer No 9) Customer listed as 'F. McClean (Navy)'. Ordered by Samson during McClean's absence to replace S.28, damaged beyond repair in naval training. Cost £600. Samson regarded it as a reconstruction of S.28, so gave it its 'Samson's Serial' of 'Navy Biplane No 2'. Started at Eastchurch 1 May 1911, delivered 23 May. Navy T2 and Navy 2. Used by Longmore for float experiments and by Samson for ship take-offs. Deleted between December 1914 and May 1915.

(15). Short S.39 Triple Twin No.1; built Eastchurch and delivered 18 September 1911, bought by navy early 1912. RN T3 and Navy 3; (**McClean No 10**). Rebuilt as S.78 with same serial, incorporating as much of S.39 as possible.

(16). Short S.40 'Biplane type 38 for McClean' (Short-Sommer No.10). Ordered 8 December 1911. Built at Eastchurch; used by Territorials. (**McClean No 13A**). Converted to floatplane April and May 1912 and used for Thames flight. (**McClean No 13B**). Reconstruction as S.58 completed 15 November 1912; see below.

(17). Birdling monoplane (Blériot XI copy by Universal Aviation Co). Bought from H J D Astley by FKM, early August 1911. (**McClean No 9**)

(18). Short S.42 Two monoplanes for McClean, but only one c/n allotted. Blériot-type, purchased by Admiralty, became M2 and 8. Second a/c begun but not completed.

(19). [Short S.48 Hydro-monoplane with tandem 70hp Gnomes for McClean (McClean's tandem-twin 'Double-Dirty' seaplane). Cancelled; not built.]

(20). [Short S.53 Twin 70hp Gnome tractor biplane for McClean. No evidence of completion.]

(21). Short S.58 Reconstruction at Eastchurch of S.40 (*q.v.*) as S.58 70hp hydroplane (wide-span S.38 nacelle type). Flying in Nov 1912, became Navy 904. (**McClean No 14**)

(22). Short S.68 100hp all-British seaplane tractor biplane, McClean's entry for 1913 Circuit of Britain (Green engine). Re-engined with Gnome while still owned by McClean and probably impressed as Navy 182. (**McClean No 15**)

(23). Short S.80 160hp Nile Seaplane, built at Eastchurch. To Grain, 1 August 1915 as dual-control trainer RNAS 905. Fitted for torpedo and 100lb bomb. Allotted to HMS *Riviera* 17 August 1914, but not taken up. Reallocated to HMS *Hermes* 28 September 1914 (maker to fit bomb gear); on board later. Re-engined with 100hp Gnome October 1914, deleted November 1914. (**McClean No 16**)

(**NB.** A military list of 30 April 1914, identifying aircraft that were candidates for impressment, lists four of McClean's aeroplanes (S.36, S.58, S.68 and S.80), and then states: 'In addition . . . Mr Maclean [*sic*] has 2 old Wrights which are about to be scrapped.' If this is accurate, it remains to be determined how McClean acquired the second Wright, and to whom it originally belonged.)

Bibliography

Note: The listing of titles in this bibliography should not be regarded as a recommendation of the books or an endorsement of their content. While some are indeed commendable works, many of the titles consulted contain errors and inaccuracies, and in numerous instances research subsequent to their publication has shed new light on the events in question. For example, it is now known that the aeroplane McClean flew under the Thames bridges on 10 August 1912 was S.40, not S.33 as stated by many sources, S.33 having been lost in the Channel on 22 December 1911.

Much of the material in this book was gleaned from British aeronautical magazines of the pre-First World War era, namely *The Aero, Aerocraft, The Aeronautical Journal, Aeronautics, The Aeroplane* and *Flight*. In most important instances the issue concerned is cited in the appropriate place in the text.

Books

Air Ministry, *A Short History of the Royal Air Force*, Air Publication 125, 2nd edition (Air Ministry, London, 1936).

Ashworth, C, *Action Stations No.9: Military Airfields of the Central South and South-East* (Patrick Stephens, Wellingborough, 1985) ISBN 0-85059-608-4.

Axten, J W, *The Hon. Charles Stewart Rolls 1877-1910* (Monmouth Historical and Educational Trust, Monmouth, Gwent, 1977).

Barker, R, *The Schneider Trophy Races* (Chatto and Windus, London, 1971) ISBN 0-7011-1663-3.

Barnes, C H, *Shorts Aircraft since 1900* (Putnam, London, 1967).

Boughton, T, *The Story of the British Light Aeroplane* (John Murray, London, 1963).

Brabazon of Tara, Lord, *The Brabazon Story* (William Heinemann, London, 1956).

Brett, R Dallas, *History of British Aviation 1908-1914* (John Hamilton, London, 1934).

Brewer, G, *50 Years of Flying* (Air League of the British Empire, London, 1946).

Brockett, P, *Bibliography of Aeronautics* (Vol I) (Smithsonian Institution, Washington, D.C., 1910).

_____, *Bibliography of Aeronautics* (Vol II) (Smithsonian Institution, Washington, D.C., 1921).

Brooks, R J, *Aviation in Kent: A Pictorial History to 1939* (Meresborough Books, Rainham, Kent, 1983) ISBN 0-90527-068-1.

Bruce, G, *Charlie Rolls – Pioneer Aviator* (Rolls-Royce Heritage Trust, Derby, 1990) Historical Series No 17. ISBN 1-872922-01-5.

_____, *C.S. Rolls: Pioneer Aviator* (Monmouth District Museum Service, Monmouth, Gwent, 1978).

Bruce, J M, *Britain's First Warplanes* (Arms and Armour Press, Poole, Dorset, 1987) ISBN 0-85368-852-4.

_____, *The Aeroplanes of the Royal Flying Corps Military Wing*, second revised edition (Putnam, London, 1992) ISBN 0-85177-854-2.

Cole, C, and Cheesman, E F, *The Air Defence of Britain 1914-1918* (Putnam, London, 1984) ISBN 0-370-30538-8.

Cronin, D, *Royal Navy Shipboard Aircraft Developments 1912-1931* (Air-Britain, Tonbridge, Kent, 1990) ISBN 0-85130-165-7.

Crossland, Prof Sir B, and Moore, J S (eds), *The Lives of Great Engineers of Ulster, Vol II* (N.E. Consultancy for Belfast Industrial Heritage, Belfast, 2008) ISBN 780 956 040 107.

Croydon, Air Commodore B, *Early Birds: A Short History of how Flight Came to Sheppey* (Publicity Matters, Sheerness, Kent, 2003) ISBN 0-95327-393-8.

Dorman, G, *Fifty Years Fly Past: From Wright Brothers to Comet* (Forbes Robertson, London, 1951).

Draper, Major Christopher, *The Mad Major* (Air Review, Letchworth, UK, 1962).

Driver, H, *The Birth of Military Aviation: Britain,*

1903-1914 (The Royal Historical Society/The Boydell Press, Woodbridge, Suffolk, 1997) ISBN 0-86193-234-X.

Empson, R H W, *The History of the Eastchurch Air Station, Sheppey, 1909-1926* (Bonner & Co, London, ca.1927; reprinted in two parts in the *Royal Aero Club Gazette* for January and February 1955, Vol 9 No 1, pp 6–17 and Vol 9 No 2, pp 35–45, and also in *Cross & Cockade International Quarterly Journal*, Vol 40 No 2, Summer 2009, pp 40.071–40.087, as 'Eastchurch: The Early Years', with many additional illustrations.)

Gamble, C F S, *The Air Weapon* (Oxford University Press, Oxford, 1931).

——————, *The Story of a North Sea Air Station* (Oxford University Press, 1928).

Gibbs-Smith, C H, *Aviation: An Historical Survey from its Origins to the End of World War II* (HMSO, London, 1970).

——————, *The Invention of the Aeroplane 1799-1909* (Faber and Faber, London, 1966).

——————, *The Rebirth of European Aviation* (HMSO, London, 1974) ISBN 0-11-290180-8*.

Goodall, M H, and Tagg, A E, *British Aircraft Before the Great War* (Schiffer, Atglen, Pennsylvania, USA, 2001) ISBN 0-7643-1207-3.

Grahame-White, C, and Harper, H, *The Aeroplane: Past, Present, and Future* (T Werner Laurie, London, 1911).

Harper, H, *My Fifty Years in Flying* (Associated Newspapers, London, 1956).

Hughes, D T, *Flying Past: A History of Sheppey Aviation* (The History Press, Stroud, Gloucestershire, 2009) ISBN 978 0 7524 5228 9.

Hurren, B J, *Fellowship of the Air: Jubilee Book of the Royal Aero Club 1901-1951* (Iliffe & Sons, London, 1951).

Jackson, A J, *British Civil Aircraft since 1919, Vol 3*, 2nd edition (Putnam, London, 1974) ISBN 0-370-10014-X.

Kent Aviation Historical Research Society, *Wings over Kent*, No 1 (undated), containing Mac-Dougall, P, 'The Navy Takes to the Air', pp 13–16; and Collyer, D, 'Early Club Pioneers', pp 17–21.

King, B, *Royal Naval Air Service 1912-1918* (Hikoki, Hampshire, 1997) ISBN 0-9519899-5-2.

Lautrec, J de *et al*, *Dans le Ciel de Pau; 1909 Les Débuts de l'aviation: Wright* (Éditions Cairn, Pau, France, 2007) ISBN 978-2-35068-092-7.

Long, A, 'John Robinson McClean 1813-1873', in Crossland, Prof Sir B, and Moore, J S, *The Lives of Great Engineers of Ulster, Vol II (q.v.)*.

Longmore, Sir Arthur, *From Sea to Sky 1910-1945* (Geoffrey Bles, London, 1946).

McFarland, M W (ed), *The Papers of Wilbur and Orville Wright, Vols 1 and 2* (McGraw-Hill, New York, USA, 1953).

Meynell, L, *Men of Speed: The Hon. C.S. Rolls* (Newnes Educational Publishing, London, 1955).

Montague of Beaulieu, Lord, *Rolls of Rolls-Royce: A Biography of the Hon. C.S. Rolls* (Cassell, London, 1966).

Morris, A, *The Balloonatics* (Jarrolds, London, 1970).

Penrose, H, *British Aviation: The Pioneer Years* (Putnam, London, 1967).

Raleigh, W, *The War in the Air, Vol 1* (Oxford University Press, Oxford, 1922).

Renstrom, A G, *Wilbur and Orville Wright: A Chronology Commemorating the Hundredth Anniversary of the Birth of Orville Wright, August 19, 1871* (Library of Congress, Washington, D.C., 1975) ISBN 0-8444-0131-5.

Riddle, B, and Sinnott, C (eds), *Letters of the Wright Brothers* (Tempus, Stroud, Gloucestershire, 2003) ISBN 0-7524-2584-6.

Roskill, Captain S W, *Documents Relating to the Naval Air Service, Vol 1 1908-1918*, (Navy Records Society, 1969).

Samson, Air Commodore C R, *Fights and Flights* (Ernest Benn, London, 1930).

Short Brothers Limited, 1903-1978: *Seventy Five Years of Powered Dynamic Flight* (Short Brothers, Belfast, 1978).

Sturtivant, R, and Page, G, *Royal Navy Aircraft Serials and Units 1911-1919* (Air-Britain, Tonbridge, Kent, 1992) ISBN 0-85130-191-6.

Thetford, O, *British Naval Aircraft since 1912*, sixth revised edition (Putnam, London, 1991) ISBN 0-85177-849-6.

Travers, E, *Cross Country* (Hothersall & Travers, Sittingbourne, Kent, 1990) ISBN 0-9515461-0-4.

Turner, Major C C, *The Old Flying Days* (Sampson, Low, Marston & Co, London, 193?).

Wallace, G, *Flying Witness: Harry Harper and the Golden Age of Aviation* (Putnam, London, 1958).

Wright, Bishop Milton, *Diaries 1857-1917* (Wright State University, Dayton, Ohio, 1999) ISBN 0-9676359-0-X.

Articles

Aeroplane, The, 'For Their Work Continueth . . .', editorial, Vol 89 No 2297 (29 July 1955).

Aeroplane, The, 'Commemorating a Birthplace', picture and caption, Vol 89 No 2297 (29 July 1955), p 163.

Aeroplane, The, 'Pioneers' Memorial', Vol 89 No 2298 (5 August 1955), p 197.

Aeroplane, The, 'Godfather to Naval Aviation', Vol 89 No 2300 (19 August 1955), p 262.

Anon. 'Sir Francis McClean, AFC', *Royal Aero Club Gazette*, Vol 9 No 10 (October 1955), pp 331–4.

Baker, D, and Roffe, M, 'Great Moments in Aviation–No 12', *Aeroplane Monthly* (August 1995), pp 54–5

Brabazon of Tara, Lord, 'Sir Francis McClean', *The Times* (16 August 1955).

Brewer, Griffith, 'The Life and Work of Wilbur Wright', *The Aeronautical Journal*, Vol 20 No 79 (July–September 1916), pp 68–135.

Brooks, R J, and Ellis, K, 'Kent's Cradle of Aviation', *Flypast* (April 2009), pp 32–7.

Carroll, T J, and Carroll, T R, 'Wright Brothers' Invention of 1903 Propeller and Genesis of Modern Propeller Theory', American Institute of Aeronautics and Astronautics *Journal of Aircraft*, Vol 42 No 1, pp 218–23.

Cheshire History, 'A Pioneer Aviator from Cheshire: The Logbook of Maurice Egerton', Part 1 in No 25 (Spring 1990); Part 2 in No 26 (Autumn 1990); Part 3 in No 27 (Spring 1991); Part 4 in No 28 (Autumn 1991).

Ellis, K, 'Kent's Shrine', *Flypast* (July 2009), pp 104–6.

Flight, 'A Dinner to Some Pioneers', Vol 23 No 18 (1 May 1931), p 380.

Flight, 'Remembering the Eastchurch Pioneers', Vol 67 No 2406 (4 March 1955), p 266.

Flight, 'The Eastchurch Memorial', Vol 68 No 2428 (5 August 1955), p 182.

Flight, 'Sir Francis McClean', Vol 68 No 2430 (19 August 1955), pp 246–7.

Freeman, J W, 'The Birthplace of British Aviation', *Aviation News* (23 January–5 February 1987), pp 870–2.

Grey, C G, 'On the King's Gifts', *The Aeroplane*, Vol 31 No 5 (4 August 1926), pp 141–6.

Harper, H, 'Makers of Flying Machines: Visit to a British Factory', *Daily Mail* (4 April 1910), p 4.

Hobbs, D, 'Wait and See: The Origins of British Naval Aviation', *Air Enthusiast*, No 131 (September/October 2007), pp 2–7.

Jarrett, P M, 'The Flying Philanthropist', *Aeroplane Monthly*, Vol 37 No 9 (September 2009), pp 34–8, and Vol 37 No 10 (October 2009), pp 40–4.

McClean, F K, 'The Gordon Bennett Balloon Race, 1908', *Royal Aero Club Gazette*, Vol 9 No 12 (December 1955), pp 410–15.

_____, 'From Zurich to Bohemia by Balloon. Being an account of the Gordon-Bennett Balloon Race, 1909', *Flight*, Vol 1 No 48 (27 November 1909), p 763.

_____, 'Lighter-than-Air Days', *Royal Aero Club Gazette* (March 1950), pp 77–81; 'Heavier-than-Air Days', *Royal Aero Club Gazette* (April 1950), pp 94–8; 'Alexandria to Khartoum, 1914', *Royal Aero Club Gazette* (May 1950), pp 125–30.

_____, 'Trials and Errors, Being Tales of the Air', *The PD Review* (house magazine of Powell Duffryn Associated Collieries Ltd), No 34 (April 1938), pp 31–4; No 35 (July 1938), pp 16–19; and No 36 (October 1938), pp 39–41.

Porter, M, 'Pigs Might Fly', *SAGA Magazine* (May 2009), pp 50–5.

Preston, J, 'Pioneer Flying on Sheppey 1909-1910', *Bygone Kent*, Vol 2 No 5 (May 1981), pp 288–92.

Pritchard, J L, 'The Wright Brothers and the Royal Aeronautical Society, A Survey and Tribute', *Journal of the Royal Aeronautical Society*, Vol 57 No 516 (December 1953), pp 739–818.

_____, and Ogilvie, Lieutenant-Colonel Alec, 'Sir Francis Kennedy McClean, AFC', *The Journal of the Royal Aeronautical Society*, Vol 59 No 539 (November 1955), pp 721–6.

Royal Aero Club Gazette, 'The Eastchurch Memorial', Vol 9 No 4 (April 1955), pp 92–3.

Royal Aero Club Gazette, 'Eastchurch Memorial to Pioneer Airmen', Vol 9 No 9 (September 1955), pp 276–7.

Royal Aero Club Gazette, 'Sir Francis McClean, AFC'

(obituary) Vol 9 No 10 (October 1955), pp 331–4.

Sphere, The, 'Photographing the Sunken "Oceana": "The Sphere's" Marine Aviation Experiments', 6 July 1912, pp 11–16.

Sphere, The, McClean's flight up the Thames on August 10, 1912, was covered in the issue of 17 August 1912, being featured on the front cover and in a series of pictorial articles on pages 149–54.

Sphere, The, 'Remarkable Success of "The Sphere" Hydro-Aeroplane Flight up the Thames', *The Sphere* (24 August 1912), p 192.

The Times, obituary of Sir Francis McClean (12 August 1955).

Trend, A, 'Heir to Air' (The Hon Maurice Egerton), *Rapide*, No 6 (2003), pp 44–7, and No 7, 2003, pp 44–6.

Turner, Major C C, 'A Pioneer of Flight, Presentation to Lieut-Col F.K. McClean, Father of Naval Aviation', *Observer* (30 March 1924).

Unpublished documents and papers

The F K McClean Collection, in the archives of the Fleet Air Arm Museum at Yeovilton, records the early aviation exploits of Sir Francis Kennedy McClean. It comprises many photographs, glass slides and press cuttings, together with publications and personal items.

F K McClean, log book of balloon voyages, July 1907–October 1918. In the McClean Collection with the Fleet Air Arm Museum at Yeovilton.

F K McClean, Royal Aero Club Aviator's Certificate No 21. In the McClean Collection with the Fleet Air Arm Museum at Yeovilton.

F K McClean, diary, June 1906–July 1925. A briefly annotated listing of events, meetings and movements. In the archives of the Fleet Air Arm Museum at Yeovilton.

F K McClean, correspondence sent to acquaintances, reporting progress of the Nile flight, January to March 1914. In the archives of the Fleet Air Arm Museum at Yeovilton.

F K McClean, Nile flight photograph album held in the Royal Aero Club archive in the RAF Museum. A similar album is in the McClean Collection in the Fleet Air Arm Museum.

Rait, J, 'The Pilot's Logbook of Maurice Egerton'. A transcript of Egerton's pilot's log book, kept at Tatton Hall, Knutsford, Cheshire. 2009

Short Brothers' first Order Book, January 1909–February 1913, also including details of later aircraft production and constructor's numbers. In the company's possession.

Index